Brian
&the
Boys

Brian & the Boys

A Story of Gang Rape

MAGGIE SIGGINS

James Lorimer & Company, Publishers
Toronto 1984

ISBN 0-88862-658-4 paper
      0-88862-659-2 cloth

Design: Brant Cowie/Art Plus Ltd.

Photos courtesy of: Mrs. Lillian Amirault (1-3); Jean Elgar (4); Brian Dempsey (5); Richard Gillespie (6); Mrs. Ruby Blake (11-14).

CANADIAN CATALOGUING IN PUBLICATION DATA
Siggins, Maggie, 1942-
   Brian & the boys

1. Trials (Rape) — Ontario — Toronto. 2. Young men — Ontario — Toronto — Conduct of life. 3. Young women — Ontario — Toronto — Conduct of life. I. Title.

KE8930.R3S63 1983   345.71'02532   C83-099152-2

James Lorimer & Company, Publishers
Egerton Ryerson Memorial Building
35 Britain Street
Toronto, Ontario M5A 1R7

Printed and bound in Canada
6 5 4 3 2 1   84 85 86 87 88

Contents

Acknowledgements

Without the help of two probing researchers this book would have been a much more difficult task. My thanks to Susan Bigelow for laying the framework and to Kit Melamud for helping me complete it. My gratitude also to Lena Sperling for her detective work.

To Gerald B. Sperling

Introduction

It's ugly, the spectre of gang rape. Brutal and surly toughs using their superior strength to violate and degrade, and sometimes mutilate, an unsuspecting and helpless victim who, if she is not murdered, often never recovers from the horror. Like many feminists, I have long felt that rape symbolized the very essence of man's historic bullying of woman. We have realized for some time that rape has nothing to do with "uncontrollable" sexual impulses, and everything to do with an attempt by an inadequate and unsuccessful man to dominate and degrade someone whom he considers less a human being than he.

In the late 1970s, I began noticing more and more articles in newspapers and magazines about gang rape. What astonished me was how much more prevalent it was than I had thought. Some studies indicated there was more sexual assault committed by gangs than by men acting alone.

I found myself asking questions about this disturbing phenomenon. To begin with, what peculiar and sordid quirks in the personalities of these men resulted in this misogyny? What unhappiness in childhood, what terrible disappointments and failures in their adolescence, led to such taste for revenge?

At the same time, I knew that there must be more to gang rape than a young punk seeking to get back at the world. What societal mores and values gives him licence to believe that he can use women as punching bags on which to vent his frustration and rage? Despite the influence of the flourishing feminist movement, are young men still being brought up to believe that women are inferior beings to be violated as one pleases? Why does society produce so many young misogynists?

1

To try to find answers, I decided to look at two cases of rape allegedly perpetrated by the same group of men in Toronto in the spring of 1979. Two women, who had not known each other, claimed they were raped and brutalized by a gang of six men on separate occasions. A six-week trial was held, the men were convicted of various offences in one or both of the cases, and were sentenced to an average of twelve years. It seemed a clear-cut case, a perfect specimen for analysis.

But something strange and disturbing occurred during the researching of this book. The more I examined the evidence presented at the trial, the more I interviewed the people involved, their families and friends, the more foggy and perplexing the picture became. It was no longer a straightforward case of brutes violating innocent victims, but rather a complex and ambiguous affair. For one thing, the convicted men insist to this day that they are innocent of the offences, that they did not commit rape.

In the chapters that follow, there are two accounts of what happened at 402 Lauder Avenue in Metro Toronto on April 23 and May 15, 1979: the one each of the victims presented in court, and the one the defendants gave. These stories were reconstructed primarily from sworn statements given at the time of trial, although details were provided through the many interviews I conducted with those involved. As well, as my research progressed, a third version of what went on during those two spring nights emerged, which some of the accused men now claim is the "real" truth. It's my hope readers will sift through the ambiguities and inconsistencies presented by both sides and arrive at their own understandings of the events: what happened, why, and whether the procedure and outcome of the judicial process was suitable and fair. I think not everyone will agree with the jury's verdict.

At the start of the trials for the rapes, Mr. Justice Galligan ordered that the victims' identities not be revealed. To comply with this order, and out of fairness to the complainants, I have changed not only their names but also the names of their friends and relatives, the streets they lived on, places where they worked, and hospitals where they were treated. I have also altered a handful of inconsequential biographical details regarding some friends and relatives, and I have changed the names of other people where I thought naming them might cause them undue embarrassment.

However, the names of the convicted men, their families and legal counsel, have remained unchanged and the details of various events and histories have been rendered as accurately as possible.

Given the questions that I was trying to answer in this book, I realized that I would have to research the childhoods and adult backgrounds of both the men and the women involved in the rapes. The question of how these people — representative of an entire subculture in society — developed their values and habits was of as much interest to me as the unfortunate predicament they found themselves in. At the heart of this story is a worldview shared by the men and women alike: a twisted version of the hippy lifestyle of the Sixties, whereby "freedom" was pursued with a vengeance, providing a cloak for an utter aimlessness in life.

But this is also an attempt to analyse how the justice system worked in this particular case, and by implication in other instances where the crime is one which has been the centre of a great deal of controversy. In fact, at the time of writing, the judiciary had not finished with the matter. Leave to appeal to the Supreme Court of Canada has been granted and the appeal is likely to be heard in the spring of 1984. Should it be successful, the convictions will be overturned and a retrial ordered.

I started out to write a book in which the villains and victims were neatly etched in black and white. The picture now is considerably greyer, an indication perhaps that the ongoing war between the sexes is much more complicated and dynamic than many people are willing to acknowledge.

PART I

The Rapes

ONE

The Raid

LOOK, SHE WAS OVERJOYED

May 16, 1979

Randy "Roadside" Blake was lying fully dressed on the cement floor at the bottom of the basement stairs at 402 Lauder Avenue when he woke up with a throbbing headache and a sore neck. He dragged himself to his feet, looked around the gloom and said to no one, "Holy fuck! How did I get down here?" He felt so bad, so utterly rotten, that all he could think about was getting his hands on a beer — quick. He staggered up the stairs and into the dining room, and there stretched out on a Formica kitchen chair, like a limp and greasy rag doll, his huge shag of a head resting back on the wall, his mouth wide open, his snores sounding like a defective Harley Davidson hawg, was his good buddy Bobby Caruso.

Blake went to the refrigerator and got out two Labatt's Extras. He kicked the leg of Caruso's chair a few times to no avail and then sat down directly opposite him at the brown kitchen table. Bending forward, peering directly into Caruso's face, he shouted as loudly as he could, "Heeey Bobby! Up and at it!" Caruso's eyes snapped open and he immediately broke into a grin. He was always glad to see Blake. "Roady, remember last night when I came in? Remember me telling you about the Avenger and how I smashed his head in at the Gasworks?" Blake confessed that he had been so blasted, so wrecked on hash and grass and beer that he didn't remember too many details. He sort of recalled Caruso trying to wake him up. But that was all. Caruso though was delighted that he had another chance to tell his story — and in detail.

At about two thirty the day before he had gone to see Ivan Kristopolous,* the hairstylist he knew who worked at the Country Cut-N

---

* A pseudonym.

Curl on Yonge Street opposite the Gasworks Tavern. Caruso's hair was as kinky and coarse as steel wool and tended to stick out perpendicular to his head. He thought that if Ivan thinned it, it might grow longer. "Well, I'll try," said Kristopolous, "but, Jesus, I don't know anybody who could tame that bramble bush of a head."

Ivan had met Bobby several years earlier at the Gasworks. Both young men were part of a network of good old drinking buddies who hung out at the tavern: if you needed your van repaired, chances are you'd find someone at the Gasworks who'd do it cheap; you'd find a reasonable and reliable dope dealer there; and if you needed a present for your old lady's birthday, you'd find a booster who'd sell you a hot watch very inexpensively.

Caruso told Roadside Blake that Ivan finished with him at about four and he then went to the Gasworks. As usual he had only a couple of dollars in his pocket but that didn't cramp his drinking style. He knew practically everybody in the place — he was one of the few "citizens" who was allowed to join the Vagabonds, who habitually gathered nonchalantly, yet menacingly, at their usual table. They sat at the back of the tavern near the ladies' washroom, which meant they could make lewd remarks as a woman walked by, even grab her ass. Or Caruso could sit with the posties, the day labourers or the kids delinquent from school, who gathered closer to the front. With its large round and high tables, seating eight "cowboys," its gloom thick with smoke, and its wailing juke box music, the Gasworks could have been the set for a grade B Western.

Caruso looked around. He spotted a table laden with a newly arrived batch of draft pints and he sat there. When he was broke that was his usual modus operandi: he'd sit with one bunch until the beer ran out and then move on to another group where an order had just been placed. No one minded. He was one of those outrageous characters whom the Gasworks crowd not only appreciated but idolized. At six feet, 225 pounds, hirsute in the extreme, he had a habit of impersonating the Incredible Hulk. His whisky voice — gruff, heavy, awe-inspiring — was unavoidable. His friend Chuck Dempsey used to say, "There are only two people I know with voices like that and they are Caruso and Santa Claus." His costume was always the same: a black, often soiled T-shirt, blue jeans encrusted with grease, a striped engineer's hat which was filthy, Wellington boots, and in his pocket a huge billfold much like a trucker's, connected to his jeans by a heavy gold-coloured chain. And finally there were his tattoos — all thirty-six of them covering his arms and chest. With very little urging, he would role up his black T-shirt to reveal his coup de grace, his pride and joy. This was a masterpiece of camp located in the middle of his hairy chest, about six inches across, crafted in every colour of the rainbow. A ribald skeleton, holding aloft an over-sized bottle of whisky, rides in a coffin equipped with huge wings, the front of which is shaped like a motorcycle. Underneath it, elaborately scrolled are the words BORN TO RIDE. In fact, Caruso hadn't owned a motorcycle for about ten years — no club would have him because he was not considered to be true biker material — but he was brilliant at cultivating the image.

Caruso began frequenting the Gasworks in 1973 when he was hired as a doorman bouncer. ("Imagine, $2.75 an hour to bust heads," he often used to brag, says his friend Brian Dempsey.) He was considered a rough one even among this group of belligerent young men hired only for their muscle, whose idea of extreme pleasure was experiencing the muffled, dead sound of a knuckle smacking into a nose, a cheekbone or an eye. Caruso had moved to other jobs and other cities across Canada, but whenever he was in Toronto, the Gasworks remained his favourite spot to drink. And if the staff was short-handed or if there was a big fracas, he'd help out. For that he got free screwdrivers — orange juice and double vodkas.

As he continued to relate to Roady Blake, on this particular Monday he was enjoying himself, bebopping from one table to another. A fellow whom Caruso knew only by the name of Chouch came in with two women. When Bobby was returning from a trip to the washroom, Chouch called him over. "How you doing there, Bobby?" he inquired. "Not bad," replied Caruso. "Come over here and have a beer with us," urged Chouch, and Caruso who had already eyed one of the girls and judged her "not bad," agreed. He was having a pretty good time, watching some hockey, then listening to Foot in Cold Water, the band playing that night, and talking to the lady. "Nice band," she said. "Not bad at all," he replied. Then he noticed the two coloured guys. Blacks always spelled trouble because the bikers hated them. But a waiter known as Jimmy the Greek had already pointed them out to Jamie Vinall, the manager on duty. They were smoking dope, the waiter told Vinall, a practice strictly forbidden in the tavern. Vinall got to them just as they has sat down on the part of the stage where the equipment was located. "What the hell do you think you're doing?" demanded Vinall. "Get the fuck out of here, you asshole," responded one. With that Caruso jumped out of his chair, ready to help.

As Caruso told it to Roady Blake, with appropriate Incredible Hulk gestures, "The coloured guy says, 'What you want, fat man?' I smacked him on the head, pulled him off balance and spun him around. Then I yanked his arm right up his back and Jamie grabbed the other guy the same. Then we literally picked them up and ran them out to the sidewalk. I says 'This is what I want, fucking, skinny man, asshole, nigger.'"

Caruso told Blake that he didn't think much more about the

incident; it was rather typical of what went on at the Gasworks every night. At one point, Caruso, Chouch and the two women went out the back door of the tavern and smoked a couple of joints. The bouncers left them alone because Caruso was such a favourite with them. They then returned and continued to drink draft. Caruso told them he'd drive them home after the bar closed.

At about one thirty in the morning, Caruso got up and went to the washroom. He was relieving himself in the urinal when he felt someone bumping his back. Bobby turned around and gasped. The man in front of him looked like a wild boar: his teeth were bared in a grimace and he was snorting through his nose. "Do you know who I am?" he roared. Caruso countered, "I've never the fuck seen you before." "I am the Avenger, here to do justice." With that Caruso did what was natural and punched him in the face. Blood spurted from his nose. The Avenger grabbed Caruso by the hair and the two large men fell to the floor. Caruso told Blake, "I seen blood when I went down and went a little crazy, beating at this guy." Finally four bouncers intervened and the two were pulled apart. "That's how I got this scrape," he said, showing Blake an exposed, raw strip of flesh on one side of his nose. By the time Caruso was finished with his story it was not only Roadside who was suitably impressed: several other inhabitants of the house had gathered in the dining room to watch Bobby's performance.

Richard Gillespie had come up from the basement and grabbed a beer. A slender 145 pounds, fine featured and fair, he was handsome in a girlish way. This morning he was even more spiffily dressed than usual, having outfitted himself by means of a $110 welfare cheque that he had received a few days ago. He wore new black denim slacks, a black T-shirt with rust-coloured trim and insignia, and a black corduroy sports jacket. Gillespie made small amounts of money dealing in drugs. He was a habitual itinerant: for the last eight of his twenty-six years he'd had no fixed address to speak of, staying at cheap hotels, the Salvation Army, the Hot Tub Club — a gay steambath — and with various friends who would put up with him for short periods. The previous Sunday night he had crashed at 402 Lauder Avenue, sleeping on an inflated air mattress in the small room in the basement. He had never met Bobby Caruso before but he enjoyed his antics. He pulled out some hash from his jacket pocket and began stuffing a pipe.

Linda Brown, leggy, good-looking and seven months pregnant, came down from an upstairs bedroom to make fried eggs and toast for her common-law husband, John Beatteay. He ate them with a bottle of Molson Ex while listening to Caruso. Linda and John had not been getting along recently, primarily because he refused to hold down a job longer than a month or two. "All he ever wants to do is party and drink with the boys. That's the only thing he cares about," she told her sister. Linda was even considering returning to her parents' farm near Carlyle, Saskatchewan, to have her baby.

Charles Dempsey, the only male in the group with short-cropped hair, a clean-shaven face, and a penchant for three-piece suits and a pretentious turn of phrase, was talking with Linda in the kitchen. He worked as a short-order chef at a Fran's Restaurant.

Upstairs, Dave Bell was slowly gaining consciousness in the cubbyhole that served as his bedroom. He felt terrible. Not only was he badly hung-over but he felt guilty — he had probably been fired from yet another job. He had borrowed his mother's car and gone to Kitchener the previous morning to look over a used Chev he was thinking of buying, fully intending to make it back by two o'clock, the time his shift at Rowntree Chocolates on Dundas Street in the west end of the city, began. But he was delayed and didn't arrive in Toronto until two thirty. He decided to go into the nearby Lansdowne hotel, phone his supervisor and tell him he was sorry he was late and he'd be there in an hour and a half. But Dave got drinking and playing pool, and by four he thought, "The hell with it." He wanted to party. He phoned the guys at 402 Lauder and they agreed to come over. By midnight Dave had consumed enormous quantities of bottle and draft beer, lemon gin and scotch. And he'd smoked grass and hash. Someone had sold him the biggest bottle of cheapo wine he'd ever seen and he recalled placing it on the kitchen table at 402 Lauder, but after that he only vaguely remembered passing out in bed. "Oh well, that's life," he thought to himself and decided to go back to sleep.

In the adjoining bedroom Jean Elgar shook Brian Dempsey and asked him what he wanted for breakfast. He mumbled something incoherently. Like many people who knew Dempsey, Jean was both fascinated by him and a little frightened of him. As aggressive and short-tempered as a bantam cock, he was the kingpin of the house, the acknowledged leader of the pack. He looked a little like Charlie Manson, with brown piercing eyes and Jesus-like hair. In fact, he had read the biography of the mass murderer four times. While he would strongly deny that the violence Manson and company had inflicted appealed to him, Brian was intrigued by the iron grip by which Charlie had controlled his "family."

Jean got dressed and went downstairs. What she saw made her very angry. The house was a mess from the party the previous night. Beer bottles were strewn everywhere, the place stank of booze, there were stains on the rug and floor. And the four dogs were running about like crazy; they were supposed to be outside or in the basement.

When she opened the refrigerator door, she discovered Linda had used all the eggs, bacon and bread. It wasn't the first time this had happened and she was annoyed. In an attempt to placate Jean, Linda said she'd drive to the store with her. They could take the four German shepherds out for some air at the same time. The two women picked up what they needed at a supermarket on St. Clair Avenue West and returned to Lauder in Brian's Ford LTD, a battered, green station wagon. Linda had both arms full of groceries, so Jean held the front door open for her and the dogs. As she was about to enter herself, she turned briefly to look over her shoulder at the street. She gasped, then hurried inside, slammed the door and ran to the window, screaming, "There's cops all over the place! We're being surrounded by police!" Randy Blake lunged for his black leather jacket, dug out a wad of hash and threw it under the table. Upstairs, Brian frantically yanked on his jeans. He ran into the next bedroom and found Dave Bell looking out the window over the backyard. "Holy shit," Dave gasped, "a fuckin' army."

In the next instant the front door burst open and what indeed did seem like an invasion force of police officers spilled in. Jean Edgar could hear unbelievably loud banging, like a sledgehammer, and she ran to the back door. "Wait a minute! Wait a minute! I'll open it," she yelled. But it was too late. The police were already charging into the kitchen.

A couple of hours earlier the details of the raid had been hastily worked out by Sergeant David Grinnell. At 10:20 that morning he had conferred with his superior, Staff-Sergeant William Crampton, head of the Criminal Investigation Bureau of 13 Division on Eglinton Avenue. As a result of this quick conversation, Grinnell and his partner, Sergeant Thomas Mitchell, had driven to North York Courts at 1000 Finch West, and had quickly got a signed search warrant from Justice of the Peace Gordon Santocono. They were back at 13 Division by 10:59. By that time twenty police officers were waiting in the conference room on the second floor of the Division. While the proceedings were technically headed by Crampton, it was Sergeant Grinnell, a veteran of seventeen years service, who gave the officers most of their instructions. Grinnell told them roughly what had allegedly transpired. He could see the look of disgust distort each man's face.

By 11:31 a convoy of thirteen police cars, both marked and unmarked, left the Division. Their destination was a quiet neighbourhood only a few blocks, about six minutes, away. Grinnell, Mitchell and Staff-Sergeant Crampton, all in plain clothes and in the same vehicle, were the first to reach the intersection of Lauder Avenue and Rogers Road. Grinnell had hoped there'd be a few minutes for his men to collect themselves before acting, but even as his car stopped he saw two people — he couldn't tell if they were male or female — running away from the house. To prevent others from escaping, he realized he'd have to act fast. Shouting at the rest of the men to move, he ran up the front walk of 402 Lauder. He tried the door, found it locked, then masterfully and precisely kicked it open. He ran in, closely followed by Mitchell and Crampton, the one officer who held a shotgun. The three ran down the hall and entered the living-dining room area. Grinnell still retains a vivid picture of that instant: he thought the three rough-looking young men were going to challenge him, and he mentally prepared for a fight. In a few seconds, though, the men realized they were vastly outnumbered by cops. Caruso remembers one of them yelled, "Don't move, scumbag! Get your hands up on the wall!" He, Beatteay and Blake quickly complied.

Grinnell held a blue search warrant high above his head and told them in a loud voice that the police were conducting an investigation. They were all under arrest. He repeated this two more times, then asked if anyone wanted to see the warrant. Roadside Blake was standing closest to Grinnell. He took it, looked at it, but was so upset that he couldn't comprehend a word.

While this was going on, Grinnell was surrounded by what to him seemed a pack of growling, snapping dogs. The frightened animals compounded the chaos as Jean screamed at them to stop barking and various officers attempted to contain them in one room, without much luck.

Constable Noel Lee noticed a plastic vial containing several small green pills and one orange pill sitting on the kitchen table. He put it in his pocket.

Constable Norman Cadorin had forced open the back door and run into the kitchen, where he spotted Jean, Linda and Richard Gillespie. He pushed Gillespie into the dining room area with the rest of the men. Cadorin then searched Caruso — he would say of him later that he was very, very dirty — handcuffed him and ran him to the car. Meanwhile a couple of other officers had frisked Blake, looked at his wallet and handcuffed his hands behind his back. He would later recall what happened next: a large burly officer put his arm through Blake's arms with the heel of his hand on his prisoner's shoulder. Blake claimed that as he was being pushed along, another plainclothes cop kicked him in the groin.

"What's that for?" he asked. "That's just the beginning. Wait till we get you down at the station."

Meanwhile Edward Callan was the first constable to run up the stairs. He was near the top when he saw two men stumbling out of a bedroom. They spotted him, froze and ran back in, slamming the door behind them. Callan kicked it open. David Bell and Brian Dempsey immediately put their arms over their heads, turned their backs to the police officer and placed their hands on the wall. Callan would later testify he didn't know why the two acted in this manner, that he didn't have his gun out. Both Bell and Dempsey would claim that he pointed his .38 revolver at them and told them he'd blast "their fucking heads" off if they tried anything. Callan searched Dempsey and found a wallet in the back pocket of his jeans and asked him if he had any money in it. "No, sir" was the response. In fact, Dempsey had $201 in loose bills in his pocket, proceeds from Jean's unemployment insurance cheque, but the police didn't bother with it. Callan then handcuffed him and handed him over to a uniformed officer, Brian Lawrie, who escorted him to a cruiser. Lawrie recalled that as well as the standard jeans and T-shirt, Dempsey wore a gold chain around his neck with a large circular pendant depicting Taurus, his astrological sign, which Jean Elgar had given him for his birthday. Dempsey also wore a gold ring with a genuine, large red ruby. He was particularly proud of this piece of jewellery because one night in a Vancouver bar he had talked it off a guy in exchange for a pair of sunglasses.

Dave Bell did not have his glasses on, so the situation seemed even more confused to him. He was absolutely terrified and could think only of how his family would react to the news that he had been busted for drugs. Slight in appearance, he had a long, scraggly beard and long, unkempt hair. Constable Morrison handcuffed him, grabbed both his arms and ran him out of the house. He had no socks or shoes on.

Sergeant Mitchell called the Humane Society to take the dogs away, but by the time the attendants arrived, one had already escaped out the front door. It was Brian's favourite. After an hour or so it returned, jumping into the back seat of the station wagon.

It took only a short time, seventeen minutes, to round up the seven men and two women.

Four hundred and two Lauder was situated in a neat and quiet working-class neighbourhood. Residents, standing in a knot on the sidewalk, couldn't believe their eyes; not one of them had ever seen anything like this before, even in times of war. But to a person they were relieved. The Romanos at 404 Lauder had many times called the police because of wild partying next door. Bruno Lacaria, whose house was situated at 400 Lauder, had become very nervous when his ten-year-old daughter had been invited to come over to 402 anytime. "They spoiled the neighbourhood. This was a nice neighbourhood until they came around," Lacaria told the police.

Orders were given that each of the suspects was to be placed in a separate area at 13 Division. Bobby Caruso, as ordered, began to strip for his skin search. "Wonder what he's got up his ass?" asked one of the officers. First thing off were his boots, and one cop literally gagged from the stench. The bottom of Caruso's feet were encrusted in a black muck, the boots' inner soles had completely rotted away, and the bottom of the boots were what Chuck Dempsey described as a "putrified marsh."

For the next hour and a half the male suspects sat alone, handcuffed to their chairs, waiting for something, anything, to happen.

As soon as the police convoy had left 13 Division for Lauder Avenue, two officers were sent out to comb the neighbourhood, looking for possible specimens for a line-up. They were to find men between the ages of eighteen and thirty-five, between five feet eight inches and six feet and between 160 and 210 pounds. They were all supposed to be similarly dressed: blue jeans and T-shirts. Some were to be dirtier than others. Sergeant Paul Mullin, in charge of coordinating the line-up, made a note of each volunteer as he was brought in. A few were rejected because they were deemed not suitable, and Mullin had a slight disagreement with Staff-Sergeant Crampton over one. Mullin thought that Robert Duz, a neatly dressed man of twenty with light brown hair and blue eyes, looked so unlike the suspects that he should be excluded. Crampton pulled rank on him and Duz joined the group. Frank McEachern, a young sergeant, took off his suit jacket and tie, unbuttoned his shirt to reveal his hairy, dark chest and joined the line-up. Brian Dempsey thought this was something of a joke: McEachern wore neatly pressed dress pants and shoes that shone like any cop's. But then Dempsey thought the decoys looked nothing like him or his buddies; he was convinced that the line-up was just phony, part of the put-up job to get the Lauder gang.

At 1:37 p.m. the arrested men were brought into the conference room to mingle with the eight stand-ins. Since the room was too small for all fifteen to stand shoulder-to-shoulder, they were ordered to form a horseshoe around three sides. Staff-Sergeant Crampton told them, "Gentlemen, you are free to take any place in the line-up you wish." There was some shuffling, but after a minute the seven suspects nodded that they were satisfied. Crampton signalled to the constable at the door to bring in Terri Spudic.*

---

* A pseudonym.

There was certainly nothing unusual about her. Twenty-seven years old, five-foot-five, slim, not terribly pretty, wearing blue jeans and a navy T-shirt, she looked like any number of restless and rootless young women. There was an obvious toughness about her, however, a determination and self-confidence that made Dave Bell, for one, feel very uneasy. After she stopped in front of the men, Crampton read from a sheet of paper, "Witness, this is a line-up of fifteen people. Would you look them over carefully and should you see any person or persons whom you recognize as having participated in the offence or incident for which you are a witness, please point them out numbering from left."

Terri Spudic did not hesitate. She looked at the man furthest on the left and simply said, "Him. Number one." The man named was Richard Gillespie. Her eyes moved to the right, and in a second she said, "Number four. The small one. Him." The person she was referring to was six-foot-tall Roadside Blake. She glanced at the man standing next to Blake. "Number five," she barked. Bobby Caruso winced. She waited a few more seconds. "Number seven. Yeah," counting with her index finger, "one, two , three, four, five, six, seven." Brian Dempsey could feel his stomach turn as she pointed to him. She continued, "Number nine. That one. One, two, next to number seven. No, not that one, the other one." Crampton asked her, "Number nine?" and she replied, "Yeah, number nine." In the confusion, Beatteay thought that he had not been identified; police later informed him that he had been. After that her cadence changed somewhat; she seemed less sure of herself. After a pause she finally said, "Number twelve. The one with the beard." David Bell had been nailed. Crampton then asked her, "Is there anyone else?" and she replied, "No, I don't think so." The entire exercise, from the time Terri Spudic was brought into the room until she was escorted out, took only four minutes. She had identified six of the seven men at 402 Lauder Avenue. Only Charles Dempsey was not named. He was charged anyway.

After Spudic left the room, Staff-Sergeant Crampton called out the names of the stand-ins and asked them to leave the room. Then, looking steadily at the remaining seven men, he said in a loud and authoritative voice, "You are all under arrest on a charge of rape. Further charges of gross indecency and buggery might be forthcoming." Then he cautioned them, "You are not obliged to say anything unless you wish to do so, but whatever you say will be taken down in writing and may be given in evidence." Randy Blake would later say, "I simply couldn't believe what was happening."

Richard Gillespie, so slight and boyish in appearance that he looked more like a bookkeeper than a gang rapist, was the first person to be questioned. Since there was a warrant out for his arrest on a charge of drug dealing, he lied to the police. He used the name found on a piece of identification he had bought at the Hot Tub Club for five dollars the month before: Kenneth Kane. He was interrogated by Sergeants Mullin and McEachern.

"Name?"

"Kenneth Kane."

"Address?"

"I stay off and on at 402 Lauder Avenue...."

"You heard Staff-Sergeant Crampton advise you that you were all charged with rape, buggery and gross indecency. At the same time he also cautioned you. Did you understand the charge that he advised you?"

"Yes."

"Did you understand the caution he read out?"

"Yeah.... Hey, if he is writing everything down, I am not saying a fuckin' thing."

"You have been formally charged with a serious offence and we are obliged to record all conversation."

"Yeah."

"Do you know the girl that picked you out of the line-up as being one of the ones that raped her?"

"I raped no one. She was willing. I heard no complaints."

"Then you know her?"

"Yeah, I picked her up downtown in the Station...."

"What station?"

"The Young Station Tavern on Yonge Street."

"Okay, go ahead. Continue, but not too fast. I have to write this down."

"I bought her a couple of beers."

"The Young Station, is it a licensed tavern?"

"Yeah, it's a dandy."

"Go on."

"We went back to Brian's place, had a couple of beers, then I took her to the basement and got laid. Look, she was overjoyed."

"Then what you are telling me is that she was a willing participant and you did not rape her or bugger her or indecently assault her and you didn't keep her against her will?"

"No. She could leave anytime."

"How did you get to Brian's place?"

"Subway and bus. That's where it all started. She was all over me. It started on the bus. She was all over me, grabbed me. She could hardly wait."

"Who is Rich?" (The officer was referring to Gillespie himself, who goes by "Rich" or "Dicky.")

"That's some name I gave her."

"When you were in the basement, did anyone else come down and screw her?"

"No, I was the only one."

"What did you do when you were finished in the basement?"

"I don't know. I was wiped. I fell asleep. I was asleep until you guys came in."

"Did she give you oral sex?"

"I can't remember.... Hey, look, I said too much now. I'm not saying anymore."

"Do you want to give us a statement?"

"No."

Bobby Caruso, six feet, 225 pounds, dishevelled, dirty and bearded, was the next to be interrogated. He said he was twenty-six years old and lived on Bowsprit Avenue in suburban Etobicoke at the home of his parents. When asked if he understood the charges, he answered that he did.

"Do you want to tell us what you were doing last night?"

"I was at the Gasworks until one thirty, then I went to this guy's place. At this place I had a couple of beers. Then I went to Brian's."

"Who is Brian?"

"I don't know. He lives on Lauder with his girl friend."

"Go on with your story."

"I just went to Brian's and passed out on the kitchen table by Roadside...."

"Have you ever seen that girl before?"

"No. That is the first time I saw her, when she came in and picked us out. I have never seen her before."

"Are you sure?"

"That is the first time I saw her,"

"Did you seduce her?"

"No."

"Did you bugger her?"

"No."

Roadside Blake, six feet, 215 pounds, was then brought in. He was wearing a black felt cowboy hat, a black T-shirt with gold letters reading LAST CHANCE, and a black leather jacket. His waist-length brown hair was tied back in a ponytail. He told the police he was twenty-four years old, the youngest of the accused, and that he lived on Jeffcoat Drive in suburban Rexdale.

Sergeant Mullin asked him to reply to Spudic's accusations that he had raped, indecently assaulted and buggered her. Blake answered: "Yeah. I know her. She was at the house. I was talkin' with her about Harleys, that's all."

"Do you have a nickname?"

"Yeah, Roadside."

"How did you get such a name?"

"The bike I was riding used to break down quite a bit so I was spending most of my time at the side of the road repairing it."

"Do you want to tell us what happened last night?"

"I was sitting at the kitchen table learning how to play crib. We were drinking beer and watching TV. This guy [Gillespie] came in with that girl. She had a beer and we started talking about Harleys. After she finished her beer, she went downstairs with this guy. That's the last time I saw her until today."

"What were you doing earlier in the night?"

"We were in the Lansdowne drinking."

"Who was all with you?"

"John, Chuck, Brian and Dave."

"What time did you leave?"

"We shot some pool, then we left. I don't know. About twelve. We went to Brian's...."

"What did you do at Brian's?"

"That guy came in with this broad. We talked about Harleys. That's all I seen of them. I passed out at the table. I woke up in the morning with a sore neck. I don't need this action. I got an old lady at home who would kill me. We also have a kid."

"Did you have any type of sex with her?"

"I didn't touch her at all."

While these statements were being taken, two other 13 Division sergeants were questioning three other suspects. First up was Dave Bell. He told them that he was twenty-six years old, that he worked at Rowntree Chocolates, that he was single and had no girl friend. He said he rented the house for $500 a month and earned $800 a month but that Brian Dempsey, Chuck Dempsey and John Beatteay lived with him. Of all the suspects, police felt that slender, weak-chinned Bell was most nervous, the most frightened.

"You mentioned three other people you lived with. Were there any other people there last night?"

"I don't know why the other people were there. What the fuck is going on?"

"A lady has complained that she was raped by seven men at 402 Lauder Avenue."

"There was no way I was involved. I came home last night and went straight to bed."

"Where were you last night before you came home?"

"I was supposed to be at work two till ten, but I went to the Lansdowne tavern."

"Were you at the Lansdowne tavern by yourself?"

"Yes, when I first went down at two thirty, but the other guys came in about five past four."

"How long did you stay there?"

"I came home about midnight and went straight to bed...."

"Was there anyone named Rich with you at the Lansdowne tavern?"

"Who's Rich?"

"Didn't a girl and another guy join you at your table at the Lansdowne?"

"No, there was just the five of us."

"A female who alleged that she was raped picked you out of a line-up today as one of the men who raped her. What, if anything, do you wish to say about this?"

"I guess I will have to go to court and fight it. She knows me and in fact she was in my bed when I woke up this morning...."

"What was she doing in your bed?"

"When I woke up this morning she was lying on the other side of the bed rubbing Brian's penis...."

"Who are you referring to when you say, she?"

"The broad who picked me out of the line-up."

"Did she do anything else while she was in your bed?"

"I think she was crying."

"Do you know why she was crying?"

"Well, her face was red and her eyes too. She was upset."

"Did you rape the girl?"

"No."

"Why do you suppose she picked you out of the line-up as one of the men who raped her?"

"Well, I didn't do anything, but I don't know about the rest of the guys."

"Did you urinate on her in the little room downstairs in the basement?"

"I didn't even go down to the basement last night."

"Did you let the girl go from the house this morning?"

"No. She left by herself after she gave Brian a blow job in my bed. I got up, went downstairs and I got two beers for Brian and I. When I got back to the room she was giving the blow job and she left."

"What time was this?"

"I don't know. It was really early, I think."

"Did you have sex in any way with the girl who picked you out of the line-up?"

"No."

"Did anyone else in the house have sex with her, that you are aware of?"

"How would I know? I went to bed at midnight. I just saw her giving Brian a blow job this morning."

Brian Dempsey was the next to be questioned. He was twenty-nine, the oldest of the group, excepting his brother Chuck. At five-foot-five and 140 pounds he was the smallest in stature of the Lauder gang, but he was also the most belligerent and sarcastic towards the police. They sensed immediately that he was the leader of the gang, that whatever had occurred the previous night, he was most likely the instigator. He told the detectives that he was unemployed because of an arthritic condition and that his wife was on welfare. Brian would later say that the police significantly distorted the statement he gave them.

"A female who alleged that she was raped picked you out of a line-up today as one of the men who raped her. What, if anything, do you wish to say about this?"

"Nothing. She's a liar."

"We have received information that you committed buggery on this female. What, if anything, do you wish to say about this?"

"No way, man. I was out all night. I got home about twelve o'clock. I was at the tavern with Dave and John and Chuck...."

"Did you see a guy called Rich and the girl that identified you come into the tavern last night?"

"No, but I saw them come into the house on Lauder just after I came home...."

"What did you do after you came?"

"Sat around and watched TV. Had a couple of beers and went to bed with my old lady about two o'clock."

"Our information is that you are one of several men who took Terri down to the basement and had intercourse with her. What do you have to say..."

"Bullshit! I didn't fuck her."

"Did you have anything at all to do with Terri this morning?"

"Nothing. I already told you, nothing."

"Our information is that you were upstairs this morning and that Terri was performing oral sex on you."

"So what's wrong with a blow job?"

"Our information is that Terri was crying at the time. Do you know why she would be crying?"

"Well, some broads don't like to do it that way. Hold on. That's all I am saying. I'm getting in too deep...."

John Beatteay was the last to give a statement. At five ten, 170 pounds, with dark curly hair, John was a handsome young man — a "hunk" was how his girl friends described him. He was also the quietest member of the Lauder gang, so much so that he was often called nondescript. He told police he was born on December 19, 1953, that he was single but lived with Linda Brown, and that he worked for a general contractor.

"A female who alleged that she was raped picked you out of a line-up today as one of the men who raped her. What, if anything, do you wish to say about this?"

"She didn't pick me out."

"It may have appeared that way initially, but she did speak to another officer and it was confirmed that you were identified and took an active part in this alleged rape."

"No way, the forensic guys will tell you that."

"Where were you yesterday?"

"I went to the Lansdowne tavern with Charlie and Brian and Roadside. When we got there we met Dave Bell. We stayed there and drank beer till between eight to ten o'clock. Then we went home. We started drinking about five o'clock...."

"Did you meet anyone else at the bar?"

"No."

"Did Rich come into the bar with a female?"

"Who's Rich?"

"Well then, did Dicky come into the bar with a female?"

"Oh yeah, they didn't come in until ten fifteen [at Lauder Avenue]."

"What happened after the girl and Dicky arrived at 402 Lauder Avenue?"

"I was feeling pretty good, so I watched TV and had a few more beers."

"Did you at any time have intercourse with the girl that Dicky brought to the house at 402 Lauder Avenue?"

"No, but Dicky left with the broad for a while."

"How would you account for the fact the girl picked you out of the line-up as being one of the men who raped her at 402 Lauder?"

"She's a liar. Those forensic guys will tell you. I didn't fuck her."

"What do you know about forensic?"

"All those exhibits you guys took earlier will turn out negative."

"The allegation is that you took part in the rape down in the basement."

"No way. I don't like using that air mattress in the basement. I like to get fucked in bed."

"Did you stay up all night?"

"No. I went to bed with Linda. That broad only picked me out because she saw me in the living room."

"Do you wish to say anything else at this time?"

"I got nothing else to say."

Each man had been ordered to spit on a piece of paper to preserve a sample of his saliva. They were also ordered to pluck out hairs from their beards and pubic regions. All of this material was eventually analysed by Toronto's Centre for Forensic Sciences. They were then asked to remove another piece of evidence — their jeans. Not one of the men wore underwear. But then neither did Terri Spudic.

While the various activities that would prove so injurious to the Lauder residents were under way at the police division, Sergeant Grinnell had begun laying the foundation of his extensive investigation. Eventually he would be honoured with Toronto's Policeman of the Month Award for his effort. A painstaking search of the entire house was the first step, beginning in the small basement bedroom where Terri Spudic said she had been repeatedly raped. Grinnell's investigating eye was immediately caught by a centrefold pinup in the basement washroom. This playmate was somewhat unusual, not so much because she was particularly buxom but because her pubic hair had been styled into a shamrock. The pinup was propped up in the sink facing the shower, and it was Grinnell's contention that the men used the busty nude to arouse themselves so that they could have yet another go at Terri. Grinnell wanted the crown prosecutor, Chris Rutherford, to enter the centrefold as evidence during the trial. Rutherford, however, quickly concluded that it was irrelevant; it was hardly uncommon for the North American male to have sexual relations with a nude paper doll.

Grinnell and his assistant began to systematically collect the forensic evidence — a turquoise and red air mattress obviously stained with semen, a filthy white blanket with blue trim, a pair of blue-jeans shorts that were dripping wet — all items found in the small basement bedroom. Grinnell also noticed a pile of damp blue and white towels near the laundry tubs, and he seized them. Although he didn't realize it at the time, these would be the most important physical evidence introduced at the trial.

By this time Constable Douglas Ford from the Police Identification Bureau had arrived. It was his job to look for fingerprints on the beer bottles scattered throughout the basement.

As the afternoon progressed, Grinnell and his men found other interesting items which they thought might eventually wind up as evidence — pipes and other paraphernalia obviously used to smoke grass, and a collection of snapshots taken at various riotous parties depicting bare-breasted girls, most of whom were not very attractive, and smug-looking young men with erect penises in various gymnastic sexual poses. Prosecutor Rutherford thought these were of such amateurish quality that they revealed a pathetic naivety, and he did not use them during the trial.

Before leaving the police division that evening, Grinnell left a note outlining the case on the desk of his colleague Sergeant David Campbell, a blunt-spoken Scotsman. He knew Campbell would be greatly intrigued because a month ago another case of gang rape had shown up on the occurrence sheet and Campbell was in charge of investigating it.

As they drove past 19 Northern Place, the clubhouse of the Iron Hawgs motorcycle gang, Claudine Harply* grew animated. "That's it, Carl," she yelled, pointing to a 1974 Blue Cortina parked in the driveway. "I'm almost sure that's the car." He immediately noted the licence number.

It was May 21, 1979, Victoria Day and a holiday for Constable Carl Kaye. He and his wife had met Claudine for the first time on the weekend at a Muskoka cottage owned by a mutual friend. Claudine had told them a horrifying story: a month earlier, on April 23, she had been repeatedly beaten, raped and made to have oral sex with a gang of animal-like bikers. The police had been called but as yet had not made any arrests. It had made Kaye feel sick to his stomach, and he was determined to help Claudine find her attackers. On this day they were driving around Toronto scrutinizing the premises of various motorcycle clubs.

Kaye immediately called 13 Division and reported the details about the car and the licence plate number. He was told to drive Claudine Harply around a certain area in the west end of the city. The first thing that Harply recognized was a small grocery shop on Rogers Road. "That's it. That's where I was taken the next morning to buy cigarettes." Kaye then drove south on Lauder Avenue past number 402. The house stood out in the quiet neighbourhood, not because it was shabby, indeed it was rather pretty, but because it

---

*   A pseudonym.

was the only one whose front was painted an odd purple colour. Claudine wasn't sure if that was the place or not. "If I went around to the backyard, I'd recognize it better," she said. Constable Kaye led her down the side pathway to the backyard. As soon as she saw the awning on the second floor window, she knew that was the house where she had been repeatedly raped and assaulted for over twelve hours. She thought then that she might throw up. Kaye quickly drove back to 14 Division, exchanged the patrol car for his own, and drove her to her apartment in Scarborough.

Claudine had been watching television a few hours when Sergeant Campbell phoned her. He had been trying to get hold of her all weekend without luck; she had been at the cottage. He told her he wanted her to come to 13 Division immediately and he would send a police car to transport her there. By the time she arrived, Campbell had set up two file folders, each with twenty photos, ten on each side of the folder. "I want you to look through the photos and tell me if you recognize any of them in connection with the rape you reported." Without hesitation she said, "That's the John guy. He took me for cigarettes the next day," and pointed at the picture of John Beatteay. Five seconds went by. "This is one of the guys," she indicated Dave Bell. Without pausing she said, "That's the Mike guy." Mike was the name she said Bobby Caruso had used to introduce himself. She continued, "He rings a bell. He's one of the guys," pointing at Chuck Dempsey. "That's the Doug guy. I'm sure he looks like him." She had known Brian Dempsey by the name of Doug. There followed a slightly longer period before she said, "He's one. He looks very familiar," indicating Richard Gillespie. There was a fifteen-second pause. Then she insisted, "That's the guy that twisted my leg." She had fingered Roadside Blake. To her the lone biker in the group was the ugliest of the whole lot and she knew she could never forget his face.

It had taken Claudine only four minutes to identify all seven men, exactly the time it had taken Terri Spudic to pick out all save Charles Dempsey.

Two days later Sergeant Campbell and Claudine visited the purple-faced house and discovered the interior matched drawings Claudine had made at the police station. The broken television sets in the dining room, the crippled bicycle in the hall, the untidy, small front bedroom where she had been maltreated, were all where she said they would be. They found Caruso's filthy engineer's cap and the small loose-leaf notebook that had been either stolen from Claudine or left behind by her on the night of the rapes. On the drive back to her apartment, she told a police officer, "I'll sleep better at night knowing these guys are in jail."

Six of the accused were incarcerated in the Don Jail when the news was broken to them that they had been charged with a second rape. John Beatteay and Brian Dempsey were led into a tiny room with a small desk and only one chair, which was occupied by their lawyer, Michael Caroline. Brian squatted on his haunches and John sat on the desk while their legal counsel tried to outline the ominous significance of having the two sets of charges to face.

David Bell was the only one of the group who was not in jail. He had a very minor criminal record — theft under fifty dollars committed when he was nineteen — and his brother Jim Bell had put up the $50,000 bail. When Dave heard the news of the second charge he decided not to tell his father. It was just as well. During the preliminary inquiry in June, Andrew Bell, the principal of Hollycrest Senior Public School in Etobicoke, was devastated when he heard for the first time that two women, who had not known each other, had very similar accounts of how they had been raped and brutalized. How could his son and others possibly be innocent?

The revulsion and anguish the parents and friends of the accused men felt about the charges were reinforced by the predictably sensational news coverage. The Toronto *Sun*, in particular, played the story for all it was worth. The paper ran a story on May 17 headed, "Bikers on rape, drug charges." It read, "Nine members of a Metro motorcycle gang were arrested yesterday...," and further, "The home was the headquarters of the Last Chance motorcycle gang." Members of the motorcycle club complained bitterly that the story was entirely inaccurate, and wanted the newspaper to print a retraction. The *Sun* refused to do so. But another story, printed May 23, stated:

> Police intelligence officers said Blake is a member of the Last Chance motorcycle gang but the other six, who were earlier labelled bikers, are not known as gang members.
>
> Intelligence officers also refuted earlier police reports that a Lauder Avenue house cited in last week's incident was the headquarters of the Last Chance.

The other two Toronto papers carried the same story, although they did not give it anywhere near the prominence the colourful tabloid did. This indicated that the police must have released the erroneous information themselves.

This was only the first of many instances that proved to the Lauder Avenue men that the establishment, indeed the entire judicial system, was out to get them. What Brian Dempsey could see coming down on them was "a hammer the size of the Western sky."

TWO

The Inquiries

NOTHING BUT ANIMALS

June and July, 1979

Crown Attorney Chris Rutherford thought that neither Terri Spudic nor Claudine Harply would be ideal witnesses. He regarded them as "easy-breezy, loosey-goosey" kinds of ladies. He would have preferred someone more like his mother on the witness stand — a "blue-chip" housewife who would no more consent to group sex than she would to robbing a bank, and therefore much more believable to sceptical jurors. It had been his experience that 99 per cent of the rape victims were street girls: they liked to go to bars and sometimes pick up unsavoury characters, or they simply had boy friends who'd get a little rough. He was fond of saying that "nearly every girl that gets raped doesn't do the things the ordinary Canadian housewife does and the ordinary Canadian housewife doesn't get raped." That didn't mean that he believed Harply and Spudic hadn't been repeatedly assaulted; after a lengthy interview with each, he believed every word they said, and he set out to create an ironclad prosecution. He liked to think that his better cases were as overwhelming as an onslaught of Nazi storm troopers; he planned to give the defence no opportunity to crack his onslaught.

At thirty-three, slight of build but fairly tall, Rutherford looked like a young Jimmy Stewart, although he lacked the famous actor's most famous attribute — his soft, easygoing drawl. Rutherford clipped his words, a mannerism that reflected his precise, no-nonsence and logical approach, not only to his job but to his lifestyle generally — he was, for example, famous for the deadly accuracy of his tennis game. The 402 Lauder Avenue gang referred to him as "The Cobra," and hissed at him whenever he approached. But the sharp, young criminal minds in the city considered that he was one of the very few prosecutors who was a worthy adversary. And his legal talents were recognized among his superiors as well.

In 1976 Ontario Attorney General Roy McMurtry had decided that something had to be done about rape victims: they often suffered as much abuse during their day in court as they did from the crime. McMurtry's solution was to assign either female or more mature and sensitive male Crown attorneys to specific rape cases. The designated prosecutor would stick with the case as it wove its way through the legal maze, advising the complainant of her legal rights and protecting her from the worst abuses of aggressive defence lawyers. As Rutherford had been one of eight Crown attorneys in Ontario chosen for this job, he was contacted by Sergeant Grinnell the moment the residents of 402 Lauder were formally charged.

It didn't take Rutherford very long to form an opinion about the accused: to him they were "nothing but animals," "sheer garbage," "out and out scum." He expected they would fabricate an intricate story in their defence, "a patchwork of lies" as he would put it, and he was determined to cut holes in it so large that it would unravel into a heap of nothing. His most important task in preparation for this was the rehearsal of his two prime witnesses.

Before the preliminary inquiries, he spent hours with Spudic and Harply in separate fatiguing sessions. He encouraged them to go over their stories again and again, hoping that the details would sink so deep into their minds that no badgering or trickery or even skilful cross-examination by the defence counsel would cause them to become muddled. They were to be very specific and were to use clinical, court-approved language. Claudine would say to him, "so and so raped me," and he would firmly reply, "No, Claudine, what is it I told you to say?" "Oh, yes," she would remember, "so and so took his penis and put it in my vagina. He then moved it around and ejaculated inside me." Rutherford quickly discovered that Harply had an incredible memory: once her story got thoroughly implanted, she rarely varied from the smallest detail. Spudic had more trouble with the language; she tended to use street talk — "butt" for posterior, "prick" for penis, "give face" for oral sex — but by the time the preliminary inquiry began, she had pretty well been cured of that habit. She could remember the first dozen or so occasions of brutality; after that, events and faces meshed into one horrific experience. Rutherford decided that rather than have her fumble with her evidence, she would frankly admit she couldn't remember specific details of what had happened after the first couple of hours. Anyway, for the time she could recall, she had identified all of the accused but Charles Dempsey as individuals who had forced her, against her will, to perform numerous vaginal and oral sexual acts.

Even though six of the seven had not been granted bail and were incarcerated first in Toronto's Don Jail and then in the East Detention Centre, before the preliminary inquiries many of the Lauder gang had no idea of the seriousness of their predicament. There was not as much thought and discussion about whom to select as their legal counsel as they later realized there should have been. Since all had either nonexistent or low incomes and virtually no assets, they were readily granted legal aid certificates. They could have chosen from Toronto's large coterie of experienced, big-name lawyers, most of whom were quite willing to take legal aid cases, but instead they named lawyers who had served them when they'd been involved in much lesser crimes in the past, or on some friend's recommendation, or by simply picking names from a list provided by the authorities. Harry Doan, for example, often represented members of the Last Chance Motorcycle Club, so naturally Randy Blake called on him. Randy's brother Dennis says Doan told him that Randy's alibi was airtight, at least in regard to one set of charges, and that he'd have him on the street in no time. This optimistic message was relayed to Roady's parents, Ruby and Bill Blake, so they considered that this was just another silly pickle their boisterous, but much beloved, middle son had gotten himself into. They thought a few months in jail might teach him a lesson and force him to grow up a little.

The Bells felt the same way — this was an embarrassing problem that would somehow sort itself out. David's father had not been allowed to put up the bail of $50,000 — the court insisted that it be someone more detached — so his older brother Jim had put forth his cottage as surety and had taken David under his wing. Jim and his wife owned a spacious house on the shores of Lake Ontario, and that's where Dave went to wait for the preliminary. The elder brother, however, was not very sympathetic about Dave's troubles. The previous summer Jim had dropped into his parents' lovely suburban home while they were on vacation and discovered a smashed David and stoned friends and their chaos at four in the afternoon after what looked like a twenty-four-hour booze and drugs party. Jim was mighty upset by this and had developed a deep antipathy to David's friends, including the 402 Lauder crowd. He told David after the rape charges had been laid, "Okay, look, we're going to get you out of this mess. No problem. But you're going to start to take instructions. It's no more 'I can handle my life and travel around and listen to the birds and become a rock star.' You're going to have to settle in." Very little time went by, however, before David began ignoring the curfews imposed by the court and staying out all night. Jim Bell even considered turning him over to the cops.

But there were those among the accused who realized what a dreadful jam they were in. Once the six accused were transferred to the Detention Centre, there was more opportunity to talk about their predicament. But Caruso and Blake tended to hang around together, the Dempsey brothers and John Beatteay formed a clique, while Richard Gillespie, as usual, purposely remained aloof. Very early on, Chuck pleaded with his brother and the others to tell the truth even though that meant forcing one of the group to take the blame. He had never like Caruso — he thought that he was "crude and ignorant" — and he was convinced that Caruso's actions had landed them in the mess they were in. His idea was not that they should squeal on Bobby to the authorities — he knew that he and the others wouldn't last long in the prison system once they were labelled informers. Chuck wanted the other five to somehow force Bobby to confess that he was the lone perpetrator of the crimes of which they were all accused. His pleas were ignored. As leader of the pack, Brian's word was law and he argued that they should all stick together. Chuck and John went along, although somewhat reluctantly.

The windows in the door of room number 305 of Toronto's Metro North Court were covered with brown paper in preparation for the first preliminary inquiry, which began on a sunny June 11, 1979, with Terri Spudic's evidence. Rutherford argued before Judge Charles Lewis that the public should be entirely excluded from the courtroom. He had known of other cases in which the rape victims had been so intimidated in court that they had either clammed up altogether or were thrown so off base that their testimony was rendered unbelievable. He was determined that "his girls" would not be harassed. Judge Lewis quickly ruled that such extreme measures were not necessary, and the paper was torn off the windows. It soon became apparent, however, that Rutherford had every reason to be worried. According to Brian and Roadside, the accused had managed to get their hands on some rather strong marijuana and hash — it had been smuggled into the Detention Centre disguised as a package of Player's Mild — and they were smashed throughout most of the proceedings. Any inhibitions they might have had were quickly dissipated, and Brian Dempsey in particular felt free to make outlandish facial and bodily gestures as Spudic told her story.

Just before noon on the first day, Terri was describing how as Brian Dempsey was attempting to sodomize her, she bit John

Beatteay's penis, which had been thrust into her mouth. Suddenly she blanched and said to the judge, "Your honour, could you have the two gentlemen at the back removed. I don't like being laughed at." Judge Lewis immediately ordered the men out of the courtroom. He then declared it was lunch time. Sergeant Grinnell approached Spudic and was about to warn her not to say anything about her evidence during the break, when she tearfully interrupted him. "I can't keep my story straight when those assholes keep making crazy faces at me," she complained. She was referring to both the accused and the courtroom spectators. Sergeant Grinnell told her to keep calm, to eat her ham sandwiches and he would relay her fears to Rutherford. Spudic was somewhat comforted. But as she was returning to the courtroom, she was accosted by the two individuals who had harassed her earlier. They were obviously bikers. (The Lauder gang claimed they didn't know who they were; it was assumed that they might have had some connection with Blake's motorcycle club.) "We've got your number, bitch!" one of them growled at her. "Say hello to George [Terri's former biker common-law husband] for us," laughed the other. Terrified, Spudic took refuge in a small office. Rutherford ordered the police to search the courthouse for the men but they had already fled. By two o'clock, however, Terri had recovered enough to continue her story. Terri Spudic had been working as a bartender in Ridout's Bar and Tavern in Houma, Louisiana, south-west of New Orleans. She had split up with a boy friend she had been particularly fond of, and to get her mind off things, she decided to pay a visit to Toronto, the city of her birth.

She managed to get a lift with a trucker friend for a short distance, from New Orleans to Bayou La Batre, Alabama. She hitchhiked the remaining 1,250 miles (2,000 kilometres). Her luggage consisted of a knapsack packed with two pairs of jeans and several T-shirts and a wallet containing a hundred dollars. She did not recollect the exact date she arrived in Toronto, although she thought it was likely the last week in April, 1979. She had been dropped off at Highway 401 and Warden Avenue, and phoned her old friend Marty Leibowitz,* who lived in suburban Agincourt. He picked her up, but since he lived with his parents, she suggested that she stay with Peter and Donna Nikolopolous.* Peter was the brother of George with whom Terri had lived for five years, and she felt the Nikolopolouses were like her family. But when she arrived unannounced at the door, she was hardly welcomed with open arms. The couple lived with their two young children in a small,

*A pseudonym.

two-bedroom apartment and they didn't relish an uninvited guest bedding down on their chesterfield. Not only that, Peter had never liked Terri; he thought she was insensitive and rather dumb.

Spudic was allowed to stay anyway on the understanding that she would quickly look for a job and other accommodation. After several weeks went by and she had given no sign of vacating the Nikolopolous couch, Peter couldn't stand the situation any longer. He ordered his wife to give Terri her marching papers. Donna did so.

According to Terri's testimony, the day of May 15 began with her getting up just after seven, a very early hour for her. She took the bus and streetcar to the federal government's Manpower and Immigration Employment Centre on Dundas Street in the city's downtown and registered there. At ten o'clock she kept an appointment with the personnel manager of Filter Queen vacuum cleaners, hoping she would be hired on as a salesperson. After that she went to another employment centre in Scarborough where she was already registered. None of this activity resulted in any job prospects and by noon she was thoroughly frustrated with looking. She went back downtown, had a corned beef sandwich at a deli on Yonge Street and then wandered through an underground mall where she bought a plant and some incense for the Nikolopolouses. She said she made the forty-five-minute trip back to their Scarborough apartment, dropped the gifts off and set off for the heart of the city once again.

Since she never wore a wristwatch, Terri didn't know when she arrived on Yonge Street, but she thought it was late afternoon. She had half-heartedly watched from the streetcar window for room for rent signs in the houses she passed, had written a few phone numbers down but had then decided to give up hunting for the moment. She was lonely for her boy friend, homesick for her friends at Ridout's Tavern, which might have been why she dropped into the Café New Orleans. She ordered a coffee and pulled out from her knapsack a book entitled *A Fire Power*, a rather sensational look at international terrorists and mercenaries complete with grisly pictures of Angolan natives with their heads blown off. It wasn't long, however, before she felt restless again. At about seven o'clock she headed for the Young Station Tavern.

The Young Station was the kind of place where Terri would feel comfortable. She had been there many times in the past, both on this trip and when she had visited the city before. Mostly she liked the music — some very good rock bands played there, Rush, Moxy, Max Webster — and she liked the cheap beer. She sat at the rear of the cavernous tavern near the jukebox and ordered two drafts. She sipped on the beer and thought sadly about how her former boy friend had ditched her. After about half an hour she noticed an attractive, well-dressed dude coming towards her. Richard Gillespie asked if he could sit down. She replied, "Sure."

Terri recalled for the court that he introduced himself as Rich, she told him her name was Terri, and they quickly discovered they had a love of music in common. "My husband Eric was in a rock band," she said. "He was a percussionist. We used to travel all over the States, doing gigs here and there. I was kind of like his manager." Rich replied that that was interesting because he was a composer of rock and roll music. They talked for about forty-five minutes, then he asked her if she'd like to go to the upstairs bar because he had friends there and after seven thirty the beer was cheaper. The conversation was just as pleasant and friendly there. Terri thought that Rich was real nice, a polite, sweet guy who was probably a student or something like that. They chatted with some acquaintances of Rich's for twenty or so minutes, then he made a phone call to a woman. He asked Terri if she would like to go to yet another bar because he had friends there and he wanted to sell them some music. She agreed and they took a subway and then a streetcar, arriving half an hour later at the Lansdowne hotel in the run-down Lansdowne and Dundas area. By that time the Lansdowne, a gloomy, soiled place, was pretty well deserted; none of Rich's friends were there. He made another phone call and then asked her if she'd like to come back to his place. He didn't live far and he wanted to show her some of his music. She asked him at once, "Would anybody else be there?" He replied that he lived alone. That satisfied Terri and she agreed to go.

They walked to 402 Lauder, which was Richard's "place" only insofar as he had stayed there once, two nights before. Gillespie let himself in with a key, and the moment the door was open Terri could hear loud laughing and chatting. "I thought you were living alone?" she asked. "It might be my brother and some friends" was the reply. "I didn't know you had a brother." "Yeah, I have." In the back of her mind, Terri realized that her companion had lied to her about his living arrangements, but she let it go with a shrug; later she would regret not paying attention to the warning sign.

Five or six young men were sitting around the kitchen table drinking beer when Rich and Terri walked into the dining room. Rich introduced her to everybody but nobody got up to offer her a chair. After Terri had stood there awkwardly for about five minutes, Rich finally asked, "Want a beer?" She replied, "Sure," and he told her to get herself one from the refrigerator. While she was in the kitchen, she saw two women preparing something to eat. She noticed that one of them was about seven months pregnant. Spudic nodded to them but said nothing.

Terri was dressed in a pair of faded Lee jeans and a navy blue T-shirt. On the front, white letters spelled out SARASOTA FLORIDA and on the back UNAUTHORIZED HARLEY-DAVIDSON DEALER. "Hey, where'd you get that T-shirt?" asked Bobby Caruso. Terri told him a friend of hers was a dealer in Florida and had given it to her six weeks before. They got onto the topic of New Orleans. "Ain't the pigs on strike there?" "Yeah," she replied, "it's like Mardi Gras all the time." Dave Bell was playing his guitar, but he noticed that she had a thick southern accent.

Terri told the court that after she had finished her Molson, Gillespie asked her if she would like to look at some music that he had written. "It's in my room. Come on down." Spudic followed Gillespie through the kitchen and down the cellar stairs. They were walking diagonally across the recreation room towards a smaller room when she heard scraping and shuffling upstairs. She didn't think anything of it because she thought the guys were getting ready to go home. But just as she and Gillespie reached the entrance to the bedroom "alarm bells began to go off." She heard what sounded like a herd of buffalo thumping down the stairs.

Spudic then told the court her version of the events, on which the charges were based.

Gillespie made the first move. He grabbed her by her left arm and yanked her into the little room. When she struggled to free herself, he got hold of the other arm and pulled her onto a dirty turquoise-coloured air mattress. He fell as she did. "Take your fuckin' clothes off or we'll rip them off," barked Brian Dempsey. Bobby Caruso grabbed her hair and jerked her backwards at the same time that David Bell and Dempsey began pulling off first her boots and then her jeans. By this time she was yelling, "What the fuck are you doing? Leave me alone! Leave me alone!"

Perhaps because she was his "find," Gillespie was the first to forcibly enter her vagina. At the same time Caruso was thrusting his penis into her mouth and when she wouldn't open it, he pulled her hair hard. Finally she did what he wanted. He ejaculated and said, "Now swallow it." The others were sitting and standing around watching, in varying degrees of undress.

Her next memory was of skinny David Bell walking into the small room — naked. He walked towards her head and Caruso again ordered her to open her mouth. "You love to give head, don't you, bitch," he said. She again refused and he put his knee on her throat and began to apply pressure. Soon she was seeing stars and gasping for breath. She had no choice but to obey Caruso's orders and Dave Bell entered her mouth. He climaxed.

Bobby said he was tired and was going upstairs for a beer. Meanwhile John Beatteay was having vaginal sex with her but when Bell finished, he moved to her mouth.

Caruso came back with beer for the guys and then forced sexual intercourse on Terri once again. "Jesus, you're a real girl, ain't you? You and me got to go for one hell of a weekend sometime, eh babe?" he said. Just after Brian Dempsey gleefully yelled, "Let's butt-fuck her," Blake and Bell obligingly turned her over. But Beatteay's penis was still in her mouth and when Dempsey tried to sodomize her, she felt incredible pain. She started screaming "and biting John Beatteay's prick." Brian stopped and forced vaginal intercourse on her instead. She was still lying face down.

By this time Roadside Blake had also taken his pants off. After Beatteay was finished, he forced his penis into her mouth and ejaculated.

Terri continued to describe to the court how over the next three hours she had her mouth attacked another ten to fifteen times. Caruso had sexual intercourse with her vaginally but before he finished he ejaculated into her face. At another point in the long hours of the night, he urinated on her stomach.

Spudic drifted off for a short time during this terrifying round robin of rape only to wake to two new faces. One was tall and had long brown hair and the other was shorter with curly brown hair. The taller one raped her and the shorter one forced her to have oral sex. Neither man was identified or prosecuted. After they left, Blake and Dempsey had another go at her. Brian finally fell asleep on the floor beside the mattress and Terri lapsed into a kind of trance. "I wasn't awake and I wasn't asleep, I was in a kind of state of numbness." She did, however, eventually fall into a deep slumber. When she woke, Dempsey was no longer beside her. Terri didn't have a stitch on — she thought that Brian Dempsey had taken her clothes, and naked she set out to find them. She tiptoed over Roadside Blake, who had passed out on the basement floor, walked up the stairs, through the kitchen area and into the dining room. Gillespie was lying across three kitchen chairs sleeping, and her clothing was piled underneath. She dressed as quickly and quietly as she was able — her entire body ached with pain. She put on her jeans, socks, boots and then noticed that her T-shirt was sopping wet. She slipped it over her head anyway. She grabbed her knapsack and headed for the front door. Just as she was going out, she turned her head. She saw David Bell standing at the top of the stairwell, staring down at her. He made no move to stop her.

Spudic ended her testimony by saying that once she was outside the house, she discovered that the only money she had in the world, forty dollars, had been stolen from the wallet she kept in the knapsack.

After two and a half days of Spudic's testimony, Judge Lewis committed all the men except Charles Dempsey to trial on charges of rape and gross indecency and three of the accused, Brian Dempsey, David Bell and Roadside Blake, of attempted buggery. All six elected to be tried by Supreme Court judge and jury.

By the time it was Claudine Harply's turn to tell her story at a second preliminary hearing held before Judge Lewis a month later, the accused had been reprimanded by their lawyers and strictly forbidden to pull any antics in the courtroom. So it was not so much her attackers with whom Harply had to contend but the women who had lived at 402 Lauder. Jean Elgar and Linda Brown were sticking by their men — no question of that. The two thought it was hilarious when Claudine pointed at them in court, indicating that they were both at the house during the entire time she was being molested. They were particularly amused when she described how she had stood naked, her dignity protected only by a small blanket, before Linda Brown, and had pleaded with her for help. Judge Lewis finally grew impatient with the display. "I am growing rather tired, particularly of you young lady on the left [referring to Linda Brown], of your responses to some of the evidence and your facial expressions when looking over at the accused and at this witness. I do not intend to tolerate it...." He ordered them to either stop or get out of the courtroom. He then asked Claudine to continue with her evidence. Her account of the events follows.

Weeks before, she had made plans with a friend, Mark Dorset,* to attend a concert at Maple Leaf Gardens featuring the Village People, who, as one critic put it, were "disco's answer to the Bowery Boys." Their first hit was *Macho Man*. The date meant a lot to Harply. Her life for the last year and a half consisted of one upheaval after another, most significantly the breakup of her marriage and what she considered was the kidnapping of her children by her husband. She was finally set up in a pleasant one-bedroom apartment in Scarborough, but she was still short of money and often very lonely. On this particular day, Monday, April 23, she was dying to get out.

She had woken up early, taken a Valium to calm her nerves, cleaned up the apartment a little and then had a sandwich for lunch. She decided at about one o'clock that she had better go out looking for a job. Thinking she would likely stay downtown for the concert, she put on a grey, pin-striped suit with vest, jacket and slacks, a smart white blouse and black high-heel shoes. She took a bus and

*A pseudonym.

subway downtown. She wandered into seven or eight shops — a shoe store, a restaurant, an office supplier — and asked them if they needed any help. The response was always negative, although she was asked to fill out a couple of application forms. By four thirty she was frustrated with job hunting and walked up to the Gasworks Tavern.

Claudine was a regular there. In the past year she had dropped in dozens of times and she knew lots of people. She felt quite comfortable sitting down by herself at one of the large round tables at the front. She ordered a draft and drank alone for about half an hour. She had noticed two men, Stuart Grady and a fellow known to everybody only as Igor, sitting behind her — she had seen them there before — so when they asked her to join their table, she was quite willing. Stuart and Igor worked for CPI (Concert Production International), the outfit responsible for organizing the Village People concert that evening, and they talked about the group's music. As time went on, more and more people joined the table, until at one point there were nine in the circle. Two of the group were Bobby Caruso and Brian Dempsey. Harply remembered that Caruso introduced himself to her as "Mike" and Dempsey as "Doug." She had not met either of them before.

Harply was beginning to get worried. Her friend Mark Dorset had the tickets and she had phoned him at home a number of times because she wanted him to meet her at the Gasworks rather than Maple Leaf Gardens. There was no answer. At six thirty she finally reached him but he had bad news. His car had broken down, and since he lived in Whitby, he told her he wouldn't be able to make the concert. Claudine was terribly disappointed, and when she returned to the table, she revealed her feelings to Igor. "That's a Goddamn shame," he remarked sarcastically. By this time Igor was very drunk and turned belligerent and nasty towards Claudine. He spat at her and called her a "douche bag." She sat for a few moments stunned, but when he kicked at her chair and told her to "get the fuck away," she moved to another table.

Claudine told the court she was talking with a female friend when Bobby Caruso came over. "I apologize for that Igor," he said. "He gets drunk quite a bit and whatever he says I am sure if you meet the guy tomorrow he probably wouldn't remember." Harply responded, "It's okay." Bobby sat down and after they had chatted for a while he said, "You must be real upset not getting to see the Village People." Claudine replied that she was. "How'd you like it if I took you? Igor's working the concert tonight, on security, and he says he can get us in." Claudine answered that she'd think about it. About then Brian Dempsey came over and joined the group, and everybody at the table talked for another fifteen minutes. Bobby asked Claudine again if she'd go with him and this time she agreed.

Caruso said that he had to drive Dempsey home first and anyway he wanted to pick up a couple of "J"s for the concert. The three left in Bobby's battered Corvette at about a quarter past seven. Claudine recalled that they immediately pulled out a joint. Claudine who was sitting in the front seat between the two men, passed it back and forth but didn't touch it herself. At one point during the twenty-minute drive, Caruso said to Brian, "Think I'll go to Wasaga Beach tomorrow and take a look at a Harley hawg that's for sale. Wanna come?" Brian responded, "Can't. I promised my old lady we'd go for a picnic."

They stopped at the beer store to pick up a case of heavy-duty Brador. When they arrived at 402 Lauder Avenue, Brian asked Claudine, "Wanna come in for a beer?" Caruso added, "I gotta roll the joints anyway." "Okay," said Harply, "but it's getting late and the concert starts at eight." "We won't be long," responded Caruso.

David Bell and John Beatteay were sitting at the table in the dining room playing cribbage. Claudine said hello and sat down to watch them. "Who's winning?" she asked. She was something of a card shark herself — she could play euchre almost as well as billiards and she was known for her ability with a pool cue — and so she watched the proceedings with interest. Harply had noticed two women walking around but they weren't introduced and neither said anything, although one did fetch her a beer. Caruso and David Bell both rolled a couple of joints. After about twenty minutes, Claudine said to Bobby, "We'd better get going soon. It's getting late and we don't want to miss the concert." Caruso replied, "Okay, let's go."

As the two walked down the hall, Caruso in front, Harply behind, Brian Dempsey and John Beatteay followed them. Claudine thought they were being polite and saying goodbye. She testified that suddenly she was grabbed from behind and pushed into a small bedroom at the front of the house. As she screamed "What the hell are you doing? Stop it!" she was flung onto the bed and all three — Brian Dempsey, Beatteay and Caruso — started to strip her. Crying and pleading with them to stop, she tried to fight them off. "I like the ones that struggle," yelled Brian Dempsey. With his open hand Beatteay smacked her repeatedly on her head and face. Caruso also smacked her and then put his fingers and thumbs around her neck and squeezed. At that point the room started to spin.

What followed was an ordeal as terrifying as the one Terri Spudic would undergo. Claudine would later say that she felt as though she had been assailed by a pack of starving wolves. Over a period of five to six hours, she was repeatedly and continuously molested and humiliated. Brian Dempsey, Beatteay and Caruso all raped her and then made her perform oral sex. Someone she couldn't identify tried to bugger her. Someone else poured beer all over her face and body. There was such a precision to the attacks, one after another, that Harply was reminded of a macabre choreography, and she thought they must be well practised in their routine.

Dave Bell eventually entered the fray. He was forcing vaginal intercourse on Harply when the others left the room to greet some visitors. Another five men, all laughing and talking, came into the room. Of these Claudine could later only identify Roadside Blake. "We should take her to the clubhouse," yelled one. "We should go get Igor," laughed another. By this time Roadside Blake had come up to her head and tried to put his penis in her mouth. When she refused he grabbed her and smacked her around the head a few times. Then he tried to climb on top of her. As Harply described it, "I crossed my legs and he grabbed ahold of my right leg and twisted it right around. I screamed in pain." From that point on she periodically blacked out.

At one point during the night of horror she was left alone and attempted to escape. She ran naked to the front door but was unable to free the chain lock. The three German Shepherd dogs, growling and barking, had encircled her, and Brian Dempsey came running out of the dining room. He threw her on the floor, hit her with his fist and pushed her back into the small bedroom.

Finally Caruso, Brian Dempsey, Beatteay and Bell dragged Claudine out of the bedroom. At the bottom of the staircase, she spotted Linda Brown. Crying, she begged her, "Can't you do anything about this. Can't you stop this?" Linda said not a word; she simply looked through her. As Claudine was led up the staircase, her injured leg caused her so much pain that she had to hold on to the bannister and pull herself up, stair by stair.

The group assembled in a small shoddy room upstairs which Dave Bell used to sleep in whenever he stayed at Lauder Avenue. A worn mattress on the floor and a broken chair were the only pieces of furniture. Bell was playing guitar and everybody else was singing — including Claudine Harply. She told the court she was so terrified that she thought she had better join in the party or the men might get angry and start assaulting her again. She drank somewhere between two and four beers and sang "I Wanna Be a Cowboy." Finally Caruso broke things up. "I gotta get up early, you guys, to get my bike from Wasaga Beach. So beat it please." Caruso went to sleep while Harply lay beside him. She tried hard not to doze off herself, frightened that they might come back and start all over.

Dave Bell came in and lay down on the bed next to her. He apologized. "I'm not a biker myself but you know the way bikers are." Claudine asked him, "Would they do it again?" "Well, if they come near you again, pretend that you're sleeping and they'll go away," he replied. At that moment she heard Beatteay and Brian Dempsey coming up the stairs. One of them poked his head in the door and said, "Don't they look cute." They went downstairs and Bell followed them. Finally Claudine passed out.

Claudine testified that the next thing she remembered was hearing a lot of noise in the backyard — guitar playing, singing and yelling. Caruso had his head out the window, it was already daylight, and he yelled, "Hey, you guys would wake the fuckin' dead. You want the cops here?" Brian Dempsey yelled up, "They've already been here." Then added, "You're a party-pooper, Caruso." Bobby said, "Aw shit!" and pulled his head back in. Claudine asked Caruso if he would go downstairs and get her clothes. He did.

She was dying for a cigarette. Charlie Dempsey, who hadn't had any part in the previous night's sexual shenanigans, Bell, Beatteay, Brian Dempsey and Caruso were all sitting around the kitchen table, drinking beer, but not one of them had a smoke. "Can I go to the store for some then?" she asked. "Yeah, but you have to have a bath first," declared Brian. Claudine said she badly needed a cigarette and that she wanted to go for a package first. "No," insisted Brian. "We want you to have a bath first. We don't want any evidence around." He ordered John Beatteay to run the water. When the bath was ready, John went upstairs with Harply and watched as she washed her genitalia with a washcloth, something Dempsey demanded that she do. When she was dressed, she was told that Beatteay would walk to the store with her.

Harply testified that her injured leg still pained her terribly. "If you don't stop that limping," Beatteay said, "I'm going to slap you." "Haven't you done enough to me already?" responded Harply. "You're lucky," John replied. "Most of the girls that have been at the house have gone away in a lot worse shape than you're in."

They bought several packages of cigarettes from a nearby variety shop; two elderly Chinese men waited on them. Claudine noticed at that point that the money — about ten dollars — she had had in her purse was gone. Her apartment keys and appointment book were missing as well. It dawned on her that her address was on the front cover; the men would know exactly where she lived.

Claudine dreaded the thought of going back into the Lauder house and so when she saw Caruso getting into his car, she asked if he would give her a lift. He dropped her off at the St. Clair West subway station. She told him she didn't have any money for subway fare and he gave her two dollars. As she was getting out of the car, he asked if he could phone her sometime. She gave him her correct number and he wrote it on a case of empties in the back seat of the car. "I don't know why I did that," Claudine told the court. "I was really scared. I didn't know if he was going to take me home or take me to the subway or take me to some field and kill me so I wouldn't say anything. I really don't know." So ended Harply's version of the events of April 23 and 24.

Once again Judge Lewis considered that there was enough evidence to send the accused on to trial. Caruso, Beatteay, Blake, Charles and Brian Dempsey, Gillespie and Bell were all committed on charges of gross indecency and rape. This time they elected to be tried by county court judge and jury. Interestingly, afterwards Judge Lewis told one of the defence counsel that on the basis of what he heard, and at this point he did not have access to forensic evidence or the testimony of other witnesses, he did not believe either Spudic or Harply. But it was not for him to decide whether the two women were lying; that would be left to the jury.

The defence counsel, on the other hand, all agreed that the women had been surprisingly strong witnesses. They had not broken down under often tough and repetitious cross-examination, and they had been precise and detailed in their accounts of what they claimed had gone on. Still, a number of illogicalities and inconsistencies had surfaced during their testimonies, so much so that the lawyers thought that the accused had at least a fighting chance to convince juries that they were innocent. Chris Rutherford, however, had already worked out a ploy that would pretty well eliminate any chance of that. From the moment he had looked at the police fact sheets, he had decided that Harply's and Spudic's evidence was so similar — the behaviour described so "animal-like" in each incident — that the two cases warranted one trial. Nothing could have been more devastating for the accused.

THREE

The Gang's Story

A HELL OF A PARTY

I t was Chris Rutherford's experience that it was more difficult to get a conviction on a rape charge than almost any other crime; jurors were loath to bring forth a guilty verdict unless the evidence was absolutely solid and straightforward, "staring them in the face," as he put it. The reasons for this were as complicated and profound as societal attitudes about sex itself. On one level a rape case often involved one person's word against another's, and naturally such a situation could provoke "reasonable doubt" in many jurors' minds. As well, the Criminal Code specified that life sentences could be handed out for rape, and while the punishment usually was nowhere near as severe as that, the threat sometimes played a part in a jury's determination. On another level, rape cases often revealed an illogical, dated and even mythical understanding of woman's role in the mating game. Wasn't a woman who hitchhiked twelve hundred miles asking for trouble? What was she doing in a bar like the Gasworks? Why did she go back to a strange man's house? It was the old equation: a promiscuous woman was an untrustworthy, unethical one. Rutherford could foresee what would have happened if separate trials were held involving the accusations of first Spudic and then Harply. He reasoned, "If the jury had listened to each girl individually, they may have concluded that either she was a street type who liked this sort of thing or else she was embellishing her story." Jurors might well have given the accused the benefit of the doubt. But two women who didn't know each other from Adam, relating individual tales of horror in which the details were so similar as to be uncanny — that was another matter. How could any jury *not* believe them?

The Lauder group were unaware of Rutherford's intentions to prosecute the two sets of charges together until they appeared before Mr. Justice J. G. O'Driscoll of the Ontario Supreme Court on August 23, 1979. This hearing, held months before the actual trial, was requested by the Crown attorney to rectify a situation that had occurred at the preliminary inquiries. Before each, the accused had been asked in what manner they elected to be tried. Their lawyers advised them thus: in the case of Harply, they had chosen judge and jury in the county court; in the case of Spudic, judge and jury in the Supreme Court. That meant, of course, that there would have to be two trials. Rutherford was now asking Mr. Justice O'Driscoll to ignore the expressed wishes of the accused and rule that the Crown may prefer an indictment in which both cases would be tried in the Supreme Court of Ontario.

For years serious charges such as manslaughter and rape could only be heard in the superior court in Canada. But in 1972 Parliament amended the Criminal Code to allow certain of these crimes to be tried in lower courts. The reason was a purely practical one: in rural areas the Supreme Court assizes might be scheduled for some time in the future and the accused could languish in jail if he hadn't got bail. Even if he was at large, the charge could hang over his head for months. A trial in the county court was usually more readily available.

During the hearing before Mr. Justice O'Driscoll, the defence counsel for the Lauder group argued that whatever the intent of the amendment, section 429.1 of the Criminal Code clearly gave the right to the accused to choose which court he wanted to be tried in and this choice did not depend on the consent or acquiescence of the Crown attorney.

Rutherford countered that that was not Parliament's intention at all. The amended section was meant to enlarge, rather than diminish, the Crown's choice. He argued that once the mode of trial had been decided, that is judge alone or judge and jury, then the prosecutor, if he deemed it practical, could attempt to get the accused's consent to have his trial heard in lower court. If he refused, then it would take place in the Supreme Court. The section, he said, was never meant to be used in the manner the defence counsel was attempting to use it.

Mr. Justice O'Driscoll ruled on October 2 that the Crown did not even need a judge's consent or a court order to prefer the indictment in the Supreme Court; the Criminal Code already gave him that right.

By this time, of course, the Lauder Avenue gang knew that they were in truly serious trouble. Their lawyers realized it even more, and making a deal with Chris Rutherford became the top priority. Rutherford was still uneasy about the case, simply because juries were notoriously unpredictable when it came to the crime of rape. If he could get one of the Lauder gang to squeal, then their defence would come tumbling down like a house of cards. The trial would be a much shorter one, with less stress and strain on Spudic and Harply. And more important, the outcome would be entirely predictable. For several months there was much chatter between Rutherford and the defence lawyers, often without the knowledge of the accused.

Dave Bell seemed to be the logical one to spin off from the group; he was a nice, middle-class young man from a highly respectable family, with almost no criminal record. Since he was out on bail, it was thought that his loyalty to the group might weaken; at any rate he himself had never felt a truly integral part of the Lauder gang. His lawyer, Mike McLachlan, held long and serious discussions with Rutherford, and a sentence of three to five years was discussed. Now and then Dave thought about testifying against his cohorts, but in the end he did not seriously consider it. Even though he had never been in prison before, he knew what it meant to be an informer. A sentence of three years wasn't much good if you didn't live to be paroled.

John Beatteay's counsel, André Dempsey, managed to negotiate a three-year term for his client if he would only turn informer. But quiet John, who was as close as a brother to Brian Dempsey, did not even give the offer serious consideration.

The lawyers for Roadside Blake and Bobby Caruso spent a lot of time coaxing their clients. They told them, "Come on, boys, quit being stupid. Admit it! She's just had too many things done to her for it to be one person. If it was a party then say so, 'Sure I did it. I see everybody getting it so I jumped in too.' Then we could go and make a deal for you." Blake and Caruso refused to even discuss it.

Marshall Sack formed an impression about his client Richard Gillespie that has stayed with him to this day: Dicky was only peripherally involved. He said to him, "You were like a small dog playing with a little cat, when all of a sudden the hounds came bounding down and tore the cat apart." The only thing Richard would say in reply was, "I have to live in a cell with those guys, you don't."

The lawyers might as well have been talking to a granite wall as thick as any prison's. Each member of the group refused to vary the least little bit from the story that was to form the common defence for all six. There were variations — some had alibis, some said they had sexual intercourse but that it was consensual, some said they were there but had nothing to do with the women in question — but these were different-coloured threads woven through the same tapestry. Each one's evidence overlapped and reinforced the others'; the umbrella defence remained intact, covering all of the accused throughout the trial.

The reasons for their allegiance were not obscure. They all knew of the terrible danger of being labelled an informer by fellow convicts. More important, none would shatter the solidarity of the brotherhood. These men had partied together, had drunk together and had fornicated together. Together they fuelled the common, obsessive dream of becoming famous and rich show biz personalities, stroking each other's sense of importance, assuring each other of their extraordinary musical talents. All adhered to a philosophy that was fundamentally antisocial, and they used the system expertly: some sponged off welfare, or lived rent free while the landlord fought their delinquency in court, or bought the luxuries of life with stolen credit cards. They contributed almost nothing in return — except maybe one day, they reasoned, the gift of their musical genius. Like a herd of shaggy bison inwardly turned with their backs to the storm, these men sought protection in the company of each other, not only from the criticism of next door neighbours but from the community as a whole. They were not going to break rank even in the most serious of circumstances. They would either sink or swim — but they would be together.

But there was a third reason for their solidarity: all of them maintained with a hard steadfast resolve that they were totally innocent of the charges, that they had certainly not raped Harply or Spudic, and that they would fight to the finish even if they had no chance of winning.

Their defence had been worked out in detail long before the trial. Their version of the events of April 23 follows — as recounted by Brian Dempsey and Caruso primarily but also the other accused, and some of the witnesses called on their behalf.

On April 23, 1979, Bobby Caruso, who was living with his parents in their Etobicoke house, woke up early and took his dog Trojan to the park. He was training him to be a jumper and daily put him through a routine. He ate lunch at home and then drove down to 402 Lauder. All afternoon he sat around watching TV and drinking with Jean Elgar and Linda Brown, Brian and Chuck Dempsey, John Beatteay and David Bell. Bobby and Brian finally decided that they needed a change of scene. They arrived at the Gasworks Tavern at about four thirty in the afternoon. Bobby immediately spotted some people he knew, in particular Igor and Stuart Grady. "How are you there, Stu," said Bobby. He liked Grady and he hadn't seen him in some time. They got into quite a discussion and finally Caruso said, "Hey, Stu, why don't you come to Brian's tonight? We're going to have a hell of a party." Grady responded that he couldn't because he was working the Village People concert at Maple Leaf Gardens as an equipment manager. Igor joined in to tell Bobby he was working that night as well, on security. "If you wanna come to the concert, you're welcome. Just come to the back gate." At that point, the only woman at the table piped up, "If you're going, why don't you take me?" "Who's she?" Bobby asked Grady. "Claudine Harply, this is Robert Caruso," he replied. Bobby said hello and then, "If I'm going I'll let you know."

Bobby went to chat with the bartender whom he knew and who slipped him a triple screwdriver. He then went over to the juke box, threw some money in and listened to a few songs. By the time he got back to the table, Claudine was no longer sitting with Stuart and Igor. Caruso went over to her and asked what happened. She said Igor had been rude and belligerent to her. Bobby apologized for Igor's behaviour and ordered a beer. Everybody was drinking fifty-cent mugs at her table. The two got talking and in a little while he said, "I'm going back to Brian's place to party. You're certainly welcome." Harply responded, "That's nice." Bobby said, "Come on over while I say goodbye to my friends." Harply replied that she didn't want to have anything more to do with Igor. "When you're finished come and get me," she suggested.

Bobby told Brian Dempsey that he was leaving and he'd meet him at the car in a few minutes. He then approached Claudine and she said, "Okay, I'm coming." Caruso told the court that as they were going down the stairs from the platform where their table had been located, Claudine stumbled. She went to grab the rail, missed and fell right down. She was embarrassed and grinned and said, "I'm okay, I'm okay." Bobby, who was feeling pretty good himself, thought she was getting awfully drunk.

"Lookee here, what I got." Caruso had talked a few joints off of Stuart Grady, and Brian replied, "No better time than the present." The three, all sitting in the front seat of the car, passed it back and forth. Once when Claudine took a toke, the burning ash fell on her leg. Caruso had to stop the car to help find it. According to Brian, that didn't faze Claudine; she put the joint back in her mouth and lit it.

"Hey, you think this shitbox will make it to Lauder?" Dempsey asked. "It better or I'm out fifty bucks," Caruso replied. "Fifty dollars. Is that all you paid for this?" asked Claudine. "A friend of mine," said Bob. "Satan's Choice. I got a lot of good deals from him."

At that point Brian Dempsey pulled out two hits of acid he had bought at the bar. "Want some, Bobbo?" he asked. "No thanks, I'm drivin'" was his reply. "How about you, Claudine?" "No thanks," she responded. "Well, I guess they're for me then." And Dempsey took both.

Brian and Bobby were arguing over whose turn it was to buy the beer. They finally decided to split it and Caruso bought a case of Molson Ex at the Dupont and Bathurst beer store. Brian testified that the three smoked a second joint on their way to 402 Lauder.

Dave Bell and John Beatteay were playing crib, Jean and Linda were washing the dishes, and Chuck Dempsey was watching TV when the trio arrived. Claudine introduced herself, and Chuck complimented her: "That's a real smart suit," he said. Claudine thanked him.

The beer was passed round, and eventually bottles of whisky, lemon gin and scotch appeared on the table. Claudine, who had a Molson Ex in her hand, said she loved lemon gin. "Mind if I have a shot?" she asked Brian. "Not at all," he responded. She drank it directly from the mickey. Caruso zeroed in on the whisky. "I'm in the mood," he roared in his loud Santa Claus voice, picked up the bottle of rye and guzzled three-quarters of it. He belched as if to throw up and wisely put the remainder down. There was also a bag of grass on the table. Bobby testified that he told Claudine, "At Brian's place, if there's grass out, you don't have to ask, you just roll one." He immediately rolled a spliff, a big ice cream cone of a joint, and Claudine inhaled it deep.

Everybody was feeling just fine. Brian had grabbed his guitar and was playing a selection of his own compositions when Claudine Harply yelled, "How about 'Country Comfort'!" Everyone knew that song, and they all joined in. Pretty soon John Beatteay and Dave Bell had their guitars out as well.

The party continued for two and a half to three hours. Claudine kept asking Bobby if she could have more lemon gin. "I told you, you don't have to ask in this house," he replied. He himself was nursing a whisky forty pounder. He rolled a super toke, put it between his lips and blew the smoke out in a big stream right into Claudine's open mouth. "How you doing there, babe?" Bobby asked Claudine. "I'm having a really good time. This is better than a concert any day," she replied.

Claudine gave Bobby a big kiss and he returned it. He figured she wanted to do more than this so he took her to Chuck's bedroom at the front of the house. They started necking, she kissed his neck, he put his hands on her breasts. "That feels good," she replied. When Caruso took her blouse off, he noticed she had bruises all over her arms.

According to Caruso, they helped each other get undressed. Then both got onto the bed and started making love in earnest. Caruso, however, had a big problem: he couldn't get an erection. Covered in sweat he finally gave up. "I think I drank too much," he apologized to Harply. "You're going to have to help me." She put her mouth on his penis and that did help. In a few moments they began to have intercourse. They were successful but it took Bobby a long, long time to climax. Claudine left her mark: hickeys on his neck and scratches all over his back.

Caruso said that when they were finished, both dressed and returned to the kitchen where the party was still roaring away. Bobby grabbed a seat and leaned against the wall. He was utterly exhausted. After another couple of drinks and a few tokes on a joint, he passed out right there. Claudine meanwhile was getting just as drunk; at one point she couldn't sit straight on her chair, she kept falling over. Finally she asked if there was some place she could lie down for a few minutes. Dave Bell offered his bedroom and helped her up the stairs. It was about midnight.

The party continued. Linda, Jean and Chuck Dempsey were sitting in the kitchen playing cards, John, Brian and Dave were banging away on their guitars and drinking. Caruso staggered upstairs to Dave Bell's room, and Jean and Linda also went to bed. The musicians, however, headed for the backyard. At about three in the morning Brian saw a light shining down the laneway; eventually it beamed into the eyes of the three dogs and they began to bark frantically. Two policemen said they had received a complaint from the neighbours about a lot of noise. The men responded that they would cool it.

They did for a while. But at seven in the morning their desire to perform overcame them and they began pounding away on their guitars in the backyard again. Caruso poked his head out the window and told them to shut up. Dempsey called up, "Party pooper." Caruso drew his head in and said, "Aw shit." Claudine was awake and told him the cops had already been there.

Caruso was hung-over and felt dreadful. All he wanted was a beer, and Dempsey, Bell and Beatteay joined him at the kitchen table. Claudine eventually appeared as well. "Good morning, everybody," she said. "Who's got a cigarette?" They all started rummaging through their pockets and through old cigarette packages and in various drawers to try and find one. When they finally concluded they were out of luck, John Beatteay said he would go to the store with Claudine — he usually went to get the milk in the morning anyway. Caruso asked Claudine if she would get him two packages of Export A small and gave her two dollars.

Bobby went outside to put some water in the engine of his old car and noticed Beatteay and Harply coming back around the corner. John had his arm around Claudine's shoulder and they were laughing and talking. Claudine asked Bobby if he would give her a lift home to Don Mills. "I'm sorry but I don't have enough money for gas to go all that way, but I'll give you a ride to the subway," he replied.

The traffic was so bad because of the morning rush hour, Caruso cursed and complained all the way there. "Fuckin' asshole," he screamed and gave one startled driver the finger. Harply asked him a couple of times if he wouldn't drive her all the way home and he said, "I only have a few bucks in my pocket and I have to get to my parents' place in Etobicoke." Once they arrived at the St. Clair West station, he turned the car off. "Phew, jeez, it's been quite a weekend," said Harply. Caruso replied, "Yeah, me too, just jamming like that." Claudine then said she would like his phone number. "You can usually get me at the Gasworks," Bobby said. "You mad at me?" asked Harply, "No. Why?" "You don't want my phone number." With that Bobby wrote it on an empty beer case in the back seat of the car. Claudine searched through her purse and said, "I must have spent more money at the Gasworks than I thought. Could you give me subway fare?" Caruso handed her a two-dollar bill, she kissed him goodbye on the cheek and got out of the car. Before she walked away, however, she leaned her head through the window, waved the bill at him and said, "Now you have a good reason to call me." And that was the end of Caruso's account.

Altogether the Lauder gang's version of events was drastically different than Claudine Harply's story. She claimed that it was Caruso who initiated their conversation and the plan to attend the Village People concert after dropping off at Lauder; they claimed that it was Harply who originally asked to be introduced and that once a party was discussed at 402 Lauder, no mention was made again of the concert. She said she drank in moderation and took no drugs; the men claimed that she was falling-down drunk and had partaken of marijuana and acid, both at the Gasworks and at Lauder. Harply insisted that she had been repeatedly raped and forced to perform oral sex by the six accused; they said that she willingly had sexual intercourse with a drunk Bob Caruso and nobody else. She claimed that they forced her to have a bath in the morning before going to the store for cigarettes; they remembered nothing about a bath. (This fact would gain great significance because of certain forensic evidence introduced at the trial.) She claimed that she was so terrified, indeed she thought that her very life was in danger, that she panicked and gave Caruso her correct telephone number; they said she was free to leave of her own free will anytime. As well, two of the men she had identified by their photos, Blake and Gillespie, maintained they weren't at Lauder on April 23, 1979.

Roadside Blake said that he spent the entire evening in his Rexdale garage doing what he usually did — tinkering with his motorcycle. He insisted that at that point he had never been to the Lauder Avenue house.

Richard Gillespie claimed that on the evening of April 23 he was at the Hot Tub Club — a steambath for gays — sweating out a bad case of pneumonia.

Gillespie told the court that the first time he visited 402 Lauder was on Sunday, May 13, two days before he met Terri Spudic. He was an especially good friend of John Beatteay's, although he had known Brian Dempsey just as long. They had met in 1969 in Saint John, New Brunswick, the city where they all had grown up. He had often corresponded with Beatteay, who thought that his friend had such a great talent for writing lyrics and poetry that he fondly nicknamed him "Dickens." But for the last four months or so, Gillespie had lost track of Brian and John, hadn't any idea where they were. In early May the three had bumped into each other at the Gasworks. It was a happy reunion and Brian invited Dicky to drop over to the house anytime.

Gillespie was relieved to find another place where he could occasionally crash. Most mornings he woke up not having the slightest idea where he could sleep the next night. Depending on the state of his finances — how much cash he could raise that day drug dealing — he'd stay at the Isabella Hotel, the Hot Tub Club, the Salvation Army or, if he was lucky, he'd pick up some woman and find refuge at her place for the night. If he was really desperate he could sleep at the tiny apartment of some friends on Prospect Street in Old Cabbagetown. But he knew he wasn't welcome there too often.

On the afternoon of May 15 he had gone to the Young Station to read his paper, have a couple of draft and see if he could do a little business. The Station was one of his favourite spots, but he also dealt marijuana and Benzedrine at the Gasworks and other downtown bars. He wasn't exactly getting rich through this activity. It cost him quite a few bucks — about $40 a day — just sitting around drinking and waiting for customers, so his total profit at the end of the week was usually somewhere between $110 and $150.

On this particular Tuesday business was very slow, so he left the Station after a few hours and went for a walk along Yonge Street. Around seven he returned to the tavern, and as he walked in he immediately noticed a girl sitting by herself near the juke box. He didn't know anybody in the bar at the time, so he went over. "You all by yourself?" he asked. "Can I join you?" Terri Spudic replied, "Sure."

She said she was a bartender, that she worked in New Orleans, and that she had a child. He told her that he came from the East Coast and that he wrote lyrics for musical compositions. At about twenty past seven Dicky ordered eight or nine small drafts because he knew the prices jumped from forty to seventy-five cents at seven thirty. Terri and he continued to chat. At eight they decided that the band was so lousy they would go upstairs where there were pool tables and where the beer was cheaper.

He had noticed that Terri was carrying a knapsack and at one point in the evening remarked on it. "I don't have any place to stay tonight," she told him. He replied, "There's this friend of mine and if it is fine with you, you can come up there with me." Gillespie then phoned the 402 Lauder house and spoke to Linda Brown. She told him the guys were at the Lansdowne tavern, and since he had never been there before, she gave him general directions. Gillespie then asked Terri if she would go over there with him to meet some friends.

Richard testified they'd had quite a few drafts — it was ten o'clock by this time — and on the way to the subway they walked arm and arm, giggling and talking. It took almost an hour to get to the Lansdowne, and during the subway and streetcar rides, Terri put her arm around Rich, and her hand on his thigh. She kissed his neck several times.

By the time they arrived at the Lansdowne, the Lauder gang had gone. Richard phoned the house and Roadside answered. Gillespie had never met Blake before but he asked him if it was alright to bring a girl back. He could hear Roadside talking to someone. "Sure, sure, come on over," he replied. On the bus on the way there, Richard and Terri made something of a spectacle of themselves, they were laughing and kissing so much.

At the house one of the girls let them in, as usual surrounded by the German shepherd pups. Richard said, "Hi, how are you, dogs?" He and Terri joined John Beatteay, Brian Dempsey and Roadside Blake who were all sitting around the kitchen table drinking beer and smoking dope. Dave Bell got so smashed that he had gone right to bed. Richard didn't see him at all that night. The conversation turned to motorcycles, and Gillespie was impressed that Terri seemed to know as much about them as King of the Road Blake. Roady told her, "Once I get talking about Harleys, it's hard for me to stop." "So I noticed," she said. All during the conversation, Terri kept her hand on Dicky's thigh. So when there was finally a lull, he said to her, "Let's go."

According to Gillespie's evidence, they helped each other get undressed down in the small basement bedroom. He kissed her breasts and massaged her vagina and she kissed his penis. It seemed to Dicky that she was not so much passionate as romantically affectionate. They made love and afterwards she said, "That was nice, that was great." She curled up beside him, they smoked a cigarette together and he finished off his beer. Then they went to sleep. When Gillespie woke the next morning, Terri was gone.

Meanwhile upstairs the guys were still trying to drink each other under the table. Beatteay finally gave up and went up to bed with Linda Brown. Dempsey pulled out some hash he'd bought at the Lansdowne and that did it. He barely managed to find his way up to his bedroom and Blake passed out right there in the kitchen chair.

At three in the morning the telephone rang and a sleepy Linda Brown answered it. She recognized the voice instantly and passed the receiver over to John. "Is that you, Bobbo?" he asked. "Everybody here's crashed out." "I'm over at a friend's having a few beers," Caruso said. "I had quite a night at the Gasworks," and he started telling the story about his run-in with the Avenger until he realized John Beatteay was fast asleep.

An hour later there was a loud banging noise. Jean Elgar dragged herself out of bed and opened the front door. Caruso was standing there, roaring to go. "Where's the party? Is anybody up?" Jean, who was pissed off at having been woken up in such an abrupt manner, pointed to the dining room with her thumb and mumbled, "Roady is in there."

Caruso kicked at Roadside's chair in an effort to wake him up to tell him about the Avenger but the only thing he could get out of him was, "Boy, am I wrecked." Caruso was still as hyper as a grasshopper, so he got out another beer and smoked a joint. Finally he put his feet up on the chair, turned the radio up and dozed off.

Next morning at about seven Brian Dempsey woke up and had to piss badly. He told the court he found Terri Spudic in the bathroom, combing her hair and putting on some makeup. She wore jeans and a T-shirt decorated with Harley Davidson wings. "Good morning," said Dempsey. "Are you going to be long?" "Go ahead," she responded, so Brian used the toilet. "How was your night? Did you have a good time?" Brian asked. "The flight was all right, but the landing was a little rough." Terri explained she was having strychnine pains, a result of taking LSD. Brian was surprised at that because he didn't know there were hard drugs around. "Wanta smoke a joint; it might help," he suggested. He went into his bedroom and got it, then he and Terri sat down on the nearest convenient spot — it happened to be Dave Bell's bed and he was still asleep in it — and smoked the joint. "What do you do for bread?" she asked. "I'm an entertainer, a real fine singer," he answered.

Brian said he then put one arm around Terri and grabbed her breasts with his free hand. She put her hand on his thigh. All he had on was a short, black silk robe and he quickly got an erection. He went to take her T-shirt off. She said, "No, let me," and began to perform fellatio on him.

In a few moments a surprised Dave Bell suddenly sat up and said, "Good morning, everybody." Brian looked at him. "Why don't you go and get a beer." Dave did.

After Terri was finished with Brian, she asked him where his room was and he said just down the hall. "Let's go there," she said. "My old lady's in there," responded Dempsey. "Well, maybe I better leave then." "You don't have to leave." "Yeah, I had better. I got to find a place to stay." Terri changed her T-shirt. By that time Dave Bell had returned with a couple of bottles of beer. Terri went to the washroom and then stuck her head in the bedroom door, she looked at Brian and said, "That was for the party." Then she left, or so the Lauder group's account of the events had it.

Again the two versions of what happened during that May night in 1979 were similar generally but quite different in important details. Spudic said that Gillespie told her he was a composer of lyrics and that she agreed to go back to his house to have a look at his music; he claimed that she told him that she had nowhere to live and he suggested that she spend the night with him at friends of his. Spudic insisted that there was no physical contact between them before they arrived at Lauder Avenue; Gillespie said she "was all over him." Terri said Gillespie told her that he lived alone and that was the reason she felt safe in going with him; Richard denied this. Terri remembered that she had a conversation about motorcycles with Bobby Caruso; Caruso said he was drinking at the Gasworks at the time, and that he arrived at the house about four in the morning. Spudic claimed that she was repeatedly raped and assaulted by six men; they maintained that she had voluntarily had intercourse with Gillespie and nobody else that night. Everybody else had passed out. Dempsey said that the next morning she quite willingly performed fellatio on him in David Bell's bed; Terri denied that this occurred. She said that when she left the house, Dave Bell, who had been among those who raped her, watched her walk out the door. Dave Bell said he had never seen Spudic before he woke to find her giving Brian a "blow job" in his bed, and he denied watching her leave the premises.

Once it became obvious that no entreaties, no matter how logical, would move the Lauder gang to change any part of their stories, the defence lawyers realized there was little hope for their clients unless they could persuade the judge to sever the two sets of charges. While Mr. Justice O'Driscoll had ruled that the Crown could prefer the indictment on all counts in the Supreme Court of Ontario, he made it clear that it would be up to the presiding judge to make a final decision on whether there should be one or two trials. Students in various law offices were set to work digging up legal precedents and other minutiae to shore up the defence's position.

FOUR

The Trial

CALLING THE KETTLE BLACK

November, 1979

The trial began on Monday, November 5, 1979, in the modern and elegant University Avenue Court House, where the Ontario Supreme Court assizes, Judicial District of York, Toronto, were held. The courtroom chosen was the largest in the building, since officials realized there would be many curious onlookers — those retired folk and unemployed who passed their days taking in one lascivious trial after another — as well as a large contingent from the media.

Most of the defence counsel were relieved to learn that the judge assigned to the trial was Mr. Justice Patrick Galligan. At forty-nine years old, Galligan was young compared to many of the other Ontario Supreme Court justices. He had been appointed in 1970 after a fourteen-year law career, primarily in Ottawa. He was generally considered by the legal profession to be among the most astute of all the judges, a reputation that would be enhanced by the upcoming trial. However, there were those among the defence lawyers who groaned when they learned that Galligan was to be the presiding justice; they had appeared before him before and felt that he was a hard-edged moralist who would be disgusted with the lifestyles that would be described during the trial. Indeed, when lawyer Harry Doan's assistant heard that Galligan was the judge, he said to himself, "Well, the game's lost."

It fell to twenty-seven-year-old Michael Caroline to be the first defence counsel to address the court. He put forth a motion to quash the indictment, arguing once again that in regard to the charges made by Claudine Harply, the accused had the right to choose a trial by judge and jury in the county court.

Red-headed Mike Caroline had been practising for a mere four years, but he was considered one of the brightest, up-and-coming criminal lawyers in Toronto. He had acted in the past for many of the Lauder Avenue gang — Dave Bell, Chuck Dempsey, Jean Elgar, Linda Brown, John Beatteay — on a variety of charges: stolen credit cards, drunken driving, indecent assault. But in the serious matter of rape, he was counsel for the kingpin, Brian Dempsey. His argument in regard to the indictment was similar in theme to the one previously put before Mr. Justice O'Driscoll by the defence except it was much more thoroughly supported by legal precedent. It didn't much matter. Galligan had little difficulty in agreeing with much of the logic formulated by his colleague O'Driscoll, and the motion to quash the indictment was quickly dismissed.

The ruling was not a great surprise to the defence counsel; they had expected that Galligan would likely follow O'Driscoll's lead. They did, however, have one more chance: they would bring a second motion forward to sever counts one and two, rape and gross indecency involving Harply, from counts, three, four and five, rape, gross indecency and attempted buggery related to Spudic, arguing that unless this was done, the accused's inherent right to a fair trial would be thwarted. It meant puncturing the well-thought-out argument of Crown Attorney Chris Rutherford.

The main plank supporting the Crown's position was a legal concept that to many laymen seems obscure and often arbitrary — that of similar fact evidence. Canada's Criminal Code says that charges for separate offences may be jointly tried if those charges are founded on the same facts or involve a series of offences of the same or similar character. Did the crimes represent "a systematic course of criminal conduct"? was the question which had to be addressed. Rutherford contended that this was certainly the case in the Harply and Spudic rapes and indeed that the crimes were so similar, so coincidental, that it would be an affront to common sense not to try them together. He then went on to give a long list of what he considered were similarities in the cases. Some were pretty far-fetched — that both occurred early in the week, one on Monday and one on Tuesday, was used to back his point. (Marshall Sack would argue that that was about as relevant as saying that both rapes involved sexual intercourse.) But most of Rutherford's examples did illustrate the uncanny parallels between the two incidents. There were the obvious facts: the six men were the same, all the crimes occurred at 402 Lauder, both women were picked up in Yonge Street bars. But there were more peculiar points which Rutherford would also use during the trial to great effect: Caruso attempted to

~~choke both victims, both women were physically humiliated by~~ having beer or urine poured on them, in both cases money was missing from their wallets. All of this made a convincing argument that the crimes were indeed analogous.

But the defence counsel were thoroughly prepared as well. The Criminal Code states that "the court may, where it is satisfied that the ends of justice require it, direct that the accused be tried separately upon one or more of the counts." In other words, the judge had the discretion to order two trials if he thought there was a possibility that the accused could not get a fair hearing when the two sets of charges were tried together. The difficult task of convincing Mr. Justice Galligan that this would indeed be the case fell primarily to Marshall Sack.

Sack was one of those lawyers who was passionate about his profession. He had an amazing number of criminal trials under his belt given that he was thirty-four years old and had practised law for only seven years. He was known in the legal community as being combative, highly articulate and thoroughly prepared. He was also considered something of a show-off and grandstander. It quickly became obvious that he would be the leading light among the six defence lawyers. In fact, Mr. Justice Galligan would praise his performance during the trial on several occasions.

Sack began by pointing out the many dissimilarities between the two cases. The two women were picked up by different accused — Harply by Caruso and Dempsey, and Spudic by Gillespie. Different bars, the Gasworks and Young Station, were the initial meeting places, and the methods of getting back to Lauder Avenue, car and public transit, were not the same. Harply's and Spudic's motives for going back to the Lauder house were different, and according to the defence, so were the sexual activities which occurred with each woman. Sack argued that a manifest injustice would be done if the two sets of charges were heard together because "there would be, in the determination of the guilt or innocence of the accused, an association between unrelated charges." They would all be tarred by the same big, black brush.

Sack argued that with six accused and the large number of particulars surrounding the events of two nights, it would be impossible for a jury to keep the evidence straight. He supported his argument by referring to previous court decisions and emphasized in particular the conclusion of Lord Chief Justice Goddard of the British High Court:

> Where the crown charges sexual offences at different times with different persons, it is asking too much to expect any jury when considering one charge to disregard the evidence on the others....

where counts charge different offences, that is to say break and enter
and then wounding in separate circumstances, then there is no difficulty in [a judge] directing a jury to disabuse their minds with
respect to the evidence on one count vis-à-vis the other.

The arguments regarding the severance of two sets of counts took
up the entire first day of the trial, and Mr. Justice Galligan had the
evening to mull over his decision. The Lauder group spent a restless
and difficult night in jail; they all realized that his conclusion might
prove to be as crucial as the jurors' findings of guilt or innocence.

The next morning at ten o'clock Galligan calmly gave his ruling.
He began, "I have heard careful and elaborate argument from
counsel on both sides.... Regrettably I have not had time to do
justice to the careful presentation that was made." He then described the yardstick which he had used to make his decision: "If
the evidence of the April incident is admissible in respect to the
May and vice versa, fairness and justice to the accused persons
would not require severance." His decision in this respect, he said,
would depend whether he was satisfied that the similarities in the
offences were such "as to be capable of supporting a reasonable
inference that both offences were likely committed by one man." He
went on to say, "I stress that the test is whether the similarities are
such as to be capable of supporting a reasonable inference of identity." After having read the transcript of the preliminary inquiries,
he concluded, "There are, of course, many dissimilarities in matters
of detail between the two incidents, but in my opinion there is
evidence of some very substantial similarities.... I rule the evidence of each incident is admissible respecting the other, and I
dismiss the motion to sever the counts."

At that instant Bobby Caruso's lawyer, George Wootten, thought
to himself, "The chance of my client being acquitted is now minis-
cule, negligible or nonexistent." The other defence counsel thought
the same thing.*

After such a staggering blow to the defence, it was crucial to

* Until this point Charles Dempsey had been involved in the proceedings,
although there were no charges against him in regard to the Spudic
rape. Immediately after Galligan's ruling, his lawyer brought a motion
severing him from the other accused. This was quickly granted by
Galligan. The charges connected with the Harply rape remained out-
standing and would have required a separate trial. Although Harply
urged Crown Attorney Rutherford to proceed, he decided that Chuck
Dempsey was only peripheral to events and he stayed proceedings.
Eventually all charges were dropped against him.

regroup and to follow a planned strategy. But this proved more and more difficult. Disagreement among the defence lawyers about the way the trial should be handled was threatening to reach crisis proportions. George Wootten explained it this way: "You know the old saying that a camel is a horse designed by a committee. We ended up with a trial that was a dromedary instead of a racer."

The lawyers divided into two camps. On one side were the two young, feisty and energetic defence counsel, Marshall Sack, who represented Richard Gillespie, and Michael Caroline, counsel for Brian Dempsey. In the middle and claimed by both groups was André Dempsey, a highly respected lawyer who had started acting for John Beatteay only weeks before the trial after Beatteay had fired his original counsel. Dempsey was not an overwhelming presence during the trial but his colleagues considered he had an excellent sense of judgement. "It quickly became apparent and obvious who was going to do the work — on similar fact evidence, on cross-examination of the girls and of the experts," said Marshall Sack. "It fell to those who were most suited to do it." Those considered suitable, at least in the mind of Marshall Sack, were Marshall Sack, Michael Caroline and André Dempsey. And there was no question who took charge of the trial: Sack did well over half of the cross-examining of witnesses. On the other side were George Wootten and Harry Doan, the most senior in years and experience, both former Crown attorneys, both having what they considered was a realistic outlook on the way the judicial system operated. Once Galligan had ruled that the counts would not be severed, they thought a deal should have been worked out with Rutherford at all costs. Doan could see as much as five years being chopped off their sentences if only they'd plead guilty. There was no way the Lauder gang would even consider it. They insisted that they were innocent and that was that.

Harry Doan was absent from the courtroom for hours at a time, sometimes for as long as a full day because he was involved in other trials that were going on concurrently. On these occasions he had George Wootten cover for him. When Doan was present, he often didn't cross-examine witnesses or did so in a brief manner. Wootten was not there for short periods of time as well. Doan's and Wootten's absence so infuriated some of the other counsel that after the trial they considered reporting them to the Law Society of Upper Canada for inadequately representing their clients, Randy Blake and Bob Caruso. The consensus among the accused was that "Doan and Wootten should have been dressed in full battle armour and made to swim the English Channel."

Michael McLachlan, lawyer for David Bell, belonged to no contingent. As Chris Rutherford explained, "Mike McLachlan can't be told to do anything. I could see the exasperation on the faces of the other counsel whenever McLachlan would go off on his little solo efforts." His strategy was plain from the start: he attempted to separate his client from the ignominious Lauder gang, portraying Bell as simply a rather pathetic young man who happened to find himself in the wrong place at the wrong time. He seemed to imply that probably rapes had occurred but that his client had been not involved or at least only on the periphery. But it was obvious at this point that the group would either sink or swim together; much would depend on the strength of their collective testimony. McLachlan kept trying to row in the opposite direction, so in the end the life boat, leaky as it was anyway, collapsed under the strain and all drowned.

Crown Attorney Rutherford sensed the strife among the defence lawyers right away. "With six big egos like that, there was bound to be some breakdowns in the defence. I quickly became aware there was a lot of conflict and I tried to foster it as much as I could without interfering."

Rutherford needed all the support he could get. The week the trial began he caught a bad cold which resulted in bouts of diarrhea, he was debating whether he should ask his girl friend to marry him, and most difficult of all, he alone was vying against six formidable competitors that included a couple of the nimblest legal minds in the city. He got depressed just thinking about it.

After the preliminary inquiries, Rutherford had kept in close contact with his two prime witnesses. Months before, Claudine Harply's brother had unexpectedly arrived in Toronto to fetch her home to Liverpool. For the trial she flew from Britain, at the Crown's expense. It saved Harply considerable money; having lived in Canada for some fifteen years, she found that she didn't like her native city at all. She was dying to move back.

Terri Spudic had gone back to New Orleans, but she too agreed to make the return trip to Toronto. She had been most reluctant to do so; she agreed only when Rutherford insisted, assuring her of his intention to be thoroughly prepared for the trial. When the Crown attorney saw her copy of the preliminary inquiry transcript, he breathed a sigh of relief. It was dog-eared and worn, indicating that she had reread it many times. Both women were brought to Toronto and put up at the downtown Holiday Inn at the attorney general's expense. They were also given ninety-eight dollars a week for spending money.*

---

* After trial proceedings had concluded for the day, Claudine Harply generally liked to go to a bar called Uncle's. One night, she got talking

The first jury chosen had to be dismissed because the registrar was heard to say "Remove the prisoners" in front of those already selected as well as the entire panel. This indicated to them that five of the six were in custody, knowledge which might lead them to conclude something unfavourable about the characters of the accused. The Lauder group thought the second jury, consisting of five women and seven men, were more interested in making shopping lists as Christmas approached than in listening to the facts. Most of the defence lawyers, however, sensed that the jurors were intelligent and fair. They would have an onerous task; the trial lasted six weeks and the evidence was detailed and complicated.

The accused had cleaned up considerably for the trial. Although all had had their hair cut, even Roadside Blake (although his was still long enough that he could tie it back in a neat ponytail), all either shaved or had their beards trimmed, all dressed neatly — indeed Dave Bell with his gold-rimmed glasses, his suit and tie looked like a bank clerk — they still were perceived as a sinister and frightening lot. Part of it had to do with their size: except for Gillespie and Bell, all were hefty guys, and shoulder-to-shoulder in the prisoners' box they looked a formidable gang of unrepentant ne'er-do-wells. Reporter Gary Oakes, who covered the trial for the *Toronto Star*, felt that an atmosphere of dread and nervousness prevailed in the courtroom. He even sensed that the lawyers were frightened of their clients, although they denied this vehemently.

First on the stand was Terri Spudic. On some days she wore a blouse of a flimsy gossamer material, and her friend Peter Niko-lopolous swore he could see right through it. He thought it most inappropriate for a trial. Her testimony, in response to the questioning of Rutherford, was pointed and indignant, almost to the point of being surly. With some grit, she related how she met Richard Gillespie in a bar, how she went back to the Lauder Avenue house, and how she was then repeatedly raped and assaulted. She told the jury that the morning after the assaults she was "kind of crawling along," crying and retching, as she walked along Lauder Avenue towards Vaughan Road, a main street. At one point she cleaned her face in a mud puddle in the road. She was looking for a phone booth

---

to the resident chanteuse, a beautiful Chinese-Canadian woman. The singer felt terribly sorry for Claudine; she thought she was devastated and demolished by the rapes. During the same six-week period, lawyer George Wootten, who lived in the outer suburbs, stayed at the hotel where the bar was located. He also got talking to the singer. His marriage was in the process of breaking up, and eventually she would become his companion. She made him feel very, very sorry for the women whom his client was accused of ravishing.

so that she could call the police, but when she couldn't see one, she stopped at a bus stop. "My body just hurt a lot and my legs were shaking and I just couldn't walk," she recalled. At that point a university student, Russ Fasullo, walked past her. He heard her moaning, as though she was in some kind of physical pain, and he noticed that she was crying. He stopped and asked her if anything was wrong. There was a moment of silence and then Terri said something to the effect, "I've just been raped." Fassulo looked upwards and thought, "Wow, how could this be happening right now?" He yelled at two young friends standing nearby to run home and call the police. He offered Terri his coat and asked if there was anything he could do. She remained silent. He then remembered there was a medical centre some distance. He asked if she would like to go there. When she didn't reply, he took her arm and led her along. During the ten-minute walk, she told him her name and that she came from New Orleans. She also said that she had met a guy in a bar in Scarborough who had taken her to some house nearby. "He slipped something in my drink," she mentioned to Fasullo.

Once at the medical centre as Terri sat waiting for a doctor, she put her coat over her head and had a good long cry. Dr. Ralph Masi, who had a family practice at the St. Clair Medical Group, talked to Terri but did not examine her. He noticed that she appeared unkempt and upset, and that she kept breaking into tears. But he saw no obvious injuries, cuts or bruises. Not did he see any streaks of mud on her face or smell urine or alcohol about her body.

The Toronto Western Hospital's Emergency was set up to handle rape, and Terri Spudic was soon taken there by police. Dr. Ronald Cyr had dealt with some fifteen rape victims in the past and knew the exact procedure to follow. During a thorough examination of Terri Spudic, he found no bruises or cuts on her body whatsoever. He also found the genital area to be generally normal except for some reddening around the vulva. But under cross-examination he said that any normal intercourse might result in such reddening. So, he added, would tight jeans worn without underwear.

Marshall Sack had two aims during his cross-examination of Spudic: he wanted to show she had lied about certain facts and that she was of loose moral fibre. He was as tough and unrelenting a questioner as she was a tough and indignant witness. It was a war of nerves, and not everyone thought the skilled, highly articulate and educated lawyer won all the time.

Some of the discrepancies in Spudic's story were obvious. She testified that as she was leaving 402 Lauder on May 16, Dave Bell "was standing at the top of the stairs leaning over the rail looking down at me." But there was a jog in the stairway very near the

bottom, which formed a small landing. A few more stairs then led
to the hallway. Witnesses, including several police officers, testified
that it would have been impossible for Spudic to have seen Bell in
the way she described. "I agree with you," said one of the lawyers
cross-examining Terri, "you did see Mr. Bell that morning, but at
the time you saw Mr. Bell you were in his bed." She replied, "I was
not." "And you were in his bed with Brian Dempsey?" "I was not."

Dr. Cyr testified that Spudic was asked if she had ever had
venereal disease. He wrote on her chart that she had contracted
gonorrhea three weeks before. But on the stand Terri adamantly
denied that she had ever had VD. The tetracycline, a penicillin she
had been taking, was prescribed for tonsillitis, not for gonorrhea,
she insisted. There was a great deal of confusion about this drug. At
the preliminary inquiry Spudic said it had been prescribed for her
by a doctor in New Orleans. At the trial her story changed: she had
got it from her family doctor in Sarasota, Florida, and it was filled
at Eckerts Drug Store in Venice, Florida. There was another drug
Terri Spudic was taking called Atarax which Spudic said had been
given to her for insect bites.* At the preliminary inquiry she said it
had been prescribed by a Dr. Armour of Toronto's Women's College
Hospital. During the trial she testified that she had originally had
the prescription filled in New Orleans. "I ask you again," demanded
Sack, "why are you lying?" "I'm not lying, sir," was her response.

Forensic evidence indicated that Spudic had been intoxicated
that night but not falling-down drunk. Blood tests indicated that at
one in the morning she probably had the alcohol equivalent of
between five or six bottles of beer. What was significant, however,
was the effect of taking Atarax with alcohol. Dr. Richard Frecker,
an expert in such matters, testified that the combination would
result in increasing sedation, sleepiness and fatigue. It would have
"a disinhibiting effect upon the person and the controls which are
normally exercised over thought and behaviour are lost."

Terri told the court that on May 15 she had a key to the Nikolopolouses' apartment, given her by Donna, and that she had
bought a plant and incense for the couple while she was downtown.

---

* Atarax is usually prescribed for anxiety and tension. It is often given to
acutely disturbed or hysterical psychiatric patients, to the alcoholic with
anxiety withdrawal symptoms or delirium tremens, and to women with
pre- and post-partum depression. But it is not uncommon to prescribe
this antihistamine for insect bites because while it is a sedative and
tranquillizer, it is used as an anti-allergic and to relieve itching
conditions.

She had returned that afternoon, let herself in with the key and left the gifts on the kitchen counter. Peter Nikolopolous testified that Terri had not been given a key and that there were no signs of a plant or incense in the apartment that day.

Spudic had testified that when she first met Brian Dempsey at 402 Lauder Avenue he had a full bushy beard. He had neither a beard then nor when she picked him out in the line-up the next afternoon. Michael Caroline had asked her during her testimony at the preliminary inquiry, "You are now saying that you have trouble telling Mr. Beatteay and Mr. Dempsey apart?"

"A little bit of trouble, yes."

"And in answer to my friend's question or questions, certain things that you attribute to Mr. Dempsey might have been Mr. Beatteay?"

"Might have been."

"Yes, is that a fair statement?"

"Yes."

Although Terri said that both Caruso and Blake stood before her naked during the night of the rapes, she could not remember seeing any tattoos on either of them. Caruso had thirty-six tattoos covering his arms and chest, in all colours of the rainbow; Blake had twenty-one.

A police officer testified that she had told him her T-shirt had been urinated on. Forensic tests uncovered no such substance on the shirt and Terri would deny on the stand that she had said any such thing. The same police officer and Dr. Masi both testified that she told them someone had slipped LSD into her drink. She would again claim that they were mistaken. "Of course, you never had any experience with LSD," said Sack. "You told us you don't indulge in drugs?" "No, I don't," responded Terri.

At one point Terri did break down under the relentless pressure of Sack's questioning. He asked her, "Of the fifteen to twenty acts of sexual intercourse, how many do you say Mr. Gillespie had with you?"

"I know he had at least one, at least."

"The first one?"

"And one after that."

"When was that?"

"I can't be exact when it was, but I know."

"Did you perform fellatio on Mr. Gillespie?"

"Yes, I believe I did. I cannot be exact. I don't remember the exact order. I know that these people raped me repeatedly, and that is all I know."

Terri then burst into tears. Usually when a rape victim breaks down on the stand, it's a setback for the defence because the jurors

will immediately sympathize with the victim. In this case Marshall
Sack was actually pleased when it occurred. "I don't think the jury
had sympathy for her because her crying was obviously very well
timed. She was trying to escape the boxes I had put her in."

The accused men, however, were not nearly so certain that her
tears would benefit them. When a recess was announced, Terri was
sitting on the bench just outside the courtroom. As one by one they
walked by, each juror watched the young woman sobbing uncontrollably. Brian Dempsey caught the look of pity on each of their
faces. He judged that it was a highly successful emotional scene in
the long tragic drama that was slowly destroying his life.

Quite coincidentally, lawyer Mike Caroline had gone to public
school with George Nikolopolous, the very man whom Terri had
lived with in the early 1970s. Nikolopolous told Caroline that she
had been a topless go go dancer in a Toronto tavern, she had been
heavily involved with motorcycle clubs for years, and she had had
at least one, and probably two, children born out of wedlock whom
she had given up for adoption. Except for putting specific questions
to the witness, there was no way of introducing most of the information. Under section 142 of the Criminal Code, a rape victim's past
history could not be introduced as evidence without specific per-
mission from the judge after an in camera hearing. "We would have
had to be in a position to show that she was a biker's girl used to
group sex and we simply didn't have that kind of evidence," said
Sack. He did ask her if she had ever worked for a tavern in Toronto
and she promptly denied that she had. Sack was able to get the
information from her that she had given a child up for adoption, one
important detail in an overall portrait he painted of her as a woman
of loose morals.

The defence counsel felt that there were enough contradictions
and illogicalities in her testimony that had she been the only witness, most jurors would have had enough "reasonable doubt" to
acquit the six men. But there was another accuser waiting in the
wings.

Claudine Harply's excellent memory served her well during the
trial. She recalled in detail going to the Gasworks on April 23, 1979,
meeting Brian Dempsey and Robert Caruso, who offered to take
her to the Village People concert, returning to 402 Lauder supposedly to pick up some marijuana, and then being repeatedly
raped and assaulted. The next morning after Caruso had dropped
her off at the St. Clair West station, she couldn't remember if she
had transferred from one subway line to another, but she somehow
managed to reach York Mills station. There she climbed into
Veikko Rautaualta's taxi. He noticed that her face was scratched
and bruised and she looked as though she was in a daze. She was not

so much limping, he said, as she was staggering. "Where to, Ma'm?" he asked. Claudine spoke in such a low voice that he had difficulty understanding her. He did manage to get out of her that she wanted to go to her apartment at 139 Fresen Drive. As he drove along, he could hear her mumbling something in the back seat but he thought she was probably inebriated and didn't pay much attention to her. After about five minutes, she suddenly raised her voice and said, "Driver, did you hear what I was saying?" "No," he responded. "I have been raped by twenty men!" He looked at her in astonishment, "Don't you think we had better go to the hospital instead of taking you home?" "You think so?" she asked. Rautaualta immediately made a U-turn and headed for North York General Hospital. When they got there, Claudine opened her purse and said, "My God, they didn't only rape and beat me, they robbed me too." She gave him her address and phone number and told him to pick the money up later. At that point he took her into Emergency and relayed to some nurses what she had said to him.

When Dr. Richard MacKenzie examined Claudine Harply, he noticed at once that she had multiple bruises over her entire body, particularly on her arms and legs. Many of them, however, were older than twenty-four hours; she had received some long before her experience at 402 Lauder. (Harply would say later that she got the bruises several days earlier while she was helping friends to move.) There were some recent abrasions as well: there was a fresh bruise just below her Adam's apple, and several around both shins, and there was some mild tenderness and swelling over her right cheek. But her most serious injury was to her right knee. He bandaged it and referred her for treatment to the orthopaedic department of the hospital. Two weeks later a cast was placed on her leg from thigh to ankle.

Dr. MacKenzie found that there was no evidence of any lacerations or bleeding in or around the vagina, nor did he find any discharge or foreign body in that area. But he added that that did not mean she wasn't raped. "It is quite possible for that situation [multiple rapes] to have occurred and for the findings to have been quite consistent with that found in marital introitus [normal intercourse].... Unless a sharp object was used for penetration we would not expect to see any laceration or contusions or injury to the tissue," he told the court.

The doctor also concluded that Harply was intoxicated — he could smell alcohol on her breath, and her senses were dulled. "I've been raped by twenty Vagabonds," she told him.

The main strategy defence lawyers used in cross-examining Harply was not to illustrate that she was lying while giving her testimony, although discrepancies between her evidence at the trial and that at the preliminary inquiry were repeatedly referred to. What they emphasized over and over again was that she had been so inebriated on April 23 that she could not possibly remember what had happened or who did what to her. She had responded on several occasions to that accusation with great indignation, insisting, "I wasn't drunk, I wasn't intoxicated."

But the defence had plenty of ammunition to prove that Claudine had been very drunk indeed. The yardstick used was the legal drinking limit for driving in Ontario — 80 milligrams of alcohol per 100 millilitres of blood. When a sample of Harply's blood was taken at nine thirty in the morning on April 24, it contained 220 milligrams of alcohol per 100 millilitres of blood. Taking into account the average metabolism rate of a woman of Harply's weight, it was calculated that at one o'clock the previous morning, the time she testified that she had consumed her last drink, she had a blood alcohol level of 360 milligrams per 100 millilitres of blood — or four and a half times the legal drinking limit. This represented eleven or twelve beers consumed all at once. Dr. Bhushan Kapur of the Addiction Research Foundation told the court that with a blood alcohol reading of 360 "that person would be very near a coma."

Dr. Richard Frecker, the expert on the effects of alcohol who was called as a defence witness, testified that towards 300 milligrams double vision, numbing, lost of sensation and slipping into a state of stupor or coma are common. "Somewhere between 300 and 400 milligrams you approximate a limit which may result in death, depending on the history of drinking and tolerance of the person." He continued, "If a person had a blood alcohol level of 300, it is entirely possible that the recollection would be either fragmented or distorted and the estimation of time could be significantly impaired." He added that taking Valium and alcohol would have had a "potentiating effect."

The defence seemed to have scored a major coup with this evidence until Rutherford, jumping on a question that lawyer Michael McLachlan had earlier put to Dr. Frecker, asked whether if the events were of great seriousness, a person, even with that high a blood alcohol level, would tend to remember them. Frecker responded, "If an event occurred that was terribly significant, if it involved a threat to security, the violation of a person, danger of death or physical violence or fear... they tend to be fixed in our memory more firmly than trivial events and we think of them as being etched in the memory."

The defence lawyers raised some important questions about

Claudine's testimony. Why had she not phoned the police immediately after she got out of Caruso's car, or at least approached someone for help on the crowded subway? Why had she given Caruso her correct telephone number? Why had she told the doctor at the hospital that she was not willing to press charges against the Lauder group? Why had she told him that she had gone home before coming to the hospital and had taken "a few" Valium tablets and then denied this to the police? Why had she drunk so much while she was in the company of the accused if she was so terrified of them? Why had she not climbed out the window of the front bedroom onto the porch at 402 Lauder in her attempt to escape? Why could she not recognize a house with a purple front, especially since she had seen it in the daylight after she had returned from buying cigarettes with John Beatteay? All of these were answered the same way: she was too much in a state of shock to act in a way one normally would. "I was terrified. I really didn't think I was going to see the light of day again. I thought they were going to kill me," Claudine told the jury. Defence lawyer Harry Doan thought such "dynamite zinger lines" did more to affect the jury than anything else.

But there was a fuzziness to much of the evidence in this trial, and one puzzle in particular came to symbolize this. What had happened to Claudine Harply's leg? She testified that Randy Blake "tried to climb on top of me. I crossed my legs and he grabbed ahold of my right leg and twisted it right around and I screamed in pain." Dr. MacKenzie testified that the ligaments on the inside of Harply's right knee had indeed been injured. How was it caused? "It indicated that she had had a traumatic injury to the knee, which in most instances would be caused from a blow to the outer aspect of the knee...." Dr. MacKenzie said the injury could very well be consistent with a hard fall on the stairs or the floor. This testimony seemed to verify Caruso's account of her falling down the stairs in the Gasworks more than it did her story that Blake had twisted her leg. However, like so much else in this trial, it was not conclusive evidence.

Despite the defence's attempt to discredit her, after two and a half days of giving evidence, Claudine Harply was judged to have been a good witness. She broke down only once under the questioning of Michael McLachlan.

"You have already been referred to a portion of the preliminary in which you indicated that your bra is fastened at the front. Do you recall that?"

"Yes."

"But in fact the exhibit which is your bra indicates that it fastens at the back; right?"

"Yes."

"If you are on your back being stripped of your clothes, how is it this bra was taken from you?"

"The same way as the rest of my clothes were, I guess."

"You don't really specifically recall the bra being removed?"

"No, I was very surprised at the whole ordeal...."

"I think you used the word 'shock'?"

"I was shocked at what was going on."

"You then detailed some incidents to us involving Mr. Beatteay and Mr. Caruso, who appeared to take turns having oral and vaginal intercourse with you; is that correct?"

"Yes."

"Would you tell me how long that lasted for, please?"

"I can't say for sure."

"In fact this experience..."

At that point Claudine Harply burst into tears. It was late and Crown Attorney Rutherford chastised her for losing control; he had wanted her testimony to be wrapped up that day. Harply would tell a friend after the trial, "I had gone from ten in the morning until four thirty at night. Bang, bang, bang, more and more questions. A lot of nasty mean things were said by those lawyers. They were more interested in how much I had to drink than what happened that night."

The consensus among the defence lawyers was that given her state of inebriation and the illogicalities raised in some of her evidence, had this case been tried on its own merits, the men would have got off. That, of course, was mere wishful thinking. At this point, all the defence counsel could hope was that the accused themselves would prove to be respectable and believable witnesses.

Brian Dempsey was the first to give the accused's side of the story, and his performance set the tone for the entire defence.

Lawyer Mike Caroline had defended Brian in the past and so had known him for about four years. He quite liked him. "He was a perfect client in many ways. He provided input into any decision but he also respected my opinions. He never suggested that anything improper be done." Caroline thought Dempsey was a fairly good witness. "There was no question what his position was and I thought he put it forward very well." Some of the other lawyers disagreed with this assessment, but then they had taken a dislike to Brian from the beginning. George Wootten had heard him bantering with Caruso and Blake and had been appalled by the macho bravado kind of talk they engaged in. Claudine was referred to as "Harply the hippo, the dog, the pig." Spudic as "a hosebag, a douche bag, a fucked-up scrotum bag." Sack had concluded that of the entire group Dempsey had the least use for women — he hated them. Rutherford thought that Dempsey was undoubtedly the worst animal of the bunch. "He was the leader, the little Napoleon of the group."

During the lunch breaks, and after trial every day, the accused men would huddle for a strategy session. Dave Bell says there was no question that Brian Dempsey was the quarterback of these sessions. "It was amazing the mesmerizing effect he has on you. We all simply did what he said." And Bell now admits that their defence changed day by day to counteract testimony from witnesses who had been called by the Crown. Dave's lawyer pleaded with him to reveal to the court that the Lauder gang were concocting their stories. Bell refused, not only because he was terrified of being branded an informer, but because although he could reveal that the men were lying, he could not in all honesty say he had been eyewitness on either night to events that he would classify as rape. In other words, he felt that Harply and Spudic were lying just as much as his cohorts.

Harry Doan, watching Brian Dempsey in court, decided that he was a "real sleaze, a mean bugger." Doan concluded that Dempsey's testimony was too pat, too contrived. He gave the impression that he had worked hard at rigging an intricate plot.

In his testimony, Brian recounted how he and Bobby Caruso had returned to the Lauder house on April 23 with Claudine Harply "to get drunk and have a party." When he arrived, Brian gave Jean Elgar a hug and a kiss like he always did, then settled down to some hard drinking. At one point he noticed Caruso and Harply leave the room and saw them come back about a half hour later, but he was having such a good time he didn't think much of it. Claudine was really drunk, "she could hardly sit straight," said Brian. He heard Dave Bell offer her his room to sleep in and saw Dave leave with her. Next time he saw Harply was when she came into the kitchen the next morning somewhere between six thirty and seven.

One piece of evidence that Dempsey brought forth was somewhat puzzling. The night that Harply visited Lauder, Brian had a very full and long beard, a moustache and long chestnut hair. But two weeks later he was making a court appearance, on a totally unrelated matter, and to make a good impression, he shaved off his beard and Jean cut his hair neatly. Brian's brother Chuck said everybody remembered it because it was such a big event, "like the deflowering of the Crown prince." Days after, Brian was arrested

~~for the Spudic rape and had his mug shot taken. It was by this photo~~
that Harply identified Dempsey, even though his appearance had
changed dramatically since she had seen him a month before. The
defence lawyers emphasized this evidence because they hoped,
without specifically saying it, they might implant in the jury's mind
the impression that the police, in their zeal to bag rapists, might
have coached Harply and Spudic. The police vehemently deny this.

Brian told the court that on May 15 they had all gone to the
Lansdowne to meet Dave Bell and had proceeded to get falling-
down drunk. About eleven they left the tavern, bought some beer
and returned to Lauder Avenue to continue the party. Terri Spudic
came in with Dicky Gillespie. Brian did not pay much attention to
them and did not join in the conversation. He did notice that they
left the room together. Eventually everyone went to bed except him
and Roadside Blake. They smoked some hash and then Brian staggered up to bed and Jean Elgar. The next morning he met Terri
Spudic in the washroom and shortly afterwards she performed
fellatio on him in Dave Bell's bed. She left after that and Brian
testified that the next time he saw her was in a police line-up.

One of Rutherford's intentions in his cross-examination of the
accused was to paint a picture of the decadent and amoral lifestyle
they led, in the process revealing them as the "garbage" he considered they truly were. Dempsey fell into his trap. Rutherford asked
him: "You had been drinking, I take it, since that morning reason-
ably non-stop, save for the automobile trips; is that fair?"

"That is fair."

"Had you any marijuana other than the amount you had in the
car with Mrs. Harply up to that point?"

"I think I smoked a joint that morning."

"Just one?"

"I can't specifically say, I usually do."

"Then as I understand it, you started drinking beer and lemon
gin and you might have had a scotch, although you can't remember,
during the party?"

"That is correct."

"You also indicated you got pretty drunk. Could you say how long
the party had gone before you reached that state?"

"The state of pretty drunk?"

"Yes."

"Well, I drink and I reach a plateau which you could call pretty
drunk."

One of the most damaging pieces of evidence against Dempsey
was the statement he was supposed to have given to the police
shortly after he had been arrested. It revealed that he had a callous,

almost cruel, attitude towards Spudic, and by implication towards all women. He was asked, "Our information is that you were upstairs this morning and that Terri was performing oral sex on you." Dempsey responded, "So what's wrong with a blow job?" "Our information is that Terri was crying at the time. Do you know why she would be crying?" "Well, some broads don't like to do it that way. Hold on. That's all I'm saying. I'm getting in too deep." Brian insisted that the statement was erroneous. His version went something like this: The police asked, "Our information is that you were upstairs this morning and that Terri was performing oral sex on you." "So what's wrong with a blow job?" "Our information is that Terri was crying at the time. Do you know why she would be crying?" "Hold it. I don't want to talk to you any more." "Why would that girl cry about a blow job?" And Brian responded sarcastically, "Some broads don't like it that way." The police officer had jotted down all the accused's statements, and Dempsey claimed that they had got it wrong.

Jean Elgar and Chuck Dempsey both testified on Brian's behalf. Their stories matched Brian's — with a few unintentional slip-ups. Jean claimed that Caruso had been with the bunch when they went to the Lansdowne hotel on May 15, although later she corrected herself and said she let Bobby in sometime in the early morning. Chuck also made an error: he said that Dave Bell was with the group when they went to the Lansdowne but he reversed himself, remembering that Dave was already at the hotel. These were small things, but like fine cracks in a piece of antiquity, they gradually undermined the whole.

Throughout the trial the spectre of bikers, gangs and their broads, and the evil and immorality that that subculture represented to upstanding citizens, permeated the courtroom. In reality the only biker in attendance was Randy Roadside Blake. And he, as his lawyer described him, was more like a "flea-bitten circus bear" than a heavy-duty tough. Homespun or quaint best described his evidence, and what it revealed was a man whose one passion in life was his "hawg." Lawyer Harry Doan had some trouble keeping him on track. He asked him what he did in the late afternoon of April 23.

"I came back that day. I wanted to keep working on my bike constantly, the Harley takes a lot of attention. I pride my Harley a lot. I was working on it. I know I had a real problem with my clutch, it kept slipping and I was working on that and I was there in that afternoon, I was signing in, I don't like to do anything that will make me late and I wanted to make sure that I was signing in and I was there that afternoon and I had to sign in at five and I wanted to beat the traffic and got back again on that afternoon and I started up the bike to go back and sign in and I noticed oil coming out of the air valve from my motor and it isn't supposed to happen and I let it idle and it got better and I thought maybe it was just a fluke and I went to sign in and then came back."

What the jury eventually managed to learn was that Roadside had gotten in a fight outside a pub sometime in March 1979. The police had broken up the fracas, and in the process Blake was alleged to have hit one of them. He was charged with assaulting a police officer and was granted bail only on the condition that he sign in at 51 Division, in the central-east part of the city, twelve times a week. He testified that he signed in both in the morning and afternoon of April 23, returning at about four thirty to the Jeffcoat Drive house where he lived. Jeff Ismail, Blake's landlord, was an auto mechanic and was installing a water pump as a favour to a friend; Roadside helped push the car from a nearby neighbour's over to Ismail's driveway. Roadside worked on his beloved Harley until about one in the morning. He then went into the recreation room of the house, watched some TV with another resident, Willy Austin, and then went to sleep.

Willy Austin and Dave Gates, who owned the car with the crippled water pump, testified on Blake's behalf. They were not the most believable witnesses. Willy Austin claimed that Roadside had arrived at Jeffcoat that day in the company of Bobby Caruso, but at that precise time Caruso was chatting with Claudine Harply at the Gasworks. When Dave Gates was asked by lawyer Harry Doan if he had a criminal record, he replied, "No." But Rutherford revealed that Gates had two prior convictions. "I thought it [the criminal record] lasted for only five years," was Gates's reply.

Dave Gates said that he got the water pump that very day from Roadside's brother Dennis Blake. Dennis worked as a driver for General Auto Parts. Rutherford called the manager of that company, who testified that no invoice had been written on that date for a sale of a water pump to an individual. Nothing did more to puncture a large hole in Roadside's alibi. His family was furious with Harry Doan for not calling more witnesses, in particular Dennis Blake. He would have testified that it was common practice for the drivers to "borrow" various parts without an invoice and pay for them at a convenient time.

Roadside said that the first time he went to the Lauder Avenue house was sometime in early May — he rode his bike, following Caruso, who drove his car. Blake acknowledged that he had gone to the Lansdowne on May 15 with Brian and Chuck Dempsey and John Beatteay. They met Dave Bell there. Roadside described the evening for the jury: "I know that Mr. Beatteay, he went down. He disappeared shortly after we got there. He was drinking that scotch and he went pow, he was gone. We shot pool, Mr. Bell was gone too. He was getting pretty intoxicated. Then he was climbing back, he had a sandwich and it was the biggest old bottle of wine I ever saw and a big red wine bottle and he put it on the table and started drinking wine and wine makes me sick too, so I didn't indulge in that wine. I stuck to the beer and marijuana."

Back at Lauder Avenue, Blake said he and the boys continued to drink. At one point Roadside answered the telephone. It was Dicky Gillespie and he wanted to bring some girl over. When Terri Spudic arrived, she and Roady got talking about motorcycles and New Orleans. Terri admired Blake's leatherex wrist band. "I have got weak wrists and there is an impression on the band and she said that is really nice." She and Gillespie disappeared and most of the others went to bed. Blake and Brian Dempsey sat up another hour, however, drinking and smoking hash. Finally Roadside fell asleep on his chair. He remembered Caruso kicking it and wanting to talk about the Avenger. In the morning he woke up at the bottom of the cellar stairs.

Rutherford asked him, "How did you end up in the basement that night?"

"I can't tell you."

"That is a blank?"

"That is a blank."

"How can you tell us that you don't know whether you raped Mrs. Harply?"

"... presumably if I had sex, oral sex, slapped, beaten, raped a woman, that would be in my mind, that would be something that I would know."

He told the jury, "I know I didn't rape anyone and I never would."

In his cross-examination of all the accused, Crown Attorney Rutherford was not so much aggressive and bullying as he was cunning; he would wait for any contradiction or slip-up and then attack. Rutherford asked Blake how long it took him to get from 51 Division where he signed in to Jeffcoat Drive in Rexdale where he lived.

"I believe on my bike I. . . ."

"I thought you indicated in your evidence in chief that you didn't get your bike working probably until the beginning of May before you could start to drive it?"

"In May?"

"Mm-hmm."

"My bike was up in May. I started to sign in on my bike — you are getting me mixed up here."

"Yes?"

"Yes."

Lawyer Harry Doan thought Blake had been a credible witness; he had a "king of the road folksiness" and appeared to be telling the truth despite — or perhaps because of — the small errors and contradictions. But at that point in the trial, Doan could see that for Blake's alibi to be believed by the jury, "we would have needed a couple of priests and maybe a nun or two to say, 'I was there.'"

George Wootten thought Bobby Caruso was a likeable guy, loquacious and comical, with his heavy whisky voice and colourful tattoos, a genuine street character. And it was this image he tried to portray to the jury. He didn't have much success. By Wootten's own admission, Caruso came across as glib and unfeeling. The problem was that Bobby was outrageously and angrily indignant; he truly believed he had done nothing wrong, that he had been framed. The jury could perceive a chip on his shoulder the size of a tree stump.

Caruso's testimony was extremely detailed. For many months he had waited for this opportunity to tell his side of the story and he did so at great length. He recounted how on April 23 he had met Claudine Harply at the Gasworks, how the two with Brian Dempsey had gone back to 402 Lauder, how a party had ensued at which everyone drank heavily and smoked dope, how he had attempted sex with Claudine but couldn't get an erection until she performed fellatio on him, how he had passed out at the table and then somehow managed to get to Bell's bedroom on the second floor, how the next morning he had driven Harply to the subway station and had written down her telephone number. "Did you rape Claudine Harply?" asked Wootten. "No, I did not" was his reply.

Caruso then had an opportunity to relate the saga of his confrontation with the Avenger at the Gasworks Tavern on May 15. After the skirmish in the washroom, Bobby waited a half hour or so to avoid the Avenger, who was reportedly gunning for him outside. Bob then said he would drive Chouch and his two women friends, the three people he'd been sitting with all night, home. As they were cruising along Danforth, one of them said, "We would really appreciate it if we could buy your breakfast." They pulled into an all-night eatery. After that he drove them to a house in the east end of Toronto and went in for a last beer. They put the television on and watched a late movie. Caruso then phone 402 Lauder, got John Beatteay on the phone, and told him he'd be coming over.

The problem with Caruso's alibi was that he did not know the full names of the two women or of Chouch. Nor was he able to remember where the house was situated. As a result his lawyer wasn't able to contact them to verify Caruso's story, and the jury might well have surmised that it was nothing but lies. Wootten did call James Vinall, the Gasworks manager, and waiter Demetre Macheros (Jimmy the Greek). But their remembrances of that night were often different, at least in detail — dates were confused, particulars about events at the Gasworks were contradictory — and Rutherford was able to make mincemeat of their evidence. The Crown attorney was particularly proud of this because, as he said, "In all the years of my experience, I can't think of more than a handful of alibis I've been able to shoot down.... if you can show the alibi was a lie, the inference is overwhelming that he was lying about everything."

When John Beatteay was called to testify in the late afternoon, Wednesday, December 5, there was obviously something wrong with him. He was vague and unfocussed, and he admitted to being confused about the simplest of questions. Finally his lordship asked him, "Are you not feeling well?" Beatteay replied, "I am feeling alright." Galligan ordered the trial adjourned to the next morning anyway. Beatteay's mind had been fogged by marijuana; Brian later said all the accused had been indulging in heavy dope smoking during the trial. They would try to estimate when one of them would take the stand and that individual would lay off for a few hours. In the case of John Beatteay they had simply miscalculated. It damaged his testimony in the jurors' eyes, even though they didn't know why he was in the condition he was.

And the Lauder group had been counting on soft-spoken, good-looking John to make a solid impression.

When Beatteay had been told that he was charged with the rape of Claudine Harply, he couldn't even recall what she looked like. April 23 stood out only as a blank. "I don't remember too much about the day myself," he told the jury. "There has been a lot suggested to me through other people's evidence, but myself, I don't remember it as that much." He did recall, however, that he had absolutely no physical contact with Claudine. "She was falling-down drunk. She couldn't walk very well toward the end of the evening." His memory of May 15 was a bit better. He recalled going to the Lansdowne, getting dead drunk and passing out in Brian's car. He testified that after he got back to Lauder, he sat around drinking for a while — he remembered Terri Spudic coming in — then he went to bed with Linda Brown.

During his first encounter with police, immediately after the raid on Lauder, Beatteay had been questioned. "The allegation is that you took part in the [Spudic] rape down in the basement," a detective said. He wrote down Beatteay's reply: "No way. I don't like using that air mattress in the basement. I like to get fucked in bed." John insisted that this statement was not accurate. He said he did not speak in this crude fashion and that he had not mentioned an air mattress. The Crown had placed some emphasis on his statement because that was the first time an air mattress had been mentioned. How would he have known that the rapes had taken place on it unless he had been down in that small bedroom that night.

Linda Brown testified on behalf of her common-law husband, and it was a humiliating experience for her. Rutherford insisted that she reveal the most intimate details of their sex life. She testified that after Beatteay had gone to bed in the early hours of May 16, they had engaged in oral sex and he had ejaculated into her mouth and then they had had vaginal sex. Several of the defence lawyers felt that the extraction of this information was a singularly underhanded thing for Rutherford to do. It had nothing to do with the alleged rapes but it indicated that Beatteay was capable of indulging in sex acts which some jurors might think repulsive.

Michael McLachlan's approach had become clearer and clearer as the trial progressed. He portrayed Dave Bell as being several cuts above the rest of the motley Lauder crowd — simply a rather pathetic young man who had a remarkable talent for choosing unsavoury friends.

McLachlan's strategy depended on convincing the jury that both Spudic and Harply, while there was no doubt they had seen Bell at 402 Lauder, were mistaken in concluding that he had been among the gang of rapists. Bell said that on May 15 he had been so smashed from all the wine he had consumed at the Lansdowne that he passed out before Spudic had even arrived. He had spent the night of May 15 in a drunken sleep in his bedroom. McLachlan attempted to persuade the jury that Terri, having seen Dave Bell in his own bed the morning after the rapes, had unconsciously transferred her memory of him to the horrific experience of the previous evening. In the case of Claudine Harply, Bell was simply peripheral to whatever had gone on. Harply's own evidence would seem to back that up. She testified that he had not been one of the gang who had originally forced her into the small bedroom and then stripped her. He had come in later, and although she claimed that he had raped her, he had remained a shadowy figure.

The other five accused would come to despise McLachlan with a vengeance. What they interpreted he was saying to the jury was "Yes, ladies and gentlemen, my client raped Miss Harply but he was only fourth in line and she doesn't remember it too vividly so what the fuck eh let's hang the first three guys and let young Davey go."

Marshall Sack had been very surprised when he learned that his client, Richard Gillespie, had been charged with two counts of gang rape. He had always assumed that Richard was a homosexual. Says Sack, "The others were large, muscular, brawny macho men but Gillespie wasn't. He's thin almost to the point of being emaciated, and he's a sickly person. I think that Terri Spudic was a tough broad, no question about that. In fact, she was probably physically superior to Gillespie." Sack thought that Richard was an "intelligent and sensitive" young man who had had a difficult and rather tragic past. He firmly believed that Gillespie had not been at the Lauder Avenue residence in April, and he set out to present an airtight alibi.

On Sunday, April 22, Richard Gillespie had travelled by train and bus to Oshawa. Even though he didn't have tickets, he was hoping he could somehow get to see the Rolling Stones concert that was being performed there as part of Keith Richard's sentence after he had been found guilty of possession of heroin in Toronto. Gillespie had planned to deal a little Benzedrine, but when he got near the Oshawa Civic Centre, there were police all over with cameras and telephoto lenses, so Richard didn't have much luck. Nor did he have any luck getting into the concert — he couldn't afford the two-hundred-dollar scalpers' tickets.

He ran into a friend of his, whom he knew by the name of Lexi, and her boy friend, and the threesome wandered around for most of the day. Richard lay down on the grass at one point and slept for several hours. It grew quite cold and he was beginning to feel terribly sick — he was coughing badly and his chest felt constricted.

At about eleven thirty at night, Lexi and her boy friend got a ride home, but there was no room in the car for Gillespie and by that time the last bus to Toronto had left. Richard grabbed a cab, which took him to Highway 401, and he hitchhiked the rest of the way. He decided he would spend the night at the Hot Tub Club, a steam bath frequented by Toronto's gay population. He paid his six dollars and got a key to one of the small cubicles. By that time he was so very sick, he could hardly breathe.

From two in the morning on Monday, April 23, to eleven in the morning on April 25, Gillespie lay on the small cot, shaking with fever, coughing up blood and gasping for breath. "I was in pain," he told the jury. "Every time my heart beat it felt like my head would explode." The manager of the club looked in on him on several occasions and once asked if he wouldn't want an ambulance. Gillespie declined; he preferred to ride it out there. "I didn't think I was going to die or anything." On Wednesday morning he felt a little better, so he left the Hot Tub Club and walked to the Wellesley Hospital. He saw a doctor who gave him a prescription for penicillin tablets.

Marshall Sack could find neither Lexi nor her boy friend to testify on Gillespie's behalf, but he did call Robert Goodman (also known as Gordon Slee), the manager of the Hot Tub Club, who recalled that Gillespie had been very sick at the club for about three days. Goodman's evidence contradicted Richard's in some details — he said Gillespie went to a concert at Maple Leaf Gardens, that he went to the Wellesley Hospital and then returned — but Sack found another witness who would further verify Richard's story.

Dr. Edward Domovitch confirmed that he had examined Gillespie and that his condition had been diagnosed as "revolving pneumonia." The doctor testified that on April 23, 1979, the night he was supposed to have been raping Claudine Harply, Gillespie would have been very ill, "with a high fever and a persistent rasping cough."

As for the May 15 incident, Gillespie confirmed again that he had met Terri Spudic at the Young Station, had gone back to 402 Lauder and then had had sexual intercourse with her. He had not seen anybody rape Terri, he insisted.

With one important exception, the forensic evidence was not so conclusive as to finally prove guilt or innocence. Constable Douglas Ford found Brian Dempsey's fingerprints on a beer bottle taken from the small room where Spudic was allegedly raped, and he detected Caruso's prints on a bottle found sitting on top of a fridge in the basement. But Ford also said that the prints could have been put there at any time. Michael Caroline asked him, "The print could have been put on the bottle when it was taken out of the beer case?" "Yes." "When it was put in the refrigerator?" "Yes."

William Philp, an analyst in the biology department of the Centre for Forensic Sciences, testified that in the examination of vaginal washings taken from Claudine Harply, semen had been found but in a small quantity consistent with "the amount we would expect to find in a vaginal sampling taken within about forty-eight hours after intercourse." But Philp qualified his remark: "That makes the assumption that there has been no attempt to remove the contents in the vagina." Harply claimed that she was forced to take a bath and clean her genital area; the Lauder gang vehemently denied this.

The tests had identified in Harply's vaginal washing, semen of blood group A.* Blake and Bell both had this type of blood, but since group A is dominant over all others (no other type can be detected if group A is present), none of the accused could be eliminated. But then, as Philp pointed out, any male in the general population could theoretically have deposited his semen there.

Philp also found heavy reddish-brown staining located on the crotch area of Harply's underwear that was determined to be menstrual blood. Harply on several occasions had denied that she was menstruating at the time. Caruso, on the other hand, claimed that he noticed that she was. And on the outside of Harply's slacks, spots of semen, group A, were detected. But, as lawyer Michael McLachlan pointed out, that likely meant that Harply would have had to have engaged in sexual intercourse with her slacks on. And that was hardly consistent with the evidence before the court given by either side.

Because Spudic had intended to complain about the rapes from the beginning (whereas Harply at first refused to lay charges), a more thorough analysis was done in her case. For example, mouth swabs from inside the cheek were taken. Philp found no semen but he said, "Based upon twelve years of processing items at the laboratory, I have come across probably ten or fifteen cases where I have been presented with what is purported to be a swab or sample from the mouth of a person and have been asked to determine whether or not semen was present, and in the vast majority of cases, I have not been able to find any semen. I don't know what this means, whether it means semen was not deposited or if it was desposited whether it was expelled from the mouth in one way or another. Quite simply, we don't have sufficient data to determine how long semen is retained in the mouth."

Philp also analysed vaginal swabs taken from Spudic. He found indications of blood and also identified semen and a group A substance. The semen was in such quantity that Philp could determine that intercourse had occurred within twelve hours prior to the collection of the sample. That did not reveal any new evidence, since Gillespie had admitted having intercourse with Spudic. Philp described his analysis further. "The group A substance I identified on the swabs could in fact be from her [Terri Spudic]. In which case I

---

* The blood of the human population can be categorized into four basic types, group A, group B, group O and group AB. Blood groups can generally be determined from analysing other bodily fluids, such as semen. However, this is not true for about 20 per cent of the population. These types are called nonsecretors. Brian Dempsey falls into this category.

can't make any comments at all about who the semen, which obviously did not originate from the female, came from — an A secretor, an O secretor, or a nonsecretor. [The accused all fell into one of these three categories.]" That meant that none of the accused could be eliminated as possible donors, but none could be pinpointed as a donor either.

Semen was also found on the jeans that all the accused had been wearing at the time of their arrest, with the exception of John Beatteay's. These finding were particularly harmful to Robert Caruso. On the inside of his fly were found two semen stains containing indications of saliva and a group A substance. Terri's blood group was A. But Philp pointed out that 42 per cent of the population were categorized in this manner and that he could not tell how old the stains were. Caruso claimed that he had slept with his girl friend the night before the Spudic rape and had had oral sex with her. As well, there was no way of knowing with certainty whether the jeans confiscated in the police station immediately after the raid had been worn directly after the Spudic or Harply rapes. When Mike Caroline suggested that up to 90 per cent of the male population had trace amounts of semen in their pants, Philp replied, "I do not know if the figure is 90 or 70 but certainly the majority of the male population did have detectable amounts of semen on their underclothing."

Two large urine stains about six inches apart were found on the white blanket that partially covered the air mattress. Mr. Justice Galligan in his charge to the jury would say, "You might ask yourselves whether if urine were poured onto a torso lying on its back on that blanket, it would run down each side of the torso and form two stains separated by some short distance." There had been testimony that the dogs were not house-trained and might have left the urine there. And Galligan cautioned, "I remind you no one who saw Mrs. Spudic after she left 402 Lauder testified to smelling urine about her."

But the truly damaging forensic evidence involved the damp blue towels that Sergeant Grinnell had spotted in the corner of the basement at 402 Lauder Avenue. Philp had found two stains on one of the towels that contained both a great deal of faeces material and semen. He was able to determine that the semen belonged to a nonsecretor. Brian Dempsey was the only one of the accused to fall into this category, so this evidence gave great credence to Terri Spudic's claim that Dempsey had attempted to bugger her. Rutherford realized that it was one of the most important pieces in the crossword puzzle because it made Spudic's testimony fall into place.

Caroline did get Philp to say that even though semen and faeces were found together in the two stains, they were not necessarily put there at the same time. Nor could Philp say whether the faeces were human or that of an animal, such as a dog.

Brian Dempsey was enraged by this accusation directed towards him. He claimed that not only was it not true but that Spudic's account of the event would render it false. If one followed the sequence of events carefully, Dempsey maintained, there was no chance that faecal material of hers could have ended up on the towel. Questioned by Rutherford, she had told the court:

"Mr. Dempsey said something to somebody else in the room to flip me over, because he wanted to butt-fuck me."

"Did he use the words 'butt-fuck'?"

"Yes."

"Could you remember, or do your best to remember, what Brian Dempsey said with respect to that?"

"I can't remember exactly what he said, not exactly, but I can remember him asking somebody to turn me over."

"As a result of Brian Dempsey saying that, what happened next?"

"Two people turned me over."

"Are you able to say which two people turned you over?"

"Mr. Blake and Mr. Bell."

"When Mr. Blake and Mr. Bell turned you over, was there still anybody else at that time touching you?"

"Yes."

"Who was that?"

"Mr. Beatteay."

"Where is he?"

"He still had his penis in my mouth."

"As you were being turned over by Blake and Bell, Beatteay was still at your mouth?"

"Yes...."

"What happened as Blake and Bell turned you over?"

"Mr. Dempsey came in and he pulled my behind up in the air."

"How did he pull your behind up in the air?"

"He just grabbed me around my waist and kind of just pulled me up."

"During that, what if anything was Beatteay doing?"

"He still had his penis at my face."

"What happened when Dempsey pulled your behind up in the air?"

"He tried to put his penis into my anus."

"What exactly did you feel at that time?"

"A lot of pain."

"How long did that attempt by Brian Dempsey last?"

"It didn't last very long, because I was screaming and I was biting Mr. Beatteay."

"Did anything come of you biting Mr. Beatteay?"

"Mr. Beatteay just continued to be in my mouth and then he pulled out."

"Do you know why he pulled out?"

"Probably because I bit him."

"As a result of you screaming and biting Mr. Beatteay, what did Dempsey do?"

"He inserted his penis into my vagina."

"Can you say how he did that?"

"In the same position, he just moved it from one point to another."

"What position were you in at the point Dempsey put his penis into your vagina?"

"I was still face down, my butt was up in the air."

Since Dempsey was about the same weight and height as Spudic, it would have been impossible, he claimed, to first have attempted anal penetration and then to have achieved vaginal intercourse while actually holding Spudic's posterior up off the ground. Also, if he had vaginal intercourse with Spudic immediately after attempted buggery, how could there be enough faeces either on Dempsey or Spudic to leave significant stains on the towel? Dempsey asked lawyer Michael Caroline to outline his objections in his final address to the jury. But Caroline felt that might be overemphasizing some potentially damaging evidence that jurors might not have felt was so important.

By Wednesday, December 12, five and a half weeks after the trial had begun, all the evidence had at last been presented. Now was the opportunity for each of the defence counsel to address the jury, laying out in some detail, like a macabre jigsaw puzzle, the scenario that would prove their client innocent. There were general themes. Claudine Harply's drunkenness, her contradictions in testimony, and her actions after she left Lauder Avenue surely would leave "reasonable doubt" in a juror's mind, they argued. Terri Spudic had been very angry when she discovered that forty dollars, the only money she possessed in the world, had been stolen. She had wanted revenge, the lawyers speculated. She had also been in a chaotic emotional state: having been ordered to leave the Nikolopolouses' apartment, she'd had nowhere to live, and no job prospects. She had also been pining for the New Orleans boy friend who had dumped her, and she'd had a hang-over from the drugs and booze she had consumed. This all resulted in the mental anguish the police and others had witnessed when they first confronted her on May 16,

1979. The lifestyles and character of the women loomed large in these addresses, as they did throughout the trial, so much so that Mr. Justice Galligan would later remark to the jury, "You may have expected after the attacks made during cross-examination upon the characters of Mrs. Harply and Mrs. Spudic, that the accused were a group of choir boys." It might be, he added, "a case of the pot calling the kettle black."

Marshall Sack was the last of the defence lawyers up, and by all accounts he gave a magnificent performance. With some force he pieced together Gillespie's alibi on April 23 and then hinted at what he thought really happened on May 15 — Richard Gillespie and Terri Spudic had gone to the basement to have sex when the other heavies came down and raped her. Gillespie was simply too frail physically to stop them.

Crown Attorney Chris Rutherford immediately followed him. His presentation was just as powerful. Pulling out pieces of forensic evidence and testimony, he wove a tangled web around the six accused. He implied that in both cases the Lauder gang had devised a plot to lure a woman back to the house in order that their "animal instincts" could be given free rein. He suggested that while Harply and Spudic were brave enough to complain to police, there were probably many more who had been sordidly abused by the Lauder gang but who had been too terrified to approach the authorities. During Rutherford's address, the accused felt that they were in some First World War trench and that the deadly enemy bullets would never stop coming.

Finally it was the turn of Mr. Justice Galligan to summarize all the evidence and discuss points of law. It would take him a day and a half to put forth to the jury all he wanted to say. Most of the defence counsel thought he did a marvellous job in being as impartial as it was humanly possible to be.

Several vital points were made but none so important as Galligan's statement that the jury could believe all, part or none of the evidence of any particular witness. In other words, if the jurors thought someone like Spudic was lying in some instances, it didn't mean they couldn't believe her on other points. He also told them, "You must consider each and every accused separately and you must consider each of the five charges separately. There may be a human tendency on the part of all of us to lump all members of a group together. You must be on constant guard against doing that...."

The jury retired at 11:10 a.m. on Monday, December 17. Michael Caroline was surprised when they hadn't returned in a couple of hours; he believed the men didn't have a chance. At 5 p.m. the jury asked that Spudic's evidence describing how she had been buggered be outlined again. There was some indication they may have been getting confused because they thought Dempsey, Beatteay and Bell had been charged with attempted buggery, when in fact it was Dempsey, Blake and Bell. Galligan quickly went over the evidence. A short time later the court was adjourned for the day.

At 2:30 p.m. on Tuesday, December 18, another question was asked: "The jury would like to hear again Mrs. Spudic's testimony regarding the alleged sexual encounter with Mr. Gillespie and any cross-examination on this point by defence counsel and also any re-examination, if any." Mr. Justice Galligan made short work of that request. The only thing Spudic had said was "Gillespie had sexual intercourse with me one more time." Twenty-three minutes later the jury was back. They had reached a verdict on everything but the rape and gross indecency charges against Gillespie in regard to the May 15 incident; on these charges the jury was hung.

Marshall Sack asked that they go back and try again. He later conceded that he may have made a mistake: he probably should have pushed for a mistrial. "I knew at that point that they had acquitted Gillespie on the other charges and what was obviously happening was that a couple [of jurors] were holding out for the other conviction." Sack hoped they'd come back with a not-guilty verdict for Gillespie. The Lauder group had thought that Sack had done a splendid job up to that point. Then Brian Dempsey could see that "his ego exploded and down went Dicky who was the only stopper in our drain."

An hour later the jury returned once more and asked Mr. Justice Galligan if he would read again his charge regarding Gillespie and the rape and gross indecency charges in the May incident. That took two full hours; Galligan concluded his remarks at 10:21 a.m. on Wednesday, December 19. Thirty-four minutes later the jury was back again. This time they had reached a verdict.

Of the rape and gross indecency perpetrated on Claudine Harply, Beatteay, Blake, Caruso and Brian Dempsey were found guilty. Dave Bell was found guilty of rape but not gross indecency.

Of the rape, gross indecency and attempted buggery of Terri Spudic, Bell and Dempsey were found guilty. Of the two counts, rape and gross indecency, Beatteay, Blake, Caruso and Gillespie were pronounced guilty.

"The conviction was the smash, that's when the elevator dropped three feet and left your guts in your throat," Brian Dempsey wrote a friend shortly after. The others reacted in a variety of ways, from "toe to head numbness" to the urge to start crying hysterically. And their families felt the same way.

FIVE

The Sentence

EIGHTY-SEVEN YEARS

The defence lawyers warned the convicted men that unless they were going to admit to their guilt and apologize for this crimes, they had better not address Mr. Justice Patrick Galligan during their sentencing hearing to be held January 31, 1980. Brian Dempsey insisted on having his say but his speech was a much watered-down version of what he really thought. Galligan held years of his life in his hands and Dempsey was not stupid enough to offend him. What he did was make an innocuous statement thoroughly vetted by his lawyer:

> I would like first to thank my lord for conducting my trial in a fair manner. My lord has heard two stories, neither of which were black and white. The jury decided against us for whatever reasons they chose and we stand convicted.
>
> I have lived with these charges for the better part of a year. They have been constantly at the forefront of my mind. I know that whatever time is left me will be no better and probably worse. I am not a violent man, as my institutional record will attest to. To close, my lord, there is good and bad in every human being and a sense of reason to govern. Sometimes we make a mistake and we must be punished for it. I only hope that I will not be dealt with so harshly as to destroy what good there is in me, or the sense of reason I have been struggling so hard to retain. Thank you.

All the time in the back of his mind Brian was translating: "Bullshit, feedle dee, humbug, crap, human aspects tempered with claptrap and utter nonsense."

The innocuous statement was concocted for a purpose. As he

explained to John Beatteay, "When you see a hammer going down on you, you just scream out, 'Holy fuck what a big hammer!!!' in the hope that the wielder of said hammer will focus his admiration on the hammer thereby slowing its progress." Dempsey used to howl over a Richard Pryor routine during which the comedian says, "Just don't stick it in too far, your honour." It wasn't so funny anymore.

Bobby Caruso was a little more honest in his address:

> My lord, I stand here in front of you only to express my views and I thank this Court for letting me have my right to freedom of speech. How does one fight for his innocence when there is a prejudicial fog hanging over you that is blinding your innocence? I think you must trust in the laws of your country to give you a fair trial. I think our country's laws may have overlooked the prejudice in the public's mind to try two cases of this magnitude together. By no means do I have any disrespect for this Court or the judge or people involved in this case. I have merely expressed my views as I see them. I thank you for the Court's time.

John Beatteay concluded a short speech with, "I grieve mostly the loss of precious time I could be spending with my daughter and the time she could be spending with me." (Linda Brown had given birth to her baby in July, 1979.)

Dave Bell said he "would like to thank the witnesses and folks that I love that have stood behind me and at this point I am engaged in looking forward to returning to society with a different lifestyle behind me." His mother, father, brother, neighbours, school chums and acquaintances had shown up in court, and several testified as character witnesses. The picture painted of Dave Bell was of a kindly, sensitive person, a dreamer and drifter, whose only real fault was the company he kept. All said that having known David for years, they simply could not imagine he could have been involved in any kind of violent crime, particularly of a sexual nature.

Roadside Blake didn't want to have anything to do with begging a judge for mercy; he knew he was a "herring" (cornered) and that was that. He would not admit guilt or beg forgiveness for his actions — although he would have liked to apologize to his family for all he had put them through. Lawyer Harry Doan also decided against calling any character witnesses on Blake's behalf. Roadside's mother, father and uncle had taken the day off work to appear, and they were furious. In fact, Bill Blake, usually the mildest mannered of men, was so angry he had to be restrained by his brother from punching the lawyer. Ruby Blake wanted to tell the judge, 'There's nothing wrong with my son. He's an angel and wouldn't hurt a fly. He's got two sisters and he loves them and he's a big old slob where I'm concerned. He would never, never hurt anybody."

Crown Attorney Rutherford urged Mr. Justice Galligan to sentence Blake and all of the others, except Gillespie, to penitentiary terms of twenty years. He thought that for the type of crimes they had committed they ought to be severely punished. "They are animals, real animals, and I wouldn't stay in the same room with them for three seconds," he told his colleagues. "They probably got caught on one of every ten things they did. That type of scum can't go a week without doing something antisocial." Rutherford didn't even feel sorry for Dave Bell, the nice middle-class boy. He considered he was a "cold-blooded liar." "I only hope he makes another mistake and ends up back in prison. It's unfortunate that garbage like that exists."

Pre-sentence reports had been prepared for all the convicted men. And while they were not exactly pillars of their communities — all of them had criminal records — their histories revealed a lack of sexual crimes of a seriously violent nature. There seemed to be nothing so dangerous in their backgrounds that would warrant turning the courtroom into an armed fortress. And that's exactly what it resembled, so many were the police officers, both uniformed and in plain clothes, in attendance. Once the sentences were handed down, they were seen punching each other's shoulders and grinning in glee.

Neither Bell nor Blake had ever received prison sentences. Dave Bell had been fined fifty dollars for minor theft in 1970, and that was his only offence.

Roadside Blake had a couple of drug-related charges: he was given a conditional discharge for possession of marijuana in 1972 and a two-hundred-dollar fine for the possession of a narcotic in 1974. In 1977 he was found guilty of driving while drinking and obstructing police and was fined one hundred dollars; in 1979 he was convicted of common assault and causing a disturbance and fined the same amount.

John Beatteay was found guilty of break, enter and theft in Saint John, New Brunswick, in 1971 and was given a one-month sentence. In 1973 in Toronto he was charged with public mischief and given a suspended sentence, and in 1978 he was found guilty of common assault and failure to appear, and ended up in jail for five days.

Brian Dempsey was convicted of possession of stolen goods in 1970 and given one month in jail. In 1971 he was convicted twice:

attempted theft and causing a disturbance, for which he received sentences of one month and twenty days. In 1975 he was found guilty of indecent assault and sentenced to three months in jail.*

Robert Caruso's and Richard Gillespie's criminal records were more serious. In 1969 Caruso was charged in Toronto with obstructing police and fined a hundred dollars. In 1970 he was convicted of breaching the Food and Drug Act in Prince George, B.C., and given three months in jail. A few months later he was found guilty of skipping bail and dangerous driving and was sentenced again to three months. In 1974 he was convicted of assault causing bodily harm and fined two hundred dollars. In June, 1975, he was charged with assaulting police, mischief and two counts of common assault, all arising from the same incident, given a three-month sentence and fined a hundred dollars. In December, 1975, he was convicted of robbery in Winnipeg and sentenced to two years. Finally, in 1978 in Swift Current, Saskatchewan, he was charged with possession of a narcotic and fined a hundred dollars.

Gillespie's record was by far the longest, listing some twelve different criminal incidents, beginning in Saint John in 1970 with theft of an automobile and concluding in Toronto in June, 1979, with a conviction for break and enter. Most of his offences were minor: unlawfully being in a dwelling house, possession of stolen property and illegal possession of a narcotic. The most serious was common assault for which he was given a two-year sentence in Saint John in 1972.

In the end their criminal records mattered little. All were given the same sentences, except for Bell, and the leniency shown towards him was a result of his compassionate acts during the nights of the rapes rather than his previous history. He had, according to Spudic, allowed her to walk out the door of Lauder Avenue without interference, and he had apologized to Harply for the gang's actions.

Despite his fairness throughout the trial, Mr. Justice Galligan had obviously been disgusted with what he had heard in his courtroom. He believed the testimony of the women and not of the men, as was evident from the sentencing.

Robert Caruso was the first to be sentenced. Galligan began by informing him that he had decided to sentence each of the convicted men separately because "while your guilt has to some extent been

---

* Dempsey was convicted of assault causing bodily harm in May, 1979, and given a three-year prison term, but this conviction was under appeal and so was not officially an item on his criminal record.

joint, your responsibility for your own conduct is individual." Then he pulled out the guns.

> Rape is an outrageous affront to the integrity and dignity of a human being. A gang rape is an unspeakably gross repudiation of the most fundamental principles by which civilized people live in a free and open society. Members of that society are entitled to expect that their courts will clearly express their repudiation of that conduct. These gang rapes are particularly disgusting because the victims were subjected to additional acts that were calculated to degrade and insult them.... On the evidence, I must conclude that the acts of you and your friends, when viewed through the eyes of these two women, were starkly horrible. While the acts of physical violence were not great, there was terrible psychological violence inflicted upon them.... The jury believed Mrs. Harply and Mrs. Spudic and so did I. On their evidence, you all were active participants in orgies in which they were the unwilling victims. To say that one of you was more culpable than the others is impossible. I think you were all equally responsible and I am so treating you.... I refuse to add to what I think is an appropriate sentence because of your life style; but your life style does not convince me that I ought to reduce your sentence because you have lived an exemplary life. I take into account the time you have spent in custody when I impose the sentences that I do. I take into account the hope of rehabilitation or perhaps the more appropriate word would be "reclamation." I wouldn't stake my life upon the likelihood of you ever becoming a worthwhile member of society, but I cannot deny the possibility of it. The duty of the law and of the courts is to protect the individual, the small and the weak, from the actions of the mob; to protect those persons from becoming the prey of a pack. The six of you did not behave like civilized human beings. I do not know what kind of animals to compare you with, because I do not know what species of animals would band together to gratify their lust, and degrade another member of their species. The sentence that I must impose must be exemplary. It must warn you, and the others who would behave as you did, that rape, particularly gang rape, will not be tolerated....

Galligan than sentenced Caruso to six years for the rape of Claudine Harply and six years for the rape of Terri Spudic, to be served consecutively. He was also given two years for each of the gross indecency convictions, but these sentences were to be served concurrently.

Marg and Ramon Caruso, Bobby's parents, were totally unprepared for such heavy sentences. Marg thought she was going to faint right there in the courtroom. She simply did not believe that her big burly character of a son could have raped any woman. Sure he got into the odd fight and you had to nag him to take a shower and he had trouble at school, but he had been brought up to respect ladies.

Marshall Sack was surprised at the lightness of the sentence; he thought Caruso would get about eighteen years.

When Roadside appeared before Galligan, his lawyer, Harry Doan, wasn't in the courtroom. The Blakes were appalled. Ruby Blake thought to herself, "That judge is not going to say those things about my son. He's not going to call him an animal and say he'll probably never be any good. Not my Randy." But Blake was subjected to exactly the same condemnation and exactly the same sentence — twelve years for the two rape charges, and another four served concurrently for the gross indecency charges. Indeed, Galligan's remarks to each of the accused were virtually identical, with the exception of Dave Bell. Brian Dempsey and John Beatteay both got twelve years (Dempsey received a further concurrent sentence of two years for attempted buggery in the Spudic case). Richard Gillespie, who had been convicted of only one of the rapes, was sentenced to six, again with two years concurrent for gross indecency.

Of Dave Bell, Galligan remarked:

> For a man of your background, and the kind of support you have had throughout your life, the guidance and example you have had from family and friends, you are in a particularly strange position in this courtroom....
>
> Having seen a member of your family... testify much earlier, and having seen and heard your friends, who came and spoke for you so eloquently this morning, I can only say to you that you ought to have known better, and I wonder if that doesn't increase your culpability rather than decrease it.

But Galligan noted that Bell had displayed some compassion for Claudine Harply and had permitted Terri Spudic to escape. His sentence was four years for the rape of Harply and five for that of Spudic, plus four years for gross indecency to be served concurrently. Dave Bell thought nine years might as well be forever.

Altogether the sentences totalled eighty-seven years. Randy Blake, riding down in the elevator, looked at the cop who was smugly grinning at him and said, "Twelve years! Jeez, I thought I was gonna get in trouble for this beef." In reality he was trying to hold back his tears.

Brian Dempsey, however, felt relieved that the public part of the ordeal was over. He wrote a friend, "By the time he [the judge] said twenty-one years [the total number of years on all counts], I was glad to hear the fucker shut up. Relief, that part of being dragged through the mud was over."

Sergeant Grinnell phoned Claudine Harply that same day. "Have you heard the news? They got twelve years." "You're kidding," was her response. He told her that several homicide officers had attended the sentencing and had commented that guys that murdered hadn't got that much. They recalled that just a few days before a women who had stabbed her husband to death had got only three years. Said Grinnell, "We were going for life but twelve is good enough. You won't be seeing them for a long, long time." Claudine thought to herself, "Twelve years. That seems like a lifetime." She told a friend that night, "I feel like one of those executioners who wear black masks and hang people." She began to feel sorry for the Lauder gang.

The whole affair, the trial and the sentencing, left a bad taste in lawyer Michael Caroline's mouth. He thought the sentences were somewhat severe, especially since early parole would be out of the question for most of the men. Perpetrators of such heinous sex crimes did not get out of jail easily. As well, he didn't think that some of the Lauder gang had been well served by their lawyers. "It was the kind of thing that if x and y were not well represented, it reflected on the entire group. Nobody could stand back and say, 'I'm not part of this.' They rose or fell together. As it turned out they fell." But there was another thing that bothered Caroline terribly. While he knew that the Lauder gang were fudging their evidence to some degree, he was absolutely convinced that Roadside Blake had not been present on the night that Claudine Harply had been raped, that he was about to serve six years for a crime he hadn't committed. Caroline also believed that during the hours that Terri Spudic had been brutalized, Dave Bell was exactly where he said he was: sound asleep in bed.

All six of the Lauder gang were sent to Kingston Penitentiary, euphemistically called the Regional Reception Centre, to be assessed as to which pigeon hole in the prison community they would fit. It was a shock. The 134-year-old fortress, known in the prison community as the "house of hate," was considered the "pig sty" of prisons. Brian Dempsey could only think, "If there is a hell, it's gonna be just like this." They were thankful that it was only a temporary situation; as soon as they were evaluated, they would be sent to another institution. Anywhere was considered an improvement on "The Pen."

Roadside Blake and Bobby Caruso were immediately singled out as the heavies of the group and assigned to Millhaven, the maximum security facility.

Caruso hated Millhaven, and his parents were seriously concerned that he might go insane. For one thing he was terrified that he would be murdered. One day he was lying on his bunk when he noticed a piece of paper being slipped under the door of his cell. It threatened, "I'm going to get you and your partner [Blake], you mother fuckers. I had a sister who was raped by a gang and you guys will pay." Caruso immediately took the note to the warden and was quickly transferred back to Kingston Penitentiary, where he would stay for the next two and a half years.

Roadside never forgave Caruso. The threatening message was signed, and so in effect Caruso had acted as a stool pigeon, an informer. "He should have talked to the boys for protection," Roadside complained. "He brags all the time about what a big man he is and acts like he's a big shit, but he's a nothing. Some little thing happens and he runs like a chicken."

Blake's criminal record was a minor one, and his parents were upset that he would join a population of heavy-duty criminals — "murderers, mafioso and muggers." Randy explained it to his mom: "They know I'm a biker, so that's it."

Actually it was his membership in Last Chance that protected Randy in a way his hefty size and daring-do couldn't. Six members of Satan's Choice had been convicted of conspiracy to commit murder and they were doing their time in Millhaven. They let it be known that Blake was an ally. It wasn't that the "bros" would be able to guard him from physical harm in such a large prison, but anyone who attacked him knew his life wouldn't be worth a nickel on the outside.

Richard Gillespie was serving only half the sentence of the others, and that combined with his frail physique and penchant for homosexual hang-outs would have made him a sitting duck for the bullies in most of the federal penitentiary system. He was sent first to Joyceville, a minimum security institution, but after a month was deemed not suitable. He was then placed in the medium security Warkworth, which was considered by many inmates as being a safer place with a more enlightened staff than most federal prisons.

On April 13, 1980, Brian Dempsey was sent alone to Collins Bay, a medium security prison, which has been nicknamed by the Kingston citizenry "Disney World" because of its colourful red guard houses shaped like turrets. Standing about five-foot-five and down to 125 pounds, Dempsey was actually the smallest of the Lauder gang. But perhaps because of his cockiness and defiant, thumb-my-nose-at-the-world attitude, he was always described as "burly" or "hefty." A few days after he arrived, he was jumped by four prisoners, one carrying a very large pipe. "You'll fucking get yours, you rapehound, bushjumper," they screeched at him. "The footprints of these four goofs were imprinted on my back and arms but I had been tensed enough that only the skin was damaged," Brian wrote a friend afterwards. The cheekbone structure on the right-hand side of his face was smashed, and he required surgery to reposition the bone that supports the eye because "it was off like a badly aligned headlight." The muscle was torn in his knee, and a cast from hip to ankle was necessary.

Brian stayed in the hospital for three days and then was wheeled down to the segregation cells. As he wrote in a letter, "Twenty-three-hour lock up. I wonder how I deserve this special treatment. Four guys beat me up and I pay for it, beautiful."

When a few days later David Bell and John Beatteay arrived at Collins Bay, they learned that Dempsey had been beaten and locked up. They were terrified but decided they'd play it by ear, hope for the best. John and Dave were sitting at a table on the range, John with his back to the wall, Dave opposite him. They related to Brian Dempsey what happened next: "Suddenly, as calm as you please, an inmate walks up to Bell and swings at him with a lead pipe. A second swing forces Dave onto the floor. The attacker sees that it is over, his man is down, and it's time to finish him — another rape-hound bites the dust. Bell put his arms up, trying to defend himself from the blows. He notices another con coming at him with what looked like a knife. Suddenly Beatteay stands up, grabs the table, fires it about ten feet to one side, and yells, 'What the fuck is going on here?' Everyone freezes. The attacker with the pipe has been told that this was an easy job, just one skinny rape fish, no friends. Now who is this fucking gorilla? Suddenly someone yells, 'Six' [guards are coming], and everybody scatters. Dave Bell's life is saved in that instant."

When Dave's parents found out about the attack, they pleaded with Toronto lawyer David Cole to do something, anything, to get their son out of the "Bay." They truly feared he would be murdered. Cole approached Crown Attorney Chris Rutherford first to ensure that he wouldn't oppose his plan, then he asked Mr. Justice Galligan to write to the prison authorities, pointing out Bell's minor criminal record and the fact that he was a nice, middle-class young man who had really only been slumming with the Lauder gang. Galligan wrote a letter and Dave was transferred to Warkworth, which was considered preferable to all but the minimum security institutions in the prison system.

Brian was entirely convinced that the authorities had purposely set the three up so that they would be hurt, if not killed. He wrote a friend, "Do you honestly think that the police who railroaded us and fabricated so much about the rape and coached the witnesses didn't try to manipulate me out of the picture before things could be brought to light? After all every guard is just a cop that didn't make it."

For their own protection, Dempsey and Beatteay were asked if they would voluntarily return to Kingston Pen. They considered it the home of sickies, queers, true rapehounds, baby murderers, and the thought left them nauseated, but they knew that if they ever wanted to see the outside world again, they didn't have any choice. The ancient penitentiary was compact and well enough guarded to offer some security to its inmates. Even mass murderers of children, such as Clifford Olson, could remain alive in its well-guarded interior.

Brian Dempsey was sitting in his cell one day not long after he had returned to Kingston. He was still bruised, battered and frightened from the beating he had received but he was melancholy for a much different reason: he had turned thirty years old that day. He opened his mail and there was a card which read, "Happy birthday, son." For some reason Brian suddenly remembered how his mother used to wrap coins in wax paper and hide them between the layers of the birthday cake she had made. For the first time Brian felt the years stretching interminably in front of him and he began to weep uncontrollably.

PART **II**

The Men

SIX

Brian and Chuck

VERY STUBBORN, VERY DETERMINED

1950-69

To this day Lillian Amirault can remember in detail what her little boy was wearing: a pinkish mauve shirt, for which she had searched the stores of Saint John for days; a sweet, little bow tie; a smart, navy blue blazer with a gold crest on the pocket; grey pants with creases pressed to knife-edge sharpness; pink socks which almost matched the shirt; and black shoes polished to mirror perfection. When the audience collectively let out a delighted gasp at the sight of her six-year-old on stage, Lillian was thrilled. And when Brian recited perfectly, without once stumbling, the prologue that opened the entire school pageant — "Ladies and Gentlemen, it's delightful to have you here this evening. We hope you enjoy yourself" — she didn't think there would ever be a happier moment.

Lillian is fond of saying that her second son was born in the spotlight, tipping his straw hat to the audience. Brian Dempsey could sing like a thrush. On one occasion his mother came out of the grocery store where she'd been shopping to discover him surrounded by people, fascinated at the four-year-old "crooning his little heart out." Lillian loved this in Brian and encouraged him. Her first born, Charles, had been a frail baby — she used to call him "my skinny little rabbit" — but Brian was a healthy, happy child and Lillian just adored him.

Lillian's grandparents, tough, hard-working people, had migrated from Sweden. They were an affectionate, caring family but also very traditional. Lillian Ekstrom did not have much chance to escape from the working-class dictum that girls were destined to become the helpmates of men, mothers and housewives; therefore there wasn't much need for her to be educated, or indeed

99

trained for a job in the larger world. She quit school when she was sixteen and went to work as a waitress. But that didn't prevent her from having a good time. She loved sports: skating and baseball and swimming. When she was sixteen, she was given a beautiful, white, shark-skin bathing suit as a present and that's what first caught Charlie Dempsey's eye.

He was born in the small town of Jacquet River, New Brunswick, on Chaleurs Bay. His father had served in the Canadian Army for years, and it was logical that Charles should follow in his footsteps. At age seventeen he joined the Canadian Army and saw action in France at the tag-end of the Second World War.

When Charlie returned to Saint John, New Brunswick, in 1945, he wandered into the Moon Palace where the pretty Lillian Ekstrom worked as a waitress. "I used to watch you all the time at the beach," he told her. "He bugged me for a whole week to go out with him," remembers Lillian. "I finally caved in." A year later they were married in the rectory of St. Luke's Church, not far from where they would spend most of their married life. Charlie was nineteen years old, and Lillian twenty-one.

Two babies followed: Charles, born in February, 1947, was a particularly sickly and difficult child. Two and a half years later Brian, a bouncy, happy infant, arrived. "My children always come before everything," Lilly Dempsey often said to her friends.

Charles Senior had been discharged from the army after the war but had trouble finding a decent job in Saint John; so in 1950, when Brian was six months old, he re-enlisted and was sent to Korea. Upon his return home eighteen months later, he took one look at his youngest son and told his wife, "I thought I had a little boy, now I find I have a little girl. He goes to the barber's today." Lillian shed tears as Brian's beautiful curly locks fell to the floor. Her husband's attitude was common among New Brunswick's working class: men are the movers and shakers, women do what they are told. Both Brian and Chuck developed a pronounced macho streak early on.

At that time the family moved to Petawawa, an armed forces base in eastern Ontario on the Quebec border. Lillian was lonely there. "I didn't drink, and most of the people, including my husband, did." She enjoyed caring for her little boys, however. "They were such sweet little kids, I adored them — they were the best thing that ever happened to me in my life. And I wish I had them days back again," she laments.

After two years, the Dempseys decided that they'd had enough of army life, and they moved back to Saint John. Charles got a job as the service manager at a car dealership and Lillian worked part-time as a cleaning woman, work she didn't mind at all. Her eldest son did, however. As Charles grew older, he became ashamed of his mother's job. At one point Lillian was offered a good-paying position as the custodian of the parochial school attended by the Dempsey brothers. But Chuck put up such a fuss, wailing that he and Brian would be the laughingstock among his friends, that Lillian had to turn it down.

Like many working-class people, the Dempseys lived in flats in the north end of Saint John. The two- and three-storey wood-shingled houses were painted brightly, but they were often derelict and drafty. "A lot of them were cold, miserable, damp places," says Lillian.

The boys were enrolled in St. Peter's parochial school, and they did well. Principal H. P. Whalen told Lillian that they had the highest IQs in the school and great things could be expected of them. "I'd go to the school on parents' night, and the teachers would just rave about Brian, say how good and sweet he was. They'd rave about Chuck too." Lillian can only remember one discordant note. One nun wrote about Brian, "Mrs. Dempsey, don't spoil this child." In a fit of pique he had ripped up his notebook. Lillian had never seen him do anything like that at home but she began to realize he had a perverse stubborn streak in him.

The sisters quickly discovered Brian's lovely voice. During the Christmas season he was taken from one classroom to another to sing carols. And it was a big moment for the Dempsey family when Brian, at age eight, auditioned and was chosen to perform on a television talent show, *Time for Juniors*. He belted out a happy school song about autumn, and the fifty kids in the live audience gave him a solid round of applause. The MC gave him a jar of peanut butter. "There he was singing his little heart out on TV. I almost started to bawl," says Lillian.

There was one predominant feature of the north end neighbourhood — there were always kids around, hundreds of them. The Dempsey brothers, small and skinny as they were, were always at the centre of anything that was "going down." They stuck together like toffee, imagining that together they could take anyone or anything on. "Even then the Dempsey brothers were considered big shits," says Paul McGrath, who grew up in the same neighbourhood. "Even then they seemed to be saying, 'We're the kings.'" Brian in particular was a gregarious child; a sense of the importance of a bunch of guys he could kid around with, share heartbreaks with and order about became deep rooted in him early on.

In summer Charles Senior liked to take his sons for an outing to Lily lake in Rockwood Park after work, while Lillian was fixing supper. When Brian was about five he hadn't yet learned to swim, but he liked to dive in over his head, turn around, grab hold of a rock and haul himself out. One night while his father watched, he got confused and turned the wrong way. He was about fifteen feet from the shore when his head broke the surface. He took a gasp of air and went under again. He kept bobbing up and down, trying to get closer to land. Charles Dempsey, thinking Brian was fooling around, didn't realize what serious trouble his son was in. When it finally occurred to him, Brian was close enough that Charles could reach in and haul him out. It frightened the little boy terribly because he knew he had almost drowned. While his mother nearly went crazy when she heard the story, his father thought it was one of those God-given ordeals that would toughen his son up and make a man of him.

Lillian Dempsey realized that her husband had in some way suffered a deep disappointment, a sadness that was overwhelming. He was a man who thought he could do anything, and often told the world about it, and he began to feel hemmed in, stinted. Charles Senior began spending a lot of time away from home, mostly in bars, although Lillian says it never affected his work — he provided for his family — and his sons did not know about his drinking. However, he became a remote figure to them. "My father just wasn't interested in kids' games. I could approach him but he taught me how to pick my moments," remembers Brian. "He was an intense man who knew he should be somewhere, have something, but at that time he had a wife and two kids and I don't guess any prospects so he was usually in a fairly serious state of mind.... He taught me a lot of things, like the ability to magnetize, illuminate, or radiate, depending on the weather." Lillian Dempsey also thought that her husband taught her sons how to be braggarts. Charles never stopped talking about how he could conquer the world. The trouble was that while he persuaded his children that they should have great expectations, he never impressed on them that they had to work for fame and fortune. These would suddenly appear by some concocted scheme, or pure good luck, maybe even a lottery ticket.

Brian got into his first bad fight when he was nine years old. He was playing at recess time with the other grade threes when first one kid and then another came crying that some big goon had hit them. "Well, what do you want me to do?" Brian asked. At that moment the instigator, who was younger but much bigger than the others, came over and started jeering at Brian. "Who do you think you are, big man?" "Wanna fight?" "Yeah, yeah, on you." The entire school yard formed one big circle around the two and started to chant, "Brian, Brian, Brian." The big kid swung, Brian ducked and

~~punched him in the stomach.~~ The same thing happened again. Suddenly Brian thought to himself, "This goof is trying to punch me in the face." His opponent swung, Dempsey ducked and then jumped up and smashed him in the face. "It froze him like a popsicle," one of the kids watching said. Brian then proceeded to walk him the length of school yard, punching him like a bean bag until finally down he went. Brian was treated like a superhero for a long time after that — the kid had been considered a mean and rough bully. The nuns, who usually watched after their brood like mother hens, were strangely absent during the fight, and Brian was never reprimanded.

It was about this time that Brian Dempsey exploded. His mother had given him a dollar to buy firecrackers on Victoria Day, 1960. Choosing a particularly fierce-looking one, he stuffed the others in his pocket. But he couldn't get it to light properly, and unaware that it was still smouldering, he shoved it in with the others. In a few moments he was on fire. It was extinguished before it did critical damage, but Brian was in the hospital for several weeks undergoing a series of skin grafts. The doctor told Lillian that the burn was just inches short of permanently damaging her son's reproductive organs. It did leave massive scars on his left thigh area, and Dempsey always considered it a bitter irony that neither Claudine Harply nor Terri Spudic, both of whom were supposed to have seen him naked, mentioned this in any description of him.

In the late 1950s the Dempseys bought an old fishing boat, which they converted into a rather splendid white and blue yacht. It was anchored at Crystal Beach on the Saint John River, and every summer Lillian and the two boys would live on it for two months, Charles driving up on the weekends. Brian's passion was fishing and he'd get up every morning at six, take the small dinghy out and see if he could come up with the family's lunch. Most days they ate hot dogs.

Chuck Dempsey developed an aversion to holidaying on the boat; he wanted to remain in town, "girling," his mother would say. By the time he was a teenager, he had become a problem of classic proportions. A teacher told his mother that he was simply too bright for his own good. Although he was an avid reader with an easy grasp for large and pretentious words, school bored him profoundly. When he got into the senior grades, he would brag that he had read everything on the term's book list in the first week. This allowed him to be a big mouth and show-off whenever he attended class, which wasn't too often.

Chuck was small of stature, thin, wiry and driven. Brian likes to tell a story of his brother at age fifteen that demonstrates the type of character he was. Brian went to meet him at the senior school one afternoon to walk him home. He could hear him before he saw him. "You, you or you, or all three of you fuckin' jerks at the same time, it don't matter." Brian spotted the three very tall and stocky dudes with whom his brother was picking a fight but nowhere could he see the guys on Chuck's side. Chuck yelled, "C'mon Bri, lets get out of here." "Gladly," Brian thought to himself.

Chuck started for the back door, with Brian trailing behind. Suddenly one of the stocky guys was sneaking up on Chuck, first coming abreast of Brian, who was so tiny as to be considered of no more significance than an ant. Brian bodychecked him so hard he smashed into the lockers. Chuck looked at the guy, looked at Brian, looked at the guy. "My little brother can take care of you," he sneered.

Chuck and Brian got outside the building and had stopped while Chuck, with his books under one arm, put his gloves on. Suddenly the biggest guy came running through the door. Brian spotted him and yelled, "Chuck! Look out!" Chuck remained calm as a cucumber. He smoothly turned and just as the guy was tackling him, he punched him expertly in the eye. He hit him again and again, until the guy went home bawling. Brian said to the crybaby, "Big brother is very, very fast with his hands."

Chuck Dempsey liked to think of himself as a sophisticated man about town and that meant the consumption of vast quantities of alcohol. Drinking became a problem with him early on. When he was only twelve, he came home one night smashed. Brian helped him up the back stairs, past "three flights of neighbours' windows." At the top, Charles and Lillian were watching television. The two brothers put their arms around each others' shoulders. Brian pulled Chuck close and said, "When I start, you sing along, okay?" Chuck was able to nod. Then Brian opened the door and started to sing at the top of his voice in his best drunken slur, "May old acquaintance be forgot...." They staggered across the kitchen, down the hall and into the bedroom like two sailors on leave. Lillian said, "Ain't that cute. They're playing drunks," and continued to watch *Dragnet*.

Chuck's rebellious behaviour became more serious as he advanced into his teens. One day when Lillian was cleaning his room, she found an old rusty revolver among his underwear. Shocked and terrified by the weapon, she put it in her purse, walked to Rockwood Park, and threw it in the bushes. She said not a word to her eldest son when he came home from school that day. Finally he asked her if she had found anything unusual in his drawer. She responded that if he ever brought anything like that in the house again, she would call the police. Chuck immediately went out and got another gun, but this time he made sure she didn't find it.

By the time he was thirteen, Chuck had developed the philosophy he'd live by for the next twenty years. He knew there was a lot of money to be made in the big world. Without having to work very hard, one could, if one was clever and articulate, become rich. At an early age he developed some skill as a wheeler-dealer, buying and selling stolen goods, drugs, anything that was going. His attitude naturally caused a lot of conflict with his parents. "I wasn't supposed to make money. I was supposed to maintain a level of poverty that was respectable," he says. Chuck left home to make his fortune at age fifteen.

One day in 1967 Brian Dempsey was called into the principal's office and told that his brother had been charged with robbery. Chuck and a friend had held up a man, punched him and stolen fifty dollars. Chuck was sentenced to two years in jail. Brian was stunned by the news. While he knew his brother had much rebellion and some larceny in his soul, he never thought of him as a criminal. It both shocked and, in some mysterious way, excited him.

Chuck did learn his lesson from this episode. By 1981 he had seven convictions on his record, but all but the robbery were minor — fines for impaired driving, use of stolen credit cards, small-time fraud. But Chuck Dempsey would brag of sixty-five non-convictions — sixty-five times he said he had been charged but acquitted in court — and a knowledge of Canadian law that would put many rookie lawyers to shame.

Brian's transition to manhood was not nearly as traumatic. He got along famously with his mother, and he knew he had something of a soft touch. Chuck thought his parents babied their youngest son outrageously. One day Chuck and his mother were watching television in the living room when, to Chuck's dismay, Lillian wondered out loud what Brian expected from Santa Claus that year. Chuck blanched. "Come on, Mom, Brian's fourteen years old."

Two events occurred just as Brian was entering his teenage years that did scar him badly, however. Brian was caught talking in a grade eight English class, taught by a beautiful, blonde British immigrant. She called him up to the front of the class, drew a circle on the board and told him, "Put your nose in that." "I can't take it off my face," says Brian. "In!" says she. Brian would later describe the episode to a friend, "Did you ever look real close at a blackboard, I mean real close? Well there is not a lot happening, so about thirty-five minutes later I started rubbing out the circle with my nose.

Well I was bored and young and stupid." By the time he got the entire circle rubbed out, the day was over and the class dismissed. The teacher told him, "Go down and see the principal and ask him for the strap." Brian went to his locker, got his coat and went home.

The next morning the principal stuck his head in the classroom and boomed, "Brian Dempsey!" Brian met him in the locker alcove. "Why didn't you come and see me yesterday when you were told to?" Brian explained that he had stood for forty minutes with his nose in a circle and that he was not about to get strapped on top of that. "Yes, but she is the teacher and she did tell you to do something and right or wrong you should have done it." Brian responded, "Are you telling me I should be punished twice for the same thing?" The argument went back and forth in a very subdued and rational fashion for about ten minutes. Then the principal pulled out a strap. "Now hold out your hand," he demanded. "No," Brian defiantly replied. The principal told him he would take drastic measures, and Brian said he would not be punished twice for the same thing. The principal called two men teachers into the corridor. Brian was given one more chance to do what he was told. He just stared straight ahead. The two teachers grabbed him and held his hands out. Brian explained what happened next. "There was a moment's hesitation, then the principal moved in to strike. I kicked him in the nuts so hard his knees wobbled like a heat wave. He would have gone down but he fell back against the lockers and hung there while these two teachers got into a contest to see who could break my arm first. By the time the principal recovered they had me twisted into enough knots to start beating me with the strap. I got an in-step and a shin before they got me under control though." While this was going on the whole school could hear him screaming at the top of his voice — "FUCK!"

Brian returned to the class, the tears just dry on his face. Nobody said a word, some kids were white-faced. When later that afternoon the teacher finally got up enough nerve to ask him a question, Brian stared at her for a full minute before she asked someone else. He never spoke to her again. He failed that year but his mother insisted he go to summer school; so he was not held back.

But there was something much more devastating that befell Brian that year. Charles Senior left Lillian for another woman. He had become the Maritime provinces' representative for Helene Curtis, and it was on his travels that he met his second wife. Brian was devastated. He had not even known that there were any problems between his mother and father. "I didn't understand at the time. I was very, very angry because he hurt my mother and me." While Charles Senior came to visit from time to time, he was no longer a forceful presence in his sons' lives, and, as Lillian said, just at the time they needed him the most.

Like many kids in Saint John, Brian lived for the day the circus came to town. The year his father left, Brian worked there for a couple of weeks, performing his W. C. Fields impersonation while he sold cotton candy and taffee apples. His mother was terribly broke during this period, and Brian contributed his paycheque to the rent money. "It saved my life that month," says Lillian. "But then he was always generous like that."

About a year after Charles left, Lillian met Gerald Amirault, a man fourteen years her junior. He had a good job, as foreman of a food-distributing plant, and treated Lillian well. "I remember when he first asked me to a movie. I asked Brian, 'Should I go?' He was absolutely amazed at the idea of his mother having a date." They were married in 1964. He was a man without a large family or many friends, and he clung to the vivacious and outgoing Lillian. Brian naturally vied for her attention so that right from the beginning there was conflict. "They were jealous of each other," explains Lillian.

She managed to smooth things over most times, and Brian continued to live with the Amiraults. Music had become his first love. He was fascinated by the Beatles but the new music of Jimi Hendrix, the Rolling Stones, the Grateful Dead, had a profound influence on his thinking in those teen years. At sixteen he sang briefly with a band. He did "House of the Rising Sun" and then they insisted he sing the Stones' "Paint It Black." Brian didn't have that song down yet, so as he told his mother, "I fucked it up." But it gave him a delicious and addictive taste for performing before an audience.

During this period Brian was losing interest in school. He flunked grade eleven, although he went back the next year and passed it. After that he decided he'd follow in his father's footsteps and join the air force because he thought it was a "very clear path to a golden future." He took a battery of tests and felt like a total idiot. He hadn't managed to finish one. A WAC lieutenant who interviewed him afterwards asked, "What would you like to do, Mr. Dempsey?" "Oh, ah, gee, I ah, what can I have?" he responded. "We would like to find out what occupation you are interested in. What were you looking for?" "Well, what am I suited for?" he asked, still hesitating. "What would you like?" she asked again. At this point Brian thought to himself, Screw it, I'll shoot for the top. "Electronics!" he shouted. "Yes, alright," she replied. "Really? What else can I have?" "Anything, anything, except sonar, there's a minor hearing deficiency in your right ear." Brian was ecstatic. He told his mother, "There is no bullshit in the service. You get every chance to work and you get what you work for."

While he was waiting to be called up for basic training, Brian took a forty-dollars-a-week job as a messenger boy for a stock brokerage. A friend he met there introduced him to Daria Mc-Dougall,* a not very attractive twenty-year-old. One night he and a friend and Daria got drinking vodka, and when Brian woke up in the morning, he found she was lying beside him. After that he told Chuck, "She used to jump into my bed at all hours. She wasn't a beauty but I wasn't hosting the Miss America Pageant." One night Daria phoned him and said she had to see him right away. They met over Cokes in a restaurant, and she told him she was pregnant and he had to marry her. "No way," was Brian's first and final remark. Settling down with a wife and kids in Saint John, locked into a dull job, was high on Dempsey's list of terrifying nightmares.

Daria's parents complained to the authorities, and in the spring of 1969 Brian was charged under the Children of Unwed Parents Act, a New Brunswick law which required the alleged father to pay support both during pregnancy and after, thereby discouraging the unwed mother from collecting welfare. Dempsey would not acknowledge the child was his and he refused to pay support. The judge sentenced him to a fine of six hundred dollars or six months incarceration. His mother didn't have the money and his father, who had bailed him out twice before on charges of drinking underage, said a dose of prison might teach him a lesson. Chuck was in Toronto at the time and learned from an acquaintance that Brian was in jail. He phoned his parents but somehow got the idea that Brian would be released in a few days and so forgot about him. Afterwards he would say, "I've never forgiven myself for not helping him at that point because at the time I had the money."

His sentence was served at a training farm; so Brian didn't mind it all that much. But worse was in store for him. After he got home, a letter arrived from the air force telling him that his services would no longer be required. He was completely devastated. Says Chuck, "Brian felt that his life got away from him at that point. He never really recovered from the blow."

The episode crystallized in Brian's mind an attitude about women that would develop in sharper and more sinister detail as he grew older. It couldn't be said that he overtly hated women or that he was determined to injure them in some way. Rather, his history suggests he considered them as hindrances to the exciting, impor-

* A pseudonym.

tant things in life. The kind of woman he wanted was a complacent, self-denying one, a second-class citizen who would do his bidding. He grew careless and uncaring about the opposite sex. Women, he decided, were meant to be used. The strange thing was so many were willing to accept his philosophy.

SEVEN

The North End

DISTURBANCE IN A DYNAMITE ZONE

1970-73

The cop was cruising along Main Street, Saint John, at two a.m. one hot August morning in 1970. He spotted three young guys, obviously smashed, singing and carrying on. "Where're you going?" he yelled out his window. Couple of questions, couple of answers followed. "What's in the bag?" Brian Dempsey was holding an Air Canada flight bag with three bottles of whisky in it, and the cop knew that all were under drinking age. Brian tried to bluff. "Oh, ah, well, just some junk," he stammered. The officer ordered him to reveal the contents. Brian gave him a peek, nonchalantly pretending that what he had was a pair of running shoes and gym shorts. The cop was not fooled.

Later at the police station, a detective told the three that the flight bag was stolen during a recent house break and enter. Furthermore, flashlight batteries found on the property were covered with the fingerprints of Dempsey's companion, Frank. Suddenly, for reasons no one could fathom, Johnny, the young black of the trio, blurted out, "I was there too. I admit it." The detective then looked at Brian. "Not me. Honest." The cop grimaced and looked at him as if he was "some kind of salad dressing." "Oh come on, Dempsey, don't give me that shit." No, no, he wasn't there," insisted Johnny. "Just me and Frank." "Yeah, it's true," said Frank. "Dempsey wasn't anywhere near us that night."

When they were placed in the police lockup, the piss can, Brian decided to do a little serenading to please the numerous drunks around. When the sergeant stuck his head into the cell, Frank and Johnny told Brian to shut up but the cop only asked, "What was that

last one?" "The Night They Drove Old Dixie Down," replied Dempsey. "Yeah, that's the one. Sing it again, would ya." Brian obliged.

The next day he was charged with possession of stolen goods, and
he was eventually sentenced to one month in jail. The other two
were found guilty of break and enter and given two months.

By this time he was sick to the teeth of his home town. He knew
he'd get nailed for any little thing — the police had it in for him now
and Saint John wasn't big enough to disappear in for longer than a
few hours. Maybe his brother in the big city making big money
would know the way.

Over the last few years Charles Dempsey had done very nicely for
himself. He was managing a Dominion Store in suburban Toronto
— one of the youngest managers that company had ever hired — he
had a pleasant apartment, drove an Oldsmobile, and seemed to be
happily married. Although he always felt that Brian would have
lasted "a sweet, hot three weeks" in the air force, he still felt guilty
about not sending him the money to cover the fine, and he was
hoping he could make it up to his younger brother.

By shooting a few mean games of pool, Brian scratched together
enough money for the flight from Saint John to Toronto, with what
he thought was just enough left over to make it to his brother's place
in a cab. A mile before he reached his destination he ran out of cash
and had to walk the rest of the way. It was freezing, sleeting and
snowing.

Chuck was happy to see his brother but he insisted that a complete overhaul was necessary. He would have to get a haircut and
wear a suit if he was ever to find work. Brian argued a little — long
hair was very much in fashion then, even among the straights —
but was so eager to do well he agreed. He quickly found a job as a
shoe salesman at Maher's in the Yorkdale Plaza but on his first
morning at work he felt like a jerk — all the other salesmen had
hair down to their shoulders. Brian swore he'd never let anyone lay
a straight trip on him again.

It was like asking a stray alley cat to make a habit of being polite
and genteel, but Brian did very well. For one thing, he could be
exceedingly charming to the customers, even the hard-to-please
ladies. The manager's son, who worked in the men's department
where the big money was made, was the only one who sold more
shoes than he did. But the day before Christmas Brian was called
into the back room. "I know you have the second highest sales
average," said the manager, "but I'm sorry to say you have the least
seniority. I have to let you go." Brian wasn't that upset; he hadn't
exactly seen it as a life-long career anyway.

Brian, Chuck and his wife, Sherry, were enjoying themselves

during this time. Most evenings they'd get ripped on booze and grass or hash and then go shoot pool. Brian liked Sherry a lot. She was like a sister to him and they remained good friends even after she and his brother split up.

By this time Chuck had decided he was fed up with being a protégé of Dominion Stores. He disliked the nine-to-five routine, but even more passionately he hated taking orders from any boss. It was a trait that both he and Brian shared. To be under the thumb of someone in a superior position was tantamount to dissipating one's manhood and was to be avoided at all costs. If that meant never working, living on the street so to speak, then that was fine. Chuck returned to Saint John to drive a taxi and made some real money by devising various schemes, most of them fraudulent — selling stolen goods, particularly credit cards, bootlegging, minor drug dealing. Brian went with him.

Back in Saint John, Brian soon met a fascinating group of people, a travelling band of gypsies who had recently arrived in town. They were from England, intent on tripping right across Canada and the States. Brian was especially attracted to Maria Conway,* a pretty, petite blonde who had once gone out with Cat Stevens. The six in this group weren't the least bit interested in suffering the discomforts of hitchhiking and grungy youth hostels; so they devised a scheme that allowed them to go in style. It was called the great Direct Billing Scam. They would send a wire to the Ritz-Carlton in Boston: "Reserve three days March 20 21 22 for son Timothy Richards. Direct bill Dr. R. H. Richards, 12, St. Augustine St., London, S.W.1." The group would then put everything — booze, food, even clothes and jewellery — on the hotel tab. Depending on the vibes being sent out by the management, one of them would ask for and even sign the hotel bill. Other times they'd just quietly leave. Car rentals were also taken in by the direct billing ploy and the band arrived at their first stop, Boston, in a Lincoln Continental. They went on from there — New York, Philadelphia where Brian had his picture taken beside the Liberty Bell, and Washington. They celebrated his twenty-first birthday, April 21, 1971, by drinking a bottle of vodka at the bottom of the Grand Canyon. Then Tulsa, Oklahoma; Albuquerque, New Mexico; Phoenix, Arizona; on to the Promised Land, California — Los Angeles and San Francisco. It was just tripping for Brian, standing at Hollywood and Vine, Haight Ashbury, strolling around Berkeley, just to have been there, to satisfy himself that he had seen a little of the world. And as an added bonus, by this time he and Maria had become lovers. The

---

* A pseudonym.

theme song for the trip was Neil Diamond's "I Am, I Said," and they
sang it as loudly and as often as they could.

By July, 1971, the group had had several close encounters with
police in various states and decided it was time to disband. As well,
Maria had discovered she was pregnant. She and Brian flew back
to Moncton, New Brunswick, where Chuck was living at the time.
They planned that she would return to England and her family.
Brian would follow her shortly and perhaps work in her father's
pub. But she soon contracted rubella (German measles) and her
physician thought it wise to abort the baby. A few weeks later
Brian received a telegram from Maria: "I'm sorry, Brian, but I've
decided to go back with my old boy friend." Brian was truly shattered. He was miserable, at loose ends and bored.

Saint John was as much in the throes of the hippy upheaval as
anywhere else, and not coping too well. Juvenile delinquency had
always been a problem for that ramshackle port city. There had
never been enough jobs to go around for those who were qualified to
do something; unskilled workers were a dime a dozen. If the old
man got drunk and didn't show up for work one day, he was simply
fired and replaced by one from the army of unemployed. Then he
went home and abused his wife and children. Teenagers rebelled
against the sadness and monotony of having nothing to do at the
moment and no prospects for the future. They responded by getting
drunk in King Square or vandalizing Lord Beaverbrook Rink. The
traditional method of dealing with the errant young was to give
them a good taste of discipline at the Kingsclear Boys Training
Centre. There they were delighted to find guys just like themselves
and they formed stronger and more loyal bonds. When they were no
longer juveniles, they were given jail sentences of one or two years
for offences like assault or stealing a car, harsher penalties than in
many other provinces. Then, of course, the circle of hoodlums was
cemented firmly.

By 1971 a dangerous and, to many Saint John residents, terrifying element had suddenly emerged among the young crowd —
drugs. Several teenagers killed themselves from overdoses of acid,
speed, heroin, ingested or shot in various combinations. Saint
Joseph Hospital was finding it hard to cope with the number of bad
trips showing up in its emergency department. Not only that, a
rag-tag army of youths from all over Canada, knapsacks on their
backs, who were encouraged by their bored and prosperous parents
to do something adverturesome, expected to find free room and
board in the form of government-funded hostels when they arrived
in Saint John. Something had to be done, and fortunately David
Lutz was prepared to do it.

Lutz had taught school in New York and Florida before he decided to dodge the draft and come to Canada. New Brunswick was the only province that would grant him a teaching certificate, and so in 1969 at the age of twenty-seven he arrived in Saint John. Two years later he was the principal of an elementary school but didn't much like the job. Then in the spring of 1971, he and a group of sympathetic friends applied for and received a grant of $27,585 from the federal government to open up a drug crisis centre and hostel called Aware House. The building where they located was a huge, gothic stone mansion, situated on Hazen Street in downtown Saint John, which ironically had once been the offices of the Board of Education. From the moment it opened its doors, the disenchanted young flocked to it like ants to honey. Eighty per cent of them had criminal records, few had more than a grade eight education. "I think at that time we got to see all the small-time hoodlums there were in town," says Dave Lutz. His aim was simple: to somehow or other ease them back into the mainstream of society.

Aware House immediately became the hottest topic of conversation around the town's dinner tables. The news media delighted in reporting the controversy, especially when it was being ridiculed; the police superintendent called it "the biggest farce of all times" and got huge headlines in the Saint John *Telegraph-Journal*. On open-line radio shows and in letters to the editors, worthy citizens claimed that it was nothing but a legitimized drug clearing house. Asked why they thought this, they responded by saying a daughter or a son had once bought a joint there. By the young it was considered as a kind of flophouse, a place were they could crash for the night and escape the tyranny of abusive parents.

Brian Dempsey was naturally attracted to this haven for the youthful dispossessed. One evening he was out driving his brother's enormous red and while Oldsmobile. It was a dream car. Vintage '62, near mint condition. Brian had once got it up to 130 miles per hour on the Trans-Canada Highway before he backed off the pedal — there was still so far to push. This night he pulled into the parking lot of Aware House, hoping to round up some lively folk. A group of six piled in; all went looking for thrills. Amphetamines (speed) was the number one happy at the time and they found some splendid stuff. Brian was jabbering away as was usual when he was hyper on speed, and the person who seemed to appreciate his frantic, manic monologue more than anyone he had met in a long time was John Beatteay. They instantly became devoted friends.

John was the first of Mary and George Beatteay's eight children to be affected by the late 1960s youth rebellion. The five older kids had paid attention to what the teacher, priest and cop-on-the-beat said. They dressed according to regulations and had never been tempted by dope because it wasn't available. They might get in trouble for drinking under age, or speeding, but these were misdemeanours that their parents could understand. But the rebellion that the drug culture nurtured during the early Seventies, like an uncontrollable toxic fog, was another matter.

For twenty years George Beatteay worked as a truck driver. A few times he allowed Johnny to ride the big rig with him to exotic places such as Bathurst and Buctouche, New Brunswick. The little boy thought that that was just about the greatest thing that could happen to anyone. Mary Beatteay, a good-looking, strong-willed woman, held down a job as a packer at Brook Bond Company for fifteen years. Sometimes she felt a little guilty about having to leave her large family every day, but money was simply too scarce for her not to work.

The Beatteays rented a series of flats in the colourful but derelict houses of the north end, not far from where the Dempseys lived. "We were never lonely when we were kids. There was never enough room in any of the places we lived to be lonely," says John's oldest brother. And there were dozens of neighbourhood kids to play with. As John grew older, the group of playmates became the gang, a more ominous force in his life They began to get into trouble — breaking windows, stealing milk bottles, playing hookey from school. While it was just kid stuff, his mother began to worry that he was developing a taste for the criminal.

At first John did well at St. Peter's Catholic School. His teachers considered him bright enough, but as he grew older they began to tell his mother that he wasn't working at anywhere near his capacity. He flunked grade eight and never went back to school.

By the time John was fourteen, the Beatteays didn't know what to do with him. He and his buddies, who meant more to him than anything in the world, had tangled with the police once too many times. They broke a car window, with the intent of stealing, and were caught. The judge decided that a stint in training school was just what John needed. His parents at first thought this was a good idea; it might break up the mischievous north end gang. But they soon realized that most of his partners in crime were going with him. All that would be accomplished was to acquaint him with a larger circle of undesirable rogues.

His parents tried to break the hold the gang had over him. They'd impose curfews, but as his father says, "If you locked the doors, he'd go out the window." He'd be forbidden to use his father's car but he'd steal the keys. And yet through all his troubles, he retained his sunny, easygoing personality. He'd often come home from work and cook up an excellent meal for the entire family. "Everybody always loved him," says his brother.

His mother says he was a most attractive young man, and there were always girls around the house, phoning him up, inviting him to their place. Still, he wasn't much of a talker, particularly about anything relating to him personally. Says his brother, "If he doesn't want to talk about something, you won't get it out of him." None of his family can recall him ever mentioning any career ambitions, not even the childish things like being a fireman or a deep-sea diver. Yet he was a good worker, a hard worker, a trait which separated him from the rest of his friends and in later years from the Lauder gang. He found a job on the *Irving*, a sixty-bunker sea ship, helping to unload oil, and he worked on the S.S. *Nanaimo*, which carried cars and large cargo from Saint John to Newfoundland. And when he started hanging around Aware House, his parents were quite pleased. It got him off the streets, away from the gang, and they thought he might be encouraged to give up drugs and get more education.

After their initial meeting, John and Brian saw each other every day. They'd meet at the youth centre, find something to get high on. One day they were in the centre's piano room, snorting some speed and "bugging like crazy" when Dave Lutz came in. "I'm starting a street school and I want you two in it," he said. "You can have first pick of rooms." John and Brian looked at each other in astonishment, rushes going up and down their backs. "Well, it doesn't sound like a bad idea. What do you think, John?" asked Brian. "Yeah, seems okay." "But," Lutz said, "there will be no drugs in the building." John and Brian had some fine speed hidden in the piano. "Oh no, no, definitely not. No, no," they promised. So they were the first two students enrolled in the new school.

One of the first things the two did was paint their room a solid black from floor to ceiling, all the better to listen to the diabolical group Black Sabbath from morning to night. According to Brian Dempsey, there were four basic courses at Aware House — partying, women, drugs and music. The basic staple of daily life was heavy acid rock — Jim Hendrix, Grand Funk Railroad, Led Zepplin. Speed and acid were the favourite drugs. (Brian did adhere to one hard and fast rule which he never broke — no needles.) Sex was casual and carefree; they shared their partners as readily as they did their peanut butter sandwiches. Brian would later call it a period of "wanton debauchery."

Meanwhile Lutz and his staff were trying hard to accomplish something with the twenty-five young misfits. Specialists in various fields would come in and lecture about politics or religion or health. The group would talk about the meaning of Bob Dylan records. Copies of George Orwell's *Animal Farm* were handed around and lively discussions ensued. Brian Dempsey was always one of the most loquacious; he voiced an opinion on just about everything. Lutz remembers the wiry young man as being exceptionally bright. He had long and intelligent conversations with Dempsey that lasted to the early hours in the morning and that, he says, always belied Brian's lack of education. Lutz would tell him, "You're better than all of this. There are other guys who can't make out because they don't have the IQ. But you do."

One night Lutz and Dempsey played a long and involved game of Scrabble. The stakes were high: what time the nightly curfew should be. Brian beat the director hands down, even though he was stoned on acid. When Lutz was told this later, he couldn't believe that Brian could have been on drugs at the time.

Lutz thought John Beatteay was a pleasant fellow, not bright but not dull either. What struck him most about the young man was how he blindly followed Brian Dempsey. "Whatever Brian did, it was alright with John. John looked up to him in an almost abnormal way." Lutz felt that Brian was a talented manipulator of people — including David Lutz himself. One night someone shot beebee pellets from John and Brian's bedroom window, smashing the glass of windows in an office building located directly behind Aware House. Police were called. Ernie Dorin, who wasn't a resident there but visited often, confessed to the crime and received a three-week jail sentence. Lutz knew that he had not committed the misdemeanour — the fellow who had was out on parole — but Brian, always the Godfather of any group, talked Ernie into taking the rap because he had no previous criminal record and the judge would give him a lighter sentence. "If anybody was going to try and pull something off, it would be Dempsey," says Lutz. Yet he liked Brian. "He had a fine sense of humour, and when most people are dull, a guy who is brighter is a good fellow to have around."

There were a couple of other key players in the group that hung out at Aware House that year. Neddy LeBlanc, who was called by his friends "Neanderthal" because he looked like their idea of one, was a legend in his own time. As Brian said, "He was the best fuckin' booster you ever did see." Neddy was a sleight-of-hand artist of the first order. You could ask for anything from a hunting knife to a pair of lady's undies, and he would walk into Woolco and with a flick of the wrist steal it for you. Brian and Chuck had always considered him as their mascot, their own personal clown, and since, as Brian said, "everywhere that Neddy went, Dicky was sure to follow," Richard Gillespie was also considered a peripheral member of the Dempsey crowd.

When Richard Gillespie was eighteen months old, his mother worried that he had become listless and pale. She took him to a Saint John pediatrician who found two lumps at the base of his neck and ordered him into the hospital for tests. Then they told Fredeane Gillespie that her little boy had leukemia and his chances for survival were not that good. Richard's grandmother was sceptical of the diagnosis and took the child to an old country practitioner who had been the family's doctor for thirty years. He examined Richard carefully and then said, "There's absolutely nothing wrong with this child." Richard had been such an active baby that he had strained himself while he was pulling himself up on the cribs bars. That accounted for the lumps on his neck. The doctor declared that what was killing the toddler was the medicine that had been prescribed for leukemia and he threw it in the garbage. In a couple of weeks Richard was his old self again.

After that incident, Mrs. Gillespie always thought there was something fated about her only child.

As a youngster he was a sweet happy kid, and Fredeane was devoted to him. When he was only two, his father left — Gillespie has no memory of him at all — and his mother worked hard in a bakery. But she tried to spend as much time as she could with her little boy. Still, as he grew older he was left by himself often, until loneliness became his natural state of being.

He had no trouble in school until about grade two or three; then the teachers started complaining about him. The principal told Fredeane that her son had the highest IQ in the school but that he wasn't applying himself. At about age nine he began to run away from school, and nothing anybody could say to him would stop him. Mrs. Gillespie has never been able to figure out why he developed into such a problem child. While they existed on a very low income, any money she did have was spent on her son.

One trait everybody noticed in him as he approached adolescence was his odd aloofness. He was not merely shy but outright antisocial. It wasn't so much that he wasn't accepted; he simply didn't want to be part of any clique. "I just wanted to do my thing, which was nothing," he says.

At age eleven he was caught breaking into a parked car by police. As a result he joined Saint John's never-ending parade to training school, where he met John Beatteay. His mother decided he would be better off if she made him a temporary ward of the New Brunswick Children's Aid Society. It didn't do any good. He ran away

from his foster home as often as he had from school and of course
that meant more run-ins with the police. Richard's problem was a
common one: he became totally absorbed with the drug mania,
snorting, shooting, swallowing anything he could get his hands on.
"Dicky just sailed off into some other place and never came down
again," said one of the Lauder gang.

In 1967 Fredeane Gillespie remarried. Richard got along with
his stepfather but, according to Mrs. Gillespie, who divorced her
second husband after a few years, he turned out to be an alcoholic
and more of a child than her son was. To make things worse,
Richard was fighting with his mother. During his entire adolescence, she had tried hard to instil some sense of responsibility in her
strange only child. "I talked to him until I was blue in the face," she
complained. Finally at age fifteen he left home to become what he
quaintly called a "street urchin," the one mode of life that appealed
to him and that would be his for the next ten years. At this point he
latched on to Neddy LeBlanc, the only close friend he had every
made, and he stuck to him like glue. And Neddy followed the
Dempsey brothers around like a puppy.

By 1971 the gang from the north end was having serious run-ins
with the police. In February of that year John Beatteay was convicted of break, enter and theft. He was sentenced to a month in jail
and spent two and a half weeks there. In August Richard Gillespie
was found guilty of break and enter with intent to steal and sentenced to a year in jail. Brian Dempsey was also shadowboxing with
the law.

Brian and a friend were walking along Union Street one September day in 1971 when the friend said, "Keep a lookout for me,"
broke into a car and tried to yank the tape deck free. It seemed to
Brian that he was taking forever. Suddenly he spotted a blue
uniform peeking out from behind a building way down the block.
Dempsey turned around and as he started walking warned his
friend, "Cops coming." The two strolled along trying to look casual.
Two blocks later a patrol car appeared and they were busted. He
got a month-long jail sentence for that episode, for as he told a
friend, in his best French, he was "coupable."

While he was in jail in November, Brian suffered excruciating
pains in his abdomen; he was sure he was having an appendicitis
attack. He called the guard, who, looking through the slit in the
steel door, told him, "You'll keep till morning." Brian did feel better
the next day but he was furious at the guard's casual attitude. "I
could have fuckin' died," he told his friends.

Shortly after he was released from prison, Brian was standing
outside a tavern when there occurred a tremendous boom. The

streets shook. Practically every window in the downtown area was blown out. Someone yelled that the county jail had been blown up and Brian decided to go see. By the time he arrived, there were huge crowds of people surveying the chaos. The bars of the windows were twisted obscenely and Brian was told that the bomb had gone off under the guard's office. He started a conversation with Danny Barrie, one of the guys who had been in the jail. "Anybody hurt?" Brian asked. "Blew me right across the cell but I'm okay. Guard in the office got cut right down the side of his face. Name of Coby Knox." "Coby Knox," screeched Brian in delight, "Jesus, I don't want to jerk off do I?" This had been the very guard who a few weeks ago had ignored Brian as he had writhed in pain. A couple of police standing nearby were offended at this and charged Brian with creating a disturbance.

In court one of the officers testified that Brian "put his hands together like this, your honour, and said 'I don't want to jerk off do I?'" The judge responded, "Well, that's nothing that Norman Mailer wouldn't say." Brian was thinking to himself, "Right on, your honour!" when the judge continued, "However, there will be a finding of guilty, a sentence of twenty days in the county jail." Brian thought, "I must be the only guy in history found guilty of creating a disturbance in a dynamite zone."

When Brian got out of jail, he found that June Wallin,* one of the women at Aware House whom he particularly liked, had been in a car accident. He went to see how she was and from that point on they became "tight."

June Wallin's father was president of a company and her mother was considered one of the most refined and stylish women in Saint John. The Wallins never could figure out what happened to their only child. Wild as the wind was the way they described her. At fifteen years old she ran away to Toronto where she was a topless go go dancer. She was persuaded by her parents to come back to Saint John, but she adamantly refused to abandon the hippy life. Highly intelligent and sharp as a tack, she was also pretty — plump, but not unpleasantly so, blonde and blue-eyed. Brian told a friend, "She's well brought up, from the Winnie-the-Pooh school of propriety." She and Brian quickly became lovers; she would be his "old lady" for the next two years.

Because of Brian's attempted theft charges, David Lutz would not allow him back into Aware House, and John Beatteay said, "If my friend is being kicked out, I'm going too." June followed suit. The three lived together until Brian and June decided to leave Saint

---

* A pseudonym.

John. For one thing, they felt as though they were living in a gold fish bowl, with the police watching their every move.

On January 8, 1972, Neddy LeBlanc, June Wallin and Brian Dempsey took off for Toronto, hitchhiking. As Brian later told friends, "We all had a lot to learn in those days and one of the very first lessons was don't hitchhike in January." They almost froze to death as they inched their way to Toronto. It was just one short ride after another, nobody seemed to be going further than fifty miles.

Chuck Dempsey was already back there, set up in a three-room flat on Jarvis Street. The threesome stayed with him for a couple of nights and then found a basement apartment of their own.

One morning not long after they had moved in, Brian Dempsey woke up in excruciating pain. The next day he hurt worse. "Jesus H. Christ," he told June, "never could you be prepared for this type of pain — it's total." He felt as though his veins were crystallizing during the night, and when he woke, his first movements sent pangs through him, as though glass had shredded into little pieces. He could specifically feel a sharp cutting pain in his heel. Finally his one eye exploded into a red ball, like a shattered sun. He went to several doctors and all offered no solutions. Finally an ophthalmologist asked him, "Do you have a particularly bad pain in your heel?" Dempsey replied, "You're the man I want to talk to. What have I got?" The doctor wouldn't give him a direct answer but referred him to Wellesley Hospital's rheumatology department.

Brian stayed there for two weeks undergoing a variety of tests. Finally a group of medical people gathered around his bed. A doctor explained, "Mr. Dempsey, the tests indicate that you have ankylosing spondylitis. Here is a pamphlet on it. Basically it's a form of arthritis that involves a progressive weight loss and deterioration of your general physical condition. Usually the patient dies before the age of thirty." Brian at that point was twenty-two.

A week later the group returned and the same doctor said, "Mr. Dempsey, there is another disease identical to ankylosing spondylitis that strikes you for two years and then goes away. It may come back and it may not. It's called Reiter's syndrome." "Well, give me some of that," responded Brian. "What are my odds?" The doctor said there was a 50 per cent chance for spondylitis and a 50 per cent for Reiter's. "When will we know?" "In two years if it goes away," said the doctor. "Right," responded Brian. To this day Dempsey suffers attacks of Reiter's and must take medication for the ailment.

His knees had been drained of fluid because they had swollen up like balloons, and he was discharged from the hospital on crutches. By that time June had found them a nice little apartment on Euclid

Street. It was then, as Chuck Dempsey described it, that "the holiday began." Of course Brian now had an excuse not to work. Their days were spent drinking, strumming on the guitar, playing cards, watching TV, yakking. Neddy LeBlanc was still there, and now and then he and Brian would go to the Young Station Tavern or to the Gasworks. But Brian was crippled for some time, and as he said, "I can't fly with a busted wing."

In November, 1972, John Beatteay suddenly showed up. He seemed to Brian "green as an apple, and totally in awe of the big city." He had bought an old Pontiac from his father to escape the tough old city of his birth, and he was determined to make good in Toronto.

There wasn't much room in the Euclid flat, so John and Neddy LeBlanc decided to get a room together. John had always been much more industrious than his chums and he quickly latched on to a series of labouring and painting jobs for subcontractors until he was hired as a machinist for the Greening Donald Company in March, 1973. By that time he had moved away from Brian's cabal. He had met a close friend of June Wallin's, Susan Elvin, a pretty clerk-typist of Icelandic origins, and they bought a condominium together in suburban Toronto. Dempsey and the bunch used to drop in on them all the time until it got to be a real sore point with Susan. She wrote to the Beatteays that Brian was around the apartment so much, often scrounging money, that she and John didn't have any time to themselves. John, however, was always glad to see him.

Brian's aimlessness was getting on his brother's nerves as well. Brian would tell him, time and again, that he was "gonna be a rock star as great as Jimi Hendrix." Chuck would respond, "Well, that's wonderful but you gotta get out there and look for it." He felt that Brian simply wasn't "giving it his all," that he was fooling around. Brian admitted he was feeling a sense of ennui. He needed something important to happen in his life. On the spur of the moment, he told June Wallin, "Dump the pills, let's have a kid." Brian remembers that "she lit up like a Christmas tree at the idea and we began work immediately."

By January, 1973, she was pregnant and they both began reading Adelle Davis's book *Let's Have Healthy Children*. June's parents were not exactly overjoyed at the prospect of their eighteen-year-old daughter taking on the responsibility of an infant. Brian got along with her mother wonderfully, but as he told a friend, "Her father's not thrilled with me, I guess because we are from two different worlds. I believe in destiny and he believes in starting in the mail room." And of course he didn't like the idea that Brian and June were not married. Brian told him that "any day June wants to get married, well she just has to pick a date. But she didn't and we didn't."

In November June gave birth to a seven-pound, thirteen-ounce baby boy. Someone asked Brian if he was pleased. "Does a centipede have legs?" he replied. He wrote his mother, "He just blows my mind, he is so beautiful." Brian's middle name was James; his father, when he was in a rare communicative mood, would affectionately call him that. Jamie became the infant's name as well.

Brian particularly liked to sing to the baby. One day when Jamie was nine months old, he was lying in his crib, gurgling away. Brian began to sing "Don't Rock the Boat," the song playing on the radio. He wrote his mother about what happened next: "I watched him click in, he'd been off in baby land somewhere and he came around to focus on me, totally intense like he was hunting and had found something. Then he pulled his little body up using the crib rungs until he was standing almost face to face with me. His face was all the awe and wonderment and joy and happiness that you could imagine. Then, blow my mind, he let go of the crib and started clapping his hands together." Brian couldn't recall when he had experienced a happier moment.

But Brian still didn't have a full-time job. June was soon back at work trying to scrounge enough money to feed them all. The couple also begged money from the Wallins and Lillian Amirault. The beer-drinking, guitar-playing parties didn't stop either. June would arrive home after a hard day's work to find the place a mess and the dinner not prepared. She'd get mad. In fact, the situation got so bad that she and Brian hardly stopped screaming at each other. One day she simply didn't come home from work. When Brian finally tracked her down, she told him that she had been only seventeen when she started going with him and that she hadn't lived enough. She was running away with an old acquaintance, a member of the Last Chance Motorcycle Club. Brian tried to talk her out of it, but when he couldn't he said, "Okay, fine, but Jamie stays with me." She agreed. Despite his stoicism, Brian remained very bitter. And Chuck Dempsey, who had always liked June, could never forgive her for leaving the baby behind.

The Wallins, who by this time had moved to Toronto and who loved Jamie dearly, volunteered to look after him. But Brian said no, at least not at the moment. He and Chuck would look after Jamie. After a few weeks Brian felt that the baby was better fed and dressed under their care than when he was June's responsibility. The neighbours downstairs adored the little boy, and whenever Brian and Chuck wanted to go out, they would mind him. And the Dempseys as usual had lots of friends in to party. Many of them were from the East Coast, including Dicky Gillespie just out of prison.

Gillespie had been through a rough few years in Saint John. His addiction to drugs had pretty well taken control of his life. One night in May of 1971, having been high on speed for days, he broke into a store that sold workman's tools. As the police arrived, Gillespie bolted, smashing through the plate glass window at the front of the store. He badly ripped open his knee and hand. The police appeared in the hospital emergency ward. "Gotcha now, kid," they said. Richard denied that he had broken into the store, claiming that someone had attacked him with a broken pop bottle. He was granted release pending trial.

A week later while playing pool, he met one of his friends, Henry Allemand,* who told him about a huge mansion standing unoccupied because the owners were away on vacation. The two were piling precious antiques at the front door when Richard spotted a police officer's hat. The two young thieves ran into the basement laundry room, and climbed into a large hardwood cabinet, Gillespie squeezing into the hatch at the top. The cops soon discovered Henry hiding below and as they were pulling him out, the cabinet tipped over, revealing Richard. He was sentenced to a year in the Saint John county jail for both escapades.

Eight months later he was on the loose again, and this time only six weeks passed before he was in deep trouble with the law.

Most of Richard's friends had been in training school or jail and their heads were screwed up something awful. Fighting was what was important to many of them, and they kept score cards, like a debutante at her coming-out party, of the number of heads that they'd busted. Dicky didn't like violence; for one thing he was physically too frail to be good at it, but he needed his friends too much to break away from the crowd.

One warm night in May, Henry Allemand became embroiled in a fight in downtown Saint John. Gillespie and another friend happened to be walking down the street when they heard the commotion. They came running and began circling the car containing Henry's adversaries, screaming, "Come out, you chicken shits, and behave like men!" The others were wise enough to remain in their vehicle but the window on the driver's side was open. The driver had a tire iron and each time Gillespie and company made a move to get into the car, he swung it at them. When Richard and his friends got to court, they received sentences of two years. "When decent

---

* A pseudonym.

citizens can't drive down the main street without being brutally assaulted, someone has to pay," said the judge.

Gillespie was sent to Springhurst Penitentiary and it seemed to do him some good. He stopped using heavy drugs and took an eight-month course in spray painting. His girl friend wrote to him that if he promised to go straight, she'd wait for him. He pleaded with the parole board that he was prepared to be a worthy citizen. They just laughed at him and he had to wait seventeen months before he was released. By that time his girl friend had disappeared, and he became an even more embittered and bewildered young man. He lived with his mother until his probation mandatory supervision period was up, then he took off for Toronto and Neddy LeBlanc. The very day Dicky arrived in Toronto, he and Neddy bicycled over to see Brian Dempsey and friends.

Brian had got it in his mind that he wanted to drive a tractor-trailer for a living. He thought that while he was on the road for all those hours, he could write songs in his head. He applied to George Brown College of Applied Arts and Technology to take a course and was told he had to drive a truck for a certain number of hours to qualify. As a result he found several jobs — delivering flowers, driving a garbage truck, chauffeuring for a printing house until they tried to put a little "red monkey suit" on him — to obtain the needed credits. He then attended the college for six weeks.

Brian managed a B-plus average and applied to Smith Transport for a job. He felt pretty good as he shunted the big rig around, lining it up nearly perfectly in the parking area. The foreman who had overseen his test was pleased and took him into the office to make out the application. A while later, however, the personnel manager told him, "Sorry, Mr. Dempsey, but your hair is too long." Chuck Dempsey says it took Brian a year to recuperate from that. "Brian takes personal disappointments extremely hard. He's a strange guy. Sometimes he can be as hard as the shell of an armadillo and sometimes as soft as the underside of a porcupine." At about that time Brian suffered another excruciating attack of Reiter's — he could hardly get up from his bed — so he told himself that he couldn't have taken the job anyway.

In the fall of 1973 Chuck and Brian made plans to celebrate Jamie's first birthday. They would invite all of their friends — there had to be lots of beer, of course — and some neighbourhood kids. The fifteen-year-old who lived downstairs was going to bake the cake. During October Brian was spending a lot of time with Judy Avrol,* the new woman in his life. He and Judy had the use of

* A pseudonym.

the bedroom, Chuck slept on the chesterfield near the baby's crib, which was kept in the front room.

On one particularly cold night, about three weeks before Jamie's birthday, Chuck awoke suddenly, realizing something was wrong. The smoke was so thick and the heat so fierce that all he could think of was to get to a window. As he stepped out onto the roof, he heard the baby cry and climbed back in. He groped around for about a minute, then tripped over something. When he got up, he thought he saw the crib and put his hand out. Whatever he touched burned terribly. He thought to himself, "Well, I don't use my left hand so much, it doesn't matter if it gets burned." But again his hand shot back in reflex from the heat. The smoke by this point was overwhelming. He stumbled around, falling again. This time he realized that he had wandered out of the front room into the hall and had tripped over a gate at the top of the stairs. He screamed at his brother, "Get the fuck out! There's a terrible fire!" Brian awoke naked in his bed, thinking he heard something fall in the kitchen. He pulled the door open and encountered "solid, unbelievable, thick-as-dough smoke." He began crawling around trying to find Chuck. He finally felt his brother's foot but it was wedged around a table leg, and Brian by this time gasping for lack of oxygen couldn't budge him. He ran back into the bedroom and with some difficulty shook Judy awake. "I'll be okay, go back to bed," she mumbled. Brian managed to pick her up and put her head through the window. He then grabbed his pants and jumped out the back window. He had decided that the best way to get to Jamie was to run through the downstairs neighbour's place, up the stairs, into the front room.

As he reached his front door he looked up at the second-floor window, the room Jamie was sleeping in. The flames were shooting up ten feet. He wrote his mother: "I stopped cold. I knew the baby was gone. A fireman rushed by me and I screamed at him that my son was in that room. He ran in but I knew Jamie was gone." Later that evening at the Hospital for Sick Children the downstairs neighbour identified the baby's body.

Brian had also seen the fire fighters haul out his brother and lay him out on the lawn. They started to work on him, give him artificial respiration, and Brian was sure that he was dead. He sat waiting with the neighbours and when they told him that Chuck had come around, Brian wouldn't believe them. "He's dead," he kept telling them. "Chuck's dead just like my baby."

After an investigation the Toronto fire marshall said the fatal blaze had likely been caused by careless smoking — a lit cigarette had probably fallen into the chesterfield.

EIGHT

Travellin'

ON A HOLIDAY
FROM LIFE

1974-77

Jamie's death left Brian Dempsey without what little purpose he had had. After the fire, he became even more nomadic, more reckless, more cocky. He had come to realize that, for some reason he could not comprehend, he had been born under a dark and sinister cloud. "I'm living for this very moment before disaster strikes again," he told his brother.

Chuck was in the hospital for a couple of weeks; the doctors thought the lens of his eyes might have been burned during the fire and that there was a chance he might be blind. When it was obvious that Chuck was okay, he, Brian and Judy got a room together. All of them were still terribly shaken by the tragedy. "We aren't totally pieced together," he told a friend. Judy finally bowed out of the ménage à trois, and the two brothers found an apartment on Broadway Avenue.

Shortly after they moved in, Brian was introduced to Christine Brown,* a beautiful woman with long, raven-black hair. She had a four-year-old son named Luke; Brian became attached to him, although he brought back painful memories of Jamie. Christine was a musician and taught Brian his first chords on the guitar. They strummed and sang Loggins and Messina's "Danny's Song" — ironically about the joy of child rearing. The relationship lasted only two months but it made Brian feel a little better.

Chuck's best friend, Al Perry, and his girl friend, Linda, both of whom were from Saint John, had rented an apartment in the same

---

* A pseudonym.

building as the Dempseys and the foursome saw a lot of each other. One day Linda said, "Guess who's coming to visit?" Brian shrugged. "One of my best friends, Daria McDougall," Linda told him. "That's the same broad who sent me down the tube for not marrying her!" shouted Brian. "That's all in the past now, Brian. Daria says she still likes you." "Of course she still likes me, she didn't go to jail." Linda insisted that she wanted them all to party together without a lot of friction. Brian thought to himself, "Fine, I'm all grown up. I won't spoil Linda's good time," but he told her, "Don't expect me to be dancing on the table." Everybody met at the restaurant where Linda worked as a waitress, and although it was an effort for him, Brian was surprisingly nice to Daria. "I hate hating," he told his brother.

About this time another female from Brian's past showed up. June Wallin and Brian got together to exchange memories of Jamie and have a good cry. They wound up in bed. "Nothing permanent," Brian pointed out, "we just felt comfortable with each other."

Brian needed some money to get himself going after the fire — the only things that had been saved were what he had been wearing, an over-sized army coat and a pair of rubber boots. All his personal possessions — his clothes, stereo, furniture — had been destroyed. So he naturally turned to the activity he knew would yield him quick cash — poker playing. Brian usually dropped into Rochdale College, the most notorious of the country's "free-schools," a hippie haven, to indulge his gambling and on this particular day he wound up head to head with the man who taught the sport. His name was Fergie and he looked coolly confident as he sat there, his hat band full of hash oil and pot joints. After a few hands, his woman had the most amazed look on her face. "Jeez," she said, "this guy's the Last Card Kid." In the end Brian won twelve hundred dollars. As he bragged to Chuck, "Fergie wasn't hurt by the money, but you know the guy who teaches gambling at Rochdale didn't look good losing." Brian later wrote a ballad about the incident which he called "The Last Card Kid."

> I'm trying to fill an inside straight, it's a fool's move in any book,
> When the redhead there by Roy L.'s chair, she gives me a come-on look.
> My drink stood near empty, the waitress at the bar was crying about something I said.
> The crowd had surrounded the dealer cross me to see what the last card read.
>
> It wasn't the first time I've painted the floor-boards and bet on how long it would dry

But it wasn't a straight that came out of the gate and Roy L. got
a gleam in his eye.

The table was piled knee deep in the folding, the redhead was
leaving me fast.
I needed a 7, an ace floated over, the straight was a thing of
the past.

That's the Last Card Kid
Someone whispered softly,
Don't look like too much to me.
That's the Last Card Kid, the dealer said,
I knew he was talking to me.

Four up and one down, it was all we could have, he still wasn't
showing a pair.
And I had the ace high, it looked the best hand, I threw
half what I had sitting there.

He wasn't impressed and said, "Throw in the rest." I called and he
doubled the Jack.
I turned up the ace, every face in the place went totally
beautifully slack.

That's the Last Card Kid
Someone whispered softly,
Don't look like too much to me.
That's the Last Card Kid, said the dealer.
I knew he was talking about me.

After four months in the Broadway apartment, Chuck Dempsey
decided to return to Saint John to have another go at making his
marriage work. Brian moved into a rooming house on Elgin
Avenue. Shortly after, his careless and nonconforming lifestyle
would land him in more trouble. This time he was charged with the
rape of a minor.

He and a friend, Gary Lang, had been visiting Al and Linda.
They were leaving the building when Brian spotted a pretty girl
coming up the stairs. "My, we're looking good today," Brian called
out. The girl smiled.

Gary met her again — her name was Lucia Sun Manten* — and
he brought her back to the rooming house. They were all sitting
around drinking, and Gary told Brian that he had had sex with

* A pseudonym.

Lucia. Brian told a friend later, "As that night wore on it got to be me and her looking at the back seat. Gary wasn't hung up about it and her and I went down to my room to assess our compatibility factor." After that Lucia moved in with Brian, not with any understanding of a personal commitment on either of their parts, but because she had nowhere else to stay.

The next night Brian and Gary Lang went to the Gasworks where they met Neddy LeBlanc and Gary Dow, another old friend of Brian's from Saint John. According to Brian, they got drunk and all four ended up at the rooming house. They went to Gary Lang's room and were soon joined by Lucia Sun Manten. The group continued drinking and talking, and eventually Brian fell asleep on the couch. "When I woke up Lucia was humming 'O Canada' in A flat minor on Gary Lang's reproductive equipment. I looked at the scene. She saw me, she never said anything, and she sure seemed to be enjoying herself." Brian went back to sleep and when he woke up she was gone.

The following Sunday evening Al Perry and Brian were sitting around drinking Jordan's Gold Seal sherry when two policemen walked in. "You Brian Dempsey?" they asked. He nodded. "We're going to have to arrest you, Brian." "What for?" he screeched. "Raping a minor," the cop replied. Lucia Sun Manten, on the urging of a girl friend, had run to the police complaining she had been assaulted by four men. Brian, Gary Dow, Gary Lang and Neddy LeBlanc were charged, although the police were never able to track down Neddy; there's a warrant out for his arrest to this day.

Brian spent his twenty-fifth birthday, April 21, 1975, in the Don Jail. He and Gary Lang beat the rape charges at the preliminary hearing. While obviously the four men had engaged in a night of sexual play, the judge determined that there wasn't enough evidence to send Dempsey and Gary Lang to trial. For Gary Dow, however, the story was different, and Lang and Dempsey had a difficult decision to make. They knew they were probably home free, but "the deal came down that we plead guilty to indecent assault and they would not shove the rape charges up Gary Dow's ass." They agreed. Brian was sentenced to three months in jail, but by that time he had already been incarcerated for nine months waiting for the trial. This was another example of how his disregard and recklessness towards, in this case, a young girl, concluded in an unsavoury way. With indecent assault added to his criminal record, Dempsey would now be considered by the authorities as one who perpetrated violence against women.

What had particularly upset Brian was a newspaper headline which read "Four men break into room, rape 16-year-old." It caused bad vibrations in the prison, and Brian was afraid he would either be beaten or murdered. Happily he could sing. Night after night he entertained his fellow prisoners and that probably saved his skin. During his sojourn there, he wrote "Don Jail Blues," which he always considered one of his wittiest.

> When you're sittin' in the Don Jail, Baby,
>   you're in the hole.
> Thinkin' bout your life style.
>   dreamin' bout your goals.
> Saturday night gonna' roll around
>   but you won't have no beer.
> Then Hockey Night in Canada is all that you'll hear.

Brian was released on January 17, 1976. He wrote his mother about it. "They can't even let you out the front door, they let you out the garage. There were about eight guys this morning. They open the automatic garage door and it's like a school of tadpoles all escaping into the big pond."

Brian went to live with John Beatteay and Susan Elvin in their Rexdale apartment. The incident with Lucia hadn't made Sue grow any fonder of him. She wrote John's parents in Saint John that Brian had beaten the rape charge and had got a nothing sentence. "If anybody ever did anything like that to me I hope they'd get a lot more — like about twelve years," she declared. It was a pronouncement that would come back to haunt them.

Brian got a job driving a truck for a printing company, and his mother sent him fifty dollars for his birthday, so he decided he could afford to buy himself a "lovely, lovely" guitar. Although he'd been singing since he was three, he always assumed he couldn't play the instrument because he was left-handed. He set out to teach himself in earnest, and from that point on the instrument went everywhere with him.

Brian ran into Neddy LeBlanc at a bar one day. Neddy was on the run from the rape charges, and he and Brian got talking about going West. They arranged for a gas-sharing ride to Winnipeg and from there hitchhiked to Vancouver. They both got jobs sandblasting the Lions Gate Bridge, balancing 250 feet in the air on a swaying wire catwalk and blasting panels. Neither one had a clue as to what they were doing but they liked the money — eleven dollars an hour, twenty-two dollars overtime. They were granted temporary permits by the union, primarily because nobody else wanted such dangerous, dirty work.

The first thing Neddy and Brian did when they got to Vancouver was to seek out a bar, the Carlton in Gastown, which they had heard about from friends. Sure enough, the place was full of expatriot New Brunswickers, including a couple of good buddies who invited the two young men to stay at their place for a while. Brian went to the bar almost every day — played some pool, drank beer, joked with the regulars.

Sometimes Brian would work the streets of Gastown, singing and playing guitar. One night he met two lawyers, who were also musicians, from Los Angeles. They raved about Brian's voice and the three went into the Carlton for a couple of drinks. As Brian reported it, "These guys were talking studio and loose professional jamming." They invited him to look them up in L.A. and he was determined he would one day. Their business cards and his guitar are among the few possessions he has always kept with him in his prison cell.

One night in August, 1976, Brian was feeling particularly good. He had bought himself a new pair of jeans and a nifty plaid shirt. As he walked into the bar, he noticed a new girl sitting with a friend of his. It was no big thing. He shot some pool and then sat sipping a couple of beers. Suddenly an old man appeared out of nowhere and said to Dempsey, "Don't ever let her go. You two were meant for each other." Brian and Jean Elgar just looked at each other in astonishment.

The next night Jean was there with the same friend, and Brian suggested the three of them go to a party that he'd been invited to. What they found were eighty people packed into a small apartment, so stoned "they were bouncing off the walls." Brian and Jean had been feeling a strong pull towards each other and he finally looked at her and said, "You wanna get out of here?" That began the longest and most passionate romance of Brian's life.

Jean Elgar was vacationing in Vancouver and in two weeks she returned to her job in Carlyle, Saskatchewan. Brian had been assigned by the union to a job painting steel girders in Skookumchuk, near Kimberley, B.C. Things went well for a few days until he and three others got into a dispute with the hotel manager and decided to move to the town's other inn. The company, which paid the workers' hotel bill, threatened to fire them, so they all quit. Brian spent a pleasant few days in Cranbrook, "viewing the local pulchritude," and then returned to Vancouver to collect his paycheque. He stayed there only a couple of nights but managed to meet an attractive "lady" in a bar who was around in the morning to drive him to the airport. He was on his way to meet Jean. He flew to Calgary, took the train to Regina and the bus to Carlyle, a town which was known as "The Cornerstone of Saskatchewan."

During the party celebrating Jean Elgar's seventh birthday, her mother, Margaret, led the young guests into the garage and one by one whipped them. Naturally the other parents raised a terrible fuss and forbade the children from going anywhere near Jean's house. It was another bizarre incident in the gothic saga of the "crazy Elgars" of Carlyle.

Margaret and William Elgar were married in 1946 and the first of seven children arrived a year later. By 1950 Margaret had begun to show signs of the schizophrenia which would plague her for the rest of her life. By the time Jean was born on December 27, 1958, her mother was caught in a revolving door, in and out of mental hospitals. She would disappear for months on end and the household would settle down to some stability, with Jean's older sister Mary Jane acting as a surrogate mother. But then Mrs. Elgar would arrive home and mayhem would ensue.

When her husband had a debilitating stroke in 1974, Margaret believed he was dead. Carrying pillows, she kept sneaking into the room where he was convalescing, intent on smothering what she thought was the spirit that had been left behind. The family finally decided she would have to be recommitted to a mental hospital. One morning in June of 1975 she was found dead on a beach. She had been on vacation with a group of psychiatric patients and had gone for a swim at six in the morning. The coroner said she drowned but her family assumed that since she was found with all her clothes on, she had committed suicide.

Jean's position in the family dictated that she suffered the most from her mother's odd behaviour — when the older children were growing up she was not quite so erratic, and Jean's younger sister, Reena May, doesn't remember too much of her mother. As a result Jean was, as her sister describes, "a very, very lonely, sad little girl," playing mostly by herself in the ramshackle family home situated in the middle of the small prairie town.

In 1972 she began working in the Carlyle Bakery, owned by her father, part-time, and in 1975, full-time. She was described by everybody who knew her as extremely capable, with a natural bent for organization. Indeed, her brothers and sisters felt she worked too hard. She was so introverted, and since she didn't curl or drink, there was little for her to do in the small town. She was often depressed and even talked about suicide. Her family were glad when in 1976 she bought herself a sprightly, orange Chevelle and took off for a vacation in Vancouver.

Brian Dempsey moved right into Jean's pleasant apartment above the bakery. It was smack in the centre of main street and if you looked out the window you could see the Lutheran church, the

Chinese restaurant, the local co-op, the town hall. With a population of 1,074 it was a bustling centre, the gathering place for the prosperous farmers in the district. It was a pretty place. The buildings along the main street had recently been refurbished, their false fronts cut into neat T or square shapes so that they looked like children's cardboard cutouts. One of the first things Brian noticed was the number of cops around. An RCMP detachment was situated on Carlyle's main street, with twenty-one officers assigned to it. Residents were fond of saying that there were more police per capita in that small town than anywhere else in Canada.

There wasn't much for Brian to do. There were no jobs and he didn't appreciate the idea of working in the bakery. He spent a lot of time in the beverage room of the Carlyle Hotel until he got in a scuffle with one of the waitresses, an old school friend of Jean's. Brian had gotten into the habit of wearing a white straw hat; it made him feel like Cool Hand Luke. One night the waitress in question glared at him and said, "Take your hat off, you're no gentleman." "No thankee, Ma'm," he responded. The woman then pinched Brian's nipples, and he responded in kind. He ran out of the hotel, the woman's husband running and shouting after him.

He made lots of friends there, especially among the local Indians. One night he was invited to a party on the nearby White Bear Reserve. He pulled out his guitar and mesmerized the guests until early in the morning. From that time onward he was accepted on the reserve and spent most of his time hanging out there. On only one occasion did he run into trouble; it was one of the few times Brian got involved in a punch-em-out fight.

He was sitting on a stack of beer cases, chatting away with friends, including Jean Elgar. The lady of the house came in the room and joined the conversation. Brian insists that although she was one of the most beautiful Indians he had ever seen, he had absolutely no intention of making a pass at her. Suddenly out of the blue, her husband tackled him. They did about three rolls and Brian ended up on top. "Never can figure out why so many guys think I'm after their old ladies. Must think I'm some kind of a stud, huh?" Brian bragged to Jean.

That incident was the exception. The Indians of the White Bear Reserve, in particular the young, liked Brian almost as much as he liked them. For one thing they were absolutely amazed at his uncanny ability with a pool cue. He could shoot a better game one-handed than they could with two. For these occasions Brian used to often wear a T-shirt with the Royal Bank logo on the back and the slogan WHEN YOU SUCCEED, WE SUCCEED. An old woman, the wife of a chief, gave him an Indian name Brian considered a great honour. It was Maza Ska Tipi; in English, House of Money.

Despite the fact that his hair was shoulder length, his beard long and scraggly, his jeans often tattered, so that he looked every inch the hippy the good citizens of Carlyle had heard so much bad news about, Jean's family tried hard to like Brian. But it wasn't long before his cocky, bantering ways had them gritting their teeth. Mary Jane, the sister who had for so long run the large household and was particularly close to Jean, grew to loathe Dempsey. She says he was arrogant and rude to everyone, and she saw him as sinister, a criminal who would harm both her sister and the Elgar family as a whole. She was convinced that his ten-speed bike, his expensive guitar, his radio and tape decks had all been stolen. Her husband was not quite so harsh in his judgement. He considered him primarily as a mooch, always putting the arm on someone for money. However, by this time Jean had become utterly devoted to Brian. She told everybody that his presence had saved her sanity, maybe even her life. "I became a person because of him," she told Mary Jane.

Many of the townspeople suspected that Brian was selling drugs to Carlyle children and young Indians. This dealing was supposed to have taken place above the bakery, six buildings away from the RCMP detachment. But Mayor Ted Brady said he was not aware of any such activity; the RCMP had a policy of letting the town councillors know of any such illegal goings-on. He remembers a lot of loud heavy rock coming from the top of the bakery but not much else. Brian says he smoked hash during this period, and he admits he gave joints away to some of his Indian friends but denies selling it to any kids. "For one thing where could I get it in that quantity?" he asked Mary Jane.

But she was eager to get rid of him. She even offered to give him fifty dollars for his bike. He refused but shortly after disappeared for a few weeks — he went to Vancouver to round up some marijuana but only, according to him, for his own personal use. While he was there, he met his old friend Neddy LeBlanc. Brian brought Neddy back to Jean's place and then the two of them really got into the mood. They would sleep all day at the bakery and stay at the reserve until the early hours of the morning, partying, singing and drinking. One day Brian went to see some friends and got back to find the apartment ransacked and Jean fit to be tied. Neddy had stolen a very old and valuable coin collection. Brian was furious, took a shotgun owned by Jean's father and set out to "blast Neddy's legs off." Fortunately he didn't find him. "It was pure theatrics but

Jean believed him," said Mary Jane. Brian later found out that Neddy, who was still on the run from the 1975 rape charge, had "freaked" at so many Mounties walking around and had felt compelled to leave Carlyle, no matter how.

On Boxing Day, 1976, Brian and Jean and some other friends were coming home from a party at White Bear Reserve. Brian, who had had several drinks and had smoked a few joints earlier, was driving Jean's Chevelle. Suddenly he spotted a patrol car at the side of the road. Red lights began to flash and sirens roar. Brian's foot clamped down on the gas and they were off on a wild chase. Brian drove sixty-four miles in forty minutes along a gravel road and through a rutted field. The six people in the car were so shaken as Brian bumped and circled around that they suffered bruises on their arms and legs. When they finally lost sight of the cops, Brian stopped and asked Jean to take the wheel. She was the only one of the group who had been neither drinking nor smoking that day.

The vehicle limped back to town. Waiting for them in the back lane were the RCMP. "I'm charging you with attempted murder for the sake of my wife and children," one of the officers told Brian. The police then thoroughly searched the car and its occupants but found nothing. Jean was charged with failing to stop at seven stop signs. As the cops were leaving, Brian taunted, "Hey, aren't you going to charge me with attempted murder. Come on, you said you were and I insist." The officer just walked away in disgust.

A few days later Brian was stopped again on the highway by an RCMP constable whom both he and Jean knew. Again the car was searched and so was Brian. The officer found nothing, having neglected to check a zippered ammunition pocket on the sleeve of Brian's jacket. It was there that a wad of hash was stashed. "I'll get you one of these days," the cop told him. "Good luck to you," yelled Brian. "They don't know what the stuff looks like," he told Jean.

Brian was excited New Year's Eve. Kenny Shields and the Streethearts were playing at the Carlyle Hotel and Brian had been asked to sing at intermission. He was just coming out of the bakery apartment when he was stopped by two RCMP officers who searched the car. In his guitar they found one small flower top of a cannabis plant. Brian spent New Year's Eve in the Carlyle jail. He was charged with possession of marijuana but in his mind something much more serious had happened: his guitar had been confiscated.

Brian and Jean both insisted the marijuana had been planted there, and all the young people in town they knew agreed with them. Mary Jane and others retorted that that was utter nonsense. However, Brian was able to work out a deal. If he left town, he'd get his guitar back.

On a cold January morning he and Jean headed out of Carlyle in the Chevelle. Left behind were the considerable bills incurred in fixing the car and various debts owed to friends and family. The apartment above the bakery was left in such a mess that the Elgars decided never to rent it again. Jean's family was devastated by her decision to leave with Brian. Her father, who could no longer talk because of his stroke, could only shake his head sadly at the mention of his daughter. Mary Jane insists that Jean would have loved anybody who showed the slightest interest in her. Brian was smart in the way he lavished so much attention on Jean, she says.

Three hundred miles out of Toronto, Brian and Jean ran into a blizzard. It was slow going and exhausting. When it cleared a little, Brian crawled into the back seat and slept while Jean drove. There were very few drivers, especially women, with whom Brian could relax. Jean was one of them. He came to think that it was symbolic of their entire relationship.

They booked into a motel on the outskirts of Toronto and immediately phoned John Beatteay. He rushed over and they had a couple of drinks, played some music and talked about what was happening in T.O. John had just split up with Sue Elvin. For some years he had worked as a mechanic at Miami Carey in Rexdale and had made good money. But he had been laid off in November, 1976, when the company moved to Barrie, Ontario. The condo had always been a hangout for John's friends, but after he became unemployed, the parties never stopped. There was a lot of dope dealing going on there too. Sue Elvin couldn't take any more and left. It was decided that Jean and Brian would move into the Rexdale condominium.

Two months after Jean and Brian arrived in Toronto, in March, 1977, they were joined by nineteen-year-old Linda Brown. Brian had met her one night in the Carlyle Hotel and when they got talking they discovered she was an old school aquaintance of Jean's. Brian was attracted to her because "she was a good-looking broad," tall, with long, brown hair and dark, "puppy-dog" eyes. Linda had grown up on a farm a few miles from Carlyle. At sixteen she left home for Regina, where she worked as a clerk in Coles book store. She became pregnant, gave the baby up for adoption and moved back to her parents' home. She was intrigued by Brian Dempsey; he seemed so exotic compared to the conservative, rather dull folk of Carlyle, like a mango tree in a forest of oaks. While Brian and Jean were still living in Carlyle, she went everywhere with them, fascinated by Brian's panache and sophistication. When Brian and Jean were about to leave, they asked her to join them in Toronto, and she jumped at the chance to escape Carlyle. She got a job as a waitress in Saskatoon to save up the air fare and then took off for Toronto.

When she first arrived, she lived by herself, working as a bartender at the posh Town Hall. But she was mighty attracted to the handsome John Beatteay, who she felt was "a hunk of a man," and soon moved in with the ménage in Rexdale. Linda and Jean got jobs as waitresses or bartenders in various establishments and supported Brian and John while they talked about becoming musicians. The men fell into a routine — boozing, smoking and partying every day, a drunken binge which lasted for two years.

On Thursday, September 15, 1977, at 2:30 p.m., Constable Douglas MacPhail, Detective Gordon Marshall and Detective Sergeant Brian Cousineau of the Criminal Investigation Branch, York Regional Police, knocked on the door of a Dixon Road condominium. Someone inside yelled, "Fuck off." Cousineau knocked again. The door opened a crack and the marijuana smoke almost knocked the cops over. Cousineau identified himself and told the ill-kempt young man at the door that he wanted to talk to him about an investigation involving an assault in Pefferlaw, Ontario. He was refused. "What's your name?" the detective asked. "George McNulty" was the reply. "Come out into the hall so I can speak to you," requested Cousineau. "Fuck you" was the response, and Brian Dempsey slammed the door in his face.

Two hours later Cousineau and the two other detectives returned with a search warrant for narcotics. Accompanying them were eight members of the Metro Toronto Police's crack Emergency Task Force, carrying automatic rifles. They sledgehammered the door in, then rounded up eight people found in the condo. Brian Dempsey would later describe it to a friend: "Guns everywhere, absolutely everywhere, a pregnant woman made to lie on her stomach, deliberate ransacking when they weren't looking for anything."

The detectives isolated Dempsey in one of the bedrooms. Cousineau noticed that between the time he first spotted him at the door and the moment of the raid, Brian's beard had disappeared. He asked him why he had shaved. "Cause I was going out," Brian replied. Cousineau than cautioned him, "Do you wish to say anything in answer to the charge? You are not obliged to say anything unless you wish to do so, but whatever you say will be taken down in writing and may be given in evidence." Cousineau reported that Dempsey then snapped, "I don't know anything about a broad being assaulted in Pefferlaw." Cousineau claimed that he had not mentioned which sex the assaulted person was. He then asked Brian where he had been on Sunday, September 11, and was told, "I didn't leave the apartment all weekend." At a trial that was to follow, Brian denied making either statement to the police.

He was accused of so badly fracturing the left arm of a twenty-nine-year-old Toronto woman, Elaine Lagroix,* that she was permanently disabled and could not continue her job as a machine operator, sewing men's socks.

There was no disagreement about certain events that occurred that lovely Sunday afternoon. John Beatteay and Brian Dempsey started drinking beer almost from the moment they got up. An old friend, Wade Blythe, a three-hundred-pound ex-biker who wore an earring and black leather, dropped in. He owned a 1972 lemon-yellow Dart Demon, and that afternoon the trio decided to drive to Pefferlaw, situated on the south shore of Lake Simcoe, where Brian, John and two other friends had rented an old dilapidated farmhouse for the summer. On weekends the gang would drop in, drink any booze that happened to be around, smoke some hash and generally "shoot the bull."

On this particular day Brian and John had a very special prize, indeed a gold mine, in their possession. It was a Visa credit card that belonged to Kevin Livingston, who lived on the eighteenth floor of their condominium. John would later claim that he had borrowed it because he didn't have any cash on him. However, Livingston reported to the police that it had been stolen. On the way to the farmhouse, Brian, John and Wade Blythe dropped into a couple of bars and ordered double scotches or rums, paying the bill with Livingston's Visa. By three in the afternoon they arrived at the Anchor Tavern situated in Sutton, about a ten-minute drive from the farmhouse. Shortly a very drunken couple staggered over and asked if they could sit with them.

It was such a nice day that Elaine Lagroix, who was so heavy as to be considered obese, and her boy friend, Paul Pietrobon, decided to go for a car ride to Sibbald Park, situated on Lake Simcoe. The Anchor Tavern seemed like a nice place to have lunch, and while they were there, they began experimenting with some exotic cocktails which Pietrobon had earlier been trying to describe for Elaine. They each had a couple of Zombies and Harvey Wallbangers and then Paul decided he wanted to go for a swim. He went down to the lake and dove in, badly cutting his head on a rock. The couple returned to the tavern and asked the owner, Zissis Kipouros, better known as Chris, for a bandage. He couldn't find one.

Paul and Elaine had a couple more drinks, and by then they were thoroughly polluted. They began wandering around the dining room, chattering at the other customers, generally making a nuisance of themselves. Chris, the owner, told them, "If you don't sit

* A pseudonym.

down properly I call the police or throw you out." And he cut them off booze.

By the time the couple came to rest at the table where John, Brian and Wade were sitting, Paul's cut had opened up more. Blood was streaming down his face. John said, "It looks revolting, man. Why don't you go in the washroom and clean it up." Pietrobon did so but he was so smashed that in about twenty minutes he was out cold at the table. Chris came over and asked the young men if they could help him with Pietrobon. Wade and John carried the drunken man out to his van and laid him down on the front seat.

It was at this point that the stories of Elaine Lagroix and Brian Dempsey began to diverge drastically.

Lagroix recalled that after Paul had been dumped in the van, she and the three men, John, Brian and Wade, had another drink or two in the tavern. The men got talking about continuing at the farmhouse and said they would wake Paul and take him as well.

Lagroix got into Blythe's car but before she knew what was happening, they drove away leaving Pietrobon behind. "Where are we going? Where are you taking me?" she yelled. Nobody responded.

According to Lagroix, after a while Dempsey pulled his penis from his pants and said to her, "Give me a hand job." "No," she told him and pushed him away from her. He then punched her. "I got hit in the face and then I was starting to protect myself and I started moving down towards the back seat and he started punching me some more. And I was being punched over towards my shoulder.... I was just blocking my face."

The next thing she knew they had arrived at the farmhouse. One of the men, she couldn't remember which one, grabbed her and pulled her inside. "'I was just screaming as far as I know, that's all I could think of, just scream and just say I didn't want to go anywhere near them."

When they got into the house, Lagroix said that Dempsey took her into a room, took out his penis and told her, "Suck my cock." When she refused, he grabbed her left arm, twisted it back, at the same time punching her and kicking her in the back. "I was on my knees and he was kicking me around and he just kept saying 'Suck my cock.' I said no I just won't do that. And he kept twisting and beating." She then remembered hearing a large snap and feeling her shoulder burn with pain. "The next thing I knew, I was being thrown out from the back seat of the car onto the road." Lagroix says that after that she remembers waking up the next morning in the intensive care unit of York County Hospital.

Brian Dempsey's account of events (supported by John Beatteay as defence witness and Wade Blythe's) was radically different. After the two men had returned from carrying Pietrobon out to his van, Brian claimed Elaine began making passes at John and Brian, kissing and hugging them and fondling their penises. "You wanna screw?" she repeatedly asked. At one point Wade Blythe went to the washroom. Another patron was having a leak when Lagroix came in. She started playing with the man's penis and Wade told him, "Boy, you done fine on a Sunday afternoon." The man laughed. Back in the restaurant, Lagroix exposed her breasts and John and Brian fondled them. Once, they stood up, glasses in hand. That was against liquor regulations, and Chris hurried over and told them to cool it. They then all decided to continue drinking at the farmhouse. John Beatteay paid the bill with the stolen credit card, got some bones for the dogs from Chris and left.

According to John and Brian, John and Elaine got in the back of the Dart Demon, Brian sat in the front with Wade Blythe. As they were driving along Elaine took her top off, baring her breasts, and undid her slacks. She and John were necking and touching each other's genitalia. At one point, she leaned over the front seat, kissed Brian and indicated that he should come back with them. He did. According to him, Elaine managed to fondle both his and John's penis at the same time.

When they arrived at the farmhouse, they all sat around and had a few shots of lemon gin and rum. Elaine was so drunk by this time she kept falling off her chair. Eventually she grabbed Brian by the hand and said, "Let's go in the bedroom." They started kissing and then as Brian described it, "She took her pants off and laid down on the bed. And she was on her menstrual cycle which I didn't know until she pulled out a tampon which was about 13 different colours.... I gagged and said, 'No way, no way.'"

The group had another drink and then decided to take Elaine back to her friend Paul Pietrobon.

The four of them sat in the front seat, Elaine perched half on John's knee and half on Brian's. Suddenly, for no discernible reason, she "started freaking out," screaming, "Let me out of here, let me out," all the while kicking the dash and the windshield violently. Wade Blythe, furious at what she was doing to his car, testified that he stopped and said, "If you want out, get out." He then pushed her onto the gravel road.

There were many facts that undermined both Elaine Lagroix's and Brian Dempsey's accounts of events that day. Lagroix had insisted that there had been no physical contact between herself or any of the men in the restaurant. But both the restaurant owner and his daughter who worked as a waitress testified that Elaine was "all over the men." Maria Kipouros claimed that Lagroix "was hustling them," necking with them and kissing them. Her father claimed that Elaine's breasts were exposed and that Brian and John were fondling them. Finally both said that unlike Elaine Lagroix and Paul Pietrobon, Brian, John and Wade "were always polite" and "very, very gentlemen."

Elaine Lagroix described Brian Dempsey to police as having light blond hair, a beard and moustache, and "piercing blue eyes." Brian's hair colour is chestnut and his eyes are so dark that they look like two black coals. Nor could she identify either John Beatteay* or Wade Blythe. In her original statement to police, Lagroix said that Brian had demanded she perform fellatio on him and then twisted her arm in the back seat of the car; she said nothing about the farmhouse.

Brian maintained that Elaine received her injuries falling off her chair in the farmhouse and being pushed out of the car by Wade Blythe. And Blythe did admit to this. But there were a couple of fundamental flaws in Dempsey's story.

Elaine Lagroix had been seriously hurt during this episode. Her arm was so badly broken that she eventually had to undergo two major operations to correct it. And as one doctor put it, "She still was severe limitation of movement in the left hand and wrist. She will likely be left with some permanent disability." The physician also concluded that the fracture "was consistent" with her arm being forcefully twisted behind her back. She also sustained bruises and abrasions all over her body, including her face. It became obvious that the scenario painted by the accused and his cohorts could not have resulted in Lagroix being so severely injured. John Beatteay testified that Wade Blythe did not shove Elaine hard. Beatteay testified that he got out of the car as she was being pushed and that he saw her walk towards the ditch. John then said goodbye and got back into the car. Beatteay was, of course, in the awkward position of having to think of the interests not only of his good buddy Brian Dempsey but also of Wade Blythe.**

---

* Beatteay was originally charged with forceful confinement and intent to wound, but the charges were dropped after Lagroix failed to point him out in a courtroom.

** Dempsey now claims that Wade Blythe, enraged that Lagroix was damaging his beloved automobile, got out of the car, opened the passenger door, grabbed Elaine and literally threw her onto the gravel road. Dempsey says he did not testify to this in court because Blythe would have been put in an untenable position and "bros" don't squeal.

Brian Dempsey was found guilty of assault causing bodily harm. He was flabbergasted when he was convicted on May 31, 1979. "Do I have blue eyes and blond hair?" he asked anyone who would listen. And indeed, as in the case of the Spudic and Harply rapes, the testimony of Lagroix was riddled with contradictions and fuzziness, primarily because of the quantities of alcohol she'd consumed that night. But as with the Lauder rapes, the jury believed that something had happened to Lagroix and that Dempsey was chiefly responsible for it. He seemed to be developing a growing misogyny, a loathing for women, which the jurors determined should be punished. Whether it was he who had fractured the woman's arm or not, the mere fact that he stood by and let it happen indicated a deeply engrained disregard, if not loathing, for the opposite sex.

Judge Hogg sentenced him to three years in prison, stating that he had treated the unfortunate victim as if she was a bag of garbage. By that time, of course, Brian Dempsey was already in jail, awaiting trial for the rapes of Claudine Harply and Terri Spudic. After two juries found him guilty, he was eventually sentenced to a total of fifteen years.

NINE

Grenadier Road

I'D GIVE ANYTHING
TO SING LIKE THAT

Brian was able to convince Jean Elgar that he had nothing to do
with the fat woman's injuries. He explained that after Wade
pushed Lagroix from the car, "I looked back but I didn't see
anything so I looked up front and then I looked back again and I
threw myself half over the front seat looking for her. She was gone
and Wade kept saying, 'I don't have to take that.' What could I do?
Oh, I guess I could have strangled him until he drove us into a
ditch." And Brian added, "As much as I love a good blow job, if I
ever need one that bad, I'll buy it. In the meantime I got plenty of
offers." Bail was arranged for Dempsey and he was released from
jail just before Christmas, 1977, three months after his arrest.

At about that time, John Beatteay, who was still unemployed,
had financial difficulties with his condominium. Wade Blythe
found a couple of apartments for John and Linda and Brian and
Jean in the building where he was a superintendent on Albany
Street. The lifestyle didn't change; indeed the drinking became
heavier, the drugs in surplus supply. Brian and the boys would
start their mornings with a beer and a toke, usually hash, and
they'd continue to imbibe all day long. Friends would drop in,
sometimes carrying a case of beer or a mickey of whisky, and the
drinking would continue. In the evening they'd often go to a pub for
a game of pool and more boozing or else a party would develop at
Lauder that often lasted the night through.

One of the people who used to drop over all the time was Brian
Krinchuk. Beatteay and Dempsey had been involved in a few drug
deals with Krinchuk, and when they discovered what a fine musician he was, they became close friends. The two Brians often sang

together and their voices blended like "bread and butter." As Brian
Dempsey told John, "Krinchuk's guitar playing is way beyond my
ability." He played the spectrum: Elton John, the Rolling Stones,
Neil Young, the Beatles, Pink Floyd. Dempsey thought Krinchuk
was "super-talented" and maybe if they worked together their
musical careers would at last soar.

They used to like to go to a bar, a small honky-tonk, pull out their
guitars and sing for their captive audience. "Everywhere we'd go,
we would just take over. People loved it," says Krinchuk. In April,
1978, on Brian's birthday, the group hit a tavern called The Mug.
The two Brians and John began singing and playing their guitars
and before long the whole place had joined them. "Must have been
150 people just behopping and having a good time," Brian Krinchuk told a friend. By the end of the evening the group's bill was
about $150. They left without paying and management didn't say a
word. It had, after all, been an evening of cheap entertainment.

Krinchuk arranged a recording session for them in the sound
studio of an acquaintance of his. They played some rock and country and western, including Brian's own composition, "Don Jail
Blues." The entertainers were smashed on Scotch and hash and so
was the sound engineer. As a result the tape remained incomplete
and of poor quality.

It was Brian Krinchuk who introduced Dave Bell to the Dempsey
entourage. They had been adolescent friends who had remained in
touch even though both travelled around. When Dave returned
from a three-year stint out West in the summer of 1977, he immediately phoned Krinchuk, who told him, "You gotta meet these
friends of mine. You gotta hear them sing." Bell refused at first. He
knew the kind of life Krinchuk's friends were indulging in — booze,
drugs and sex — and he didn't want to be sucked into it. Krinchuk
persevered, however, and finally Dave agreed to visit the Beatteay's Rexdale condominium. He was sucked in immediately.

Dave told Brian Dempsey, "I'd give anything to sing like that."
"Well why don't ya," responded Brian. "Yeah, yeah, sure," said Dave
in his usual self-deprecating manner. "I'm serious," said Brian, "I'll
help ya if you wanna learn." Dave got in the habit of calling Brian
"Mr. Sinatra." Brian Krinchuk developed other interests at the
time and stopped visiting Dempsey and friends. But Dave began
hanging around them more and more until eventually he moved in
with them.

When Dave Bell was in his mid-teens his father had put a sticker
on his son's bedroom door which said, "Bitch a Little." "I don't think
Dave had a conflict in his life," says Andrew Bell, "and I didn't think
it was normal for anyone to be that placid. I wanted him to get a

little hot under the collar now and then." From earliest childhood Davey Bell had the nicest, sunniest personality imaginable.

Although he had friends as a young child, he played mostly with his much loved sister, Brenda. "Dave was always a really gentle child," she recalls. "And we seemed to be on the same wavelength. We've had a very special thing, Dave and I." Jim thought his younger brother was coddled far too much. "My mother is a very loving individual who puts perhaps more than a normal amount of emphasis on her children as opposed to herself or her husband." And it was often Jim who suffered from this overprotection of the baby in the family. He remembers a vivid example of this, an epsiode which occurred when he was about ten and Dave five. Jim took Dave for a toboggan ride one winter afternoon, placing the little boy up front between his legs. They hit a particularly icy patch, swerved off the trail and hit a tree. Dave's lip was split and a front tooth knocked loose. "I knew I was going to get it when I took him home," says Jim, "and I really got it."

Jim saw a big difference between his own and his brother's personality. "I had a large group of friends at school and we'd get together and play marbles or chestnuts or floor hockey. Dave was much more of a loner. He would tend to meet one individual and stay with that boy as a friend for a little while and then go to another. He didn't seem to get along well with groups, yet I sensed that he craved that kind of friendship."

While Dave was growing into adolesence, Andrew Bell was handling a heavy teaching load as well as taking courses towards his M.A. in education so that he wasn't home a lot. Says Dave's mother, Eleanor, "I didn't notice until he got older that he really wanted to do things with his father, be with his father, an awful lot." When Dave was twelve, his parents decided they would fulfil a lifelong dream and take the family to visit the Golden Gate Bridge in San Francisco. On his return to school in the fall, Dave was assigned the standard composition about what he had done during his vacation. To his parents chagrin and amazement, he wrote not a word about the Golden Gate Bridge. He and his father had gone by themselves on a weekend camping trip to Algonquin Park, and that's what had impressed David.

He didn't do brilliantly at school; he underwent speech therapy and failed grades six and ten primarily because he had trouble sitting still, but he persevered and eventually got his grade twelve at Scarlett Heights in 1972 when he was twenty.

"Jim and his father would have confrontations all the time but Dave would never get angry," says Eleanor. "He was really an easy child to mould, he had such a nice personality, but when I think about it now I guess there must have been a lot of frustration for him which he didn't express. Things were so good for him at home that I guess he wasn't challenged enough. We might have spoiled him in that he never had to take pressure, never had to prove himself."

Indeed, competition of any kind became an anathema to him. "He was a lot like I am in that regard," says Rocky Lucchetta, who knew David all through his teenage years. " He was laid-back but he has the funniest sense of humour and has been the most compassionate person." Rocky and Dave used to double-date the odd time. "Dave was kind of shy, but when he got to know the girls, he related to them real well. Even now, when he's in jail for gang rape, I still have lots of his girl friends come up and ask after him."

Dave began playing guitar at about sixteen and it quickly became an obsession with him. He dreamed about travelling with rock star Neil Young, who like Dave had a middle-class Ontario background. He and Brian Krinchuk spent a lot of time together, "just picking away on the guitar." Their goal was to become professional musicians. But Dave wasn't really working at it, "giving it his all, " as his brother said. Jim thought his brother's music was just a diversion, a means of escaping the real world.

"As children we were always involved in taking music lessons," remembers Jim Bell, "mostly piano, and we were made to practise two or three times a week and take grade two theory and grade eight conservatory. Well, Brenda and I struggled with that, but not Dave. He'd never pass any of those things and it never bothered him.

"Similarly he wasn't interested in any kind of regimentation with his guitar. I'd meet him after a long period and I'd say, 'How's your guitar?' 'Oh, I haven't practised much lately,' he'd tell me. 'Play for me,' I'd ask, but he never would."

Like many of his friends, when he was in his last years of high school, Dave got heavily involved with drugs — marijuana, speed and acid. This led to a run-in with the police, the one time David gave the Bells serious trouble. One evening in December, 1970, he and a couple of friends got high on acid. One of their favourite pastimes had been making fun of a retired, alcoholic airplane pilot who was often seen lurching drunkenly around the local park. This particular night they decided to break into his house, and while there, for reasons no one could figure out, ransacked the place by throwing fresh eggs all over the walls, floors and furniture. Some figurines and glass pieces were destroyed.

One of the young men involved had a lengthy criminal record and, as part of a plea bargaining on an unrelated offence, confessed to the episode and informed on the other two. On December 18 two plainclothes detectives arrived at the Bell home, and they and Andrew Bell had a long talk with David. For several hours he denied any knowledge of the offence, but under pressure from the three adults, he finally confessed. He was humiliated to learn that his buddy, even after being badly beaten by police, did not. So guilty did Dave feel that he tried, without success, to shoulder the entire blame.

David was locked up over Christmas, a shock his parents never quite recovered from. He pleaded guilty to theft under fifty dollars, was ordered to pay all costs in repairing the damage, and was placed on twelve months probation. It was his only brush with the law until he was convicted of two counts of rape seven years later.

After he quit school, he got menial work with O'Neil Electric and then the Sears Craft Company. "He simply wouldn't be challenged by his jobs. None of them," says his mother. His father made him take a bartending course so that he would always have the means of making a few bucks to feed himself and never have to resort to anything illegal.

In 1974 Dave set out on a lifetime dream — travellin'. He and a friend hitchhiked to Vancouver and then headed for the tiny but quite beautiful village of Sechelt on the coast. At that time it attracted a combination of hippies and artistic people, and Dave felt wonderfully at home. He made friends quickly and soon moved into an old farmhouse with half-a-dozen other adults and several children. It was Dave's first taste of communal living and he loved it. "It's so relaxed, the scenery here is so gorgeous, and we can travel around when we want," he told his mother during one of his monthly phone calls home. He got a job at the pulp and paper mills in Port Mellon and then spent one of the happiest years of his life.

After a brief trip home in the mid-Seventies to attend his brother's wedding and see his family, he set off travelling again, picking up work where he could. By the summer of 1976 he was back in B.C., working as cook for a hostel in Kamloops. It was at this point that his grandmothers, both eighty, and his mother came to visit him.

Dave found a cottage for the three women on Davis Bay, rented a car and generally made himself available. "He was most gracious and patient with the grandmothers. And they were so happy to see him. They told me it was the best holiday they had ever had," Eleanor says. They thought Dave wasn't dressed warmly enough, so they went shopping for clothes on Eleanor's Simpsons charge card.

By the summer of 1977, he decided he was homesick. He bought himself an old Ford and headed for Toronto. In North Bay he lost his beloved dog Dawg. The animal wandered away from the car and Dave spent several days trying to track him down without any luck. Without a cent in his pocket and with a half litre of gas left in his tank, he arrived at his parents' spacious Etobicoke home unannounced. They were overjoyed to see him. Then he told them that he had driven all the way without a spare tire. "My father just about died," Dave recalls.

The first thing he did was call his sister, Brenda Hikida, who had married by this time. It was her husband who answered the phone, and he and Dave decided to surprise Brenda. With a laundry basket under her arm, she came upstairs later that day to discover her brother sitting there. She let out a screech. "After I got over the tears," she recalls, "I realized we were just as close. It was as though he had never been away." She would remain a faithful defender of Dave's throughout the gang rape trial. She simply didn't believe he was capable of committing the terrible crimes of which he was accused.

Dave got a job with a building contractor near the Hikida's house in Brampton. He stayed with them for a while and got to know his two nieces, ages one and three. They quickly came to love Uncle Dave. "He always took the time for whatever they were interested in doing and he would talk to them in a very genuine way," says Brenda. "Because he and I were so close, he felt close to them too."

The contractor reneged on his promise of work but Dave was soon hired at Douglas Aircraft. That job lasted six months before he was laid off once again. During this time he lived with his parents, although at one point he and Brian Krinchuk moved into a derelict farmhouse in Flesherton, Ontario, owned by Krinchuk's father. They planned on concentrating on their music, getting an act together and maybe even going professional. In four months they were back in Toronto. The Unemployment Insurance Commission had refused to send them the payments they had been planning to live on. Since the house was in farm country, the UIC officials reasoned quite rightly that they had no intention of looking for work. It was after their return to Toronto that David began to drift more and more towards Brian Dempsey and his friends. He had always felt comfortable with a "communal" lifestyle, where the responsibility of everyday living — paying the phone bill, buying fresh lettuce, arguing with the landlord — did not rest entirely on his shoulders, where there were people who accepted him for what he was and who didn't expect him to conquer the world, and where he could live for that very moment, with a beer in his hand, and not worry about the harshness of the future.

In October of 1978, Dave, Brian and Jean Elgar, John Beatteay and Linda Brown, and Chuck Dempsey rented a four-bedroom house at 13 Grenadier Road in Toronto's west end. From the beginning there was no question that it was Brian Dempsey who was the acknowledged leader, the mastermind of the ménage. "He had such a sense of himself, was so unable to be intimidated, that he dominated everybody," says Dave Bell. "You'd be getting ready to go to work and it'd be Brian who'd say, 'Aw, come on, Dave, fuck the job bit. Let's try that new Eagles number, "King of Hollywood." Get your guitar.' And what we would do is spend the day drinking or smoking hash. Now and then Chuck would try and pull the older brother number on Brian but it never fazed him." Chuck says "We were on a holiday from life. I now feel it was a total, absolute waste of time."

To say the women were not liberated was to indulge in an understatement. Like everyone else they did what Brian said. Chuck Dempsey explained it this way: "Linda was working for John, Jean was working for Brian." What that meant was that they would hand over their paycheques or unemployment insurance to their men. They might also be called upon to take a rap for some criminal activity or other.

The group had just about everything they wanted. Jean and Linda provided the most reliable money, for rent and groceries. But John worked the odd job for a construction company, Dave was employed as a part-time chef for Anthony's Pizzeria, and Chuck was a short-order cook at a Fran's restaurant. Brian seemed always to have a pocketful of bills as well, usually obtained through a poker or pool game, and sometimes through some small-time drug dealing. By this time he wasn't even bothering to look for work. He acted as the innkeeper, collecting as much cash from each individual as he or she could afford. He was supposed to pay the rent and other bills, "but I think he often bought drugs or shot pool with the money," says Linda. "Our expenses weren't that high," says Chuck. "We had the best of everything, went to the best restaurants. Those extras were all paid for by stolen charge cards." They engaged in this practice as often as they could get their hands on any.

In the fall of 1978, Chuck had walked into a telephone booth and was amazed to find a wallet full of plastic — Visa, American Express, Master Charge, department store cards. The group had a wonderful time for a while. It was Linda who signed for most of the stuff. "Jean didn't have many clothes, so I went shopping with her. I bought toasters, records, shirts — all presents for the people in the house." When the police finally caught up to her, Linda took the rap for all the illegal activity, although the others had been involved as well. "We got her to take the beef for it," says Chuck. "We would have got life while she got a slap on the wrist. It was the price she paid for living with us." In February, 1979, she was sentenced to thirty days consecutive and put on a year's probation. On appeal, however, her sentence was reduced to a fine of $2,500. She paid it by cashing in bonds which had been given to her as a child. By that time, in 1981, she had returned to Saskatchewan and she now kicks herself that she ever bothered to pay it.

Only a few months after Linda was nabbed while using the stolen Visa, Brian and John were again in trouble with the police, charged with break and enter, theft and assault. It was a bizarre incident.

Their friend Wade Blythe had been fired from his job as building superintendent at the Albany Street apartments where John and Brian had lived and had been replaced by a Lorne Gernstein. By that time Brian and John had moved to Grenadier Road, but a few days into the new year, 1979, the three had returned "to have a few drinks with the building." They couldn't find anyone home, so they knocked on Lorne Gernstein's door. "Oh, hi," he said, "come on in." While they were sitting there drinking, Lorne's boss phoned and Brian, who knew him slightly, chatted with him.

Shortly after the phone call Gernstein suddenly became anxious for the three men to leave. Brian explained what happened next: "He was expecting a broad who had answered his ad in the paper in the 'Males in Heat' column, you know the kind, 'Established, good-looking, intellectual male seeks seven-foot female, any colour, with Master's Degree in rubber boots.' Well we said we'd finish our drinks and leave but the girl showed up and she wasn't bad at all. But she was dumbfounded by this poor excuse for a human being that Lorne Gernstein is so she beat it. There were about two or three shots left in the forty-ounce bottle. Wade kills it and tells Lorne, 'Well, now we're even for the five bucks you owe me.' Then we get up and go."

A few days later Dempsey, Beatteay and Blythe were arrested. At the trial Gernstein told a quite different story. He testified that Wade had a key to his apartment and let Dempsey and Beatteay in. Lorne claimed he was in bed at the time, sleeping in the same room as his young son. When Gernstein got up, Wade, Brian and John were supposed to have smacked him around "for the sheer pleasure of it." They took a full forty-ounce bottle of vodka out of his filing cabinet and drank it down. As Brian told Jean, "It sounded really bad at the trial — him up there looking so wimpy and us pushing him around with his kid in the room." Then Dempsey's lawyer asked Gernstein about the phone call from his boss which he'd received during the attack. Gernstein was asked if he had complained to the caller that he was being abused or intimidated in any way. Gernstein stuttered that he hadn't. "You should have seen his face," related Brian. "He screwed up so bad the judged stopped the trial and said, 'Now I know I'm not supposed to do this but what was the first thing you said to your boss on the phone?' Gernstein said something like, 'Oh yeah, so and so and so and so are here. No, nothing I can't handle.'" After that, plea bargaining began. John and Brian were told that one of them could plead guilty to theft under two hundred dollars. They had been in jail for almost two months at this point awaiting trial, so they knew the worst either one could get was time served. They flipped to see who would take the beef and John lost. But the Crown came back and said they wanted the others for assault. "Tell them they get nothing. We'll take the rest of the trial," Brian told his lawyer. They were acquitted on all counts. The judge simply had not believed Gernstein's testimony.

Dempsey and Beatteay would later learn that Lorne Gernstein was an infamous police informer in Toronto. For a decade he had worked as an operative for the morality squad of the Metro Police Department. His usual modus operandi was to go into what the police considered was a bawdy house, obtain an offer from a prostitute, and report him or her to the authorities. By 1981 Gernstein had appeared in court more than a hundred times, and often his calendar was much more fully booked than the officer in charge of the case. Dempsey frequently used this case to illustrate how he was unfairly and systematically persecuted by authorities. If Gernstein had been able to mount a more credible story, "we would have been convicted of those charges like all the rest."

The household at Grenadier Road lasted for only four months before a dispute with the landlord forced Brian and Jean, John and Linda, and Dave Bell to leave. It involved their three German shepherds. The animals messed up the back porch, and for the landlord, who had already received complaints from the neighbours about the wild noisy parties, that was the last straw. He claimed they hadn't paid him February's rent — although Jean Elgar insisted they had — and moved to have them evicted. The group thought it wise to leave and had no trouble finding a house for rent at 402 Lauder Avenue. It was Dave Bell who made the arrangements, paying the first and last month's rent and looking after the lease because by that time all the other males were in jail. Chuck was accused of fraud for one of his many money-making schemes involving stolen goods and would as usual be acquitted. John and Brian were still in jail awaiting trial on the Gernstein charges.

The one person in the group who kept her nose remarkably clean was Jean Elgar. She didn't drink at all, and only occasionally indulged in small amounts of marijuana. In her job as waitress at the Great Canadian Soup Company and as bartender at Between Friends restaurant, she was considered industrious and capable, with a flair for organization. Her friends sometimes laughingly called her a prude, so ethical and responsible did she appear. She seemed an upstanding prairie lily among a crowd of debauched dandelions, and people often wondered what she was doing with the others. For one thing, during their never-ending parties Dempsey and the others engaged in whatever sexual shenanigans where "going down." As Brian put it, "If some broad comes in and wants to give me a blow job, I'm supposed to say no?" Jean Elgar, of course, saw this happening. And she acknowledges that as these parties got wilder and more debauched, she feared the police would step in. However, she insists these women weren't raped. "They did it of their own free will," she says.

But then Jean was still totally fascinated and obsessed by Brian Dempsey. Says Chuck Dempsey, "He gave her a place in life and she reciprocated in kind. They were very close.

"For a long time she didn't believe that she even existed. She was shown by Brian that she did and her gratitude was such that she would accept the parties, and everything that transpired in them. She was fortunate enough to have what she had which was a great relationship and there was no way she would jeopardize it. And if she had complained, Brian would have shown her the door."

Life in the Lauder Avenue house was just about what it had been at the previous places — a three-ring circus with simultaneous performances by Brian's confreres going on all the time. The characters who passed through were a motley crew: old friends from the East Coast, bikers whom Brian picked up in the bars of Yonge Street, unemployed strippers, failed country and western singers, successful sleight-of-hand artists, card sharks and poker players. But few were as colourful, funny or appealing as Randy "Roadside" Blake.

TEN

Roadside
Blake

WELL, HOT DOG!

Even in the world of Red Hot, Beachball, Truck and Degenerate Jim, Roadside Blake was looked upon as something of a mythical hero. "No matter where he travelled on that big Harley of his," says his older brother Dennis, "people would say, 'Are you Roadside Blake? Well, hot dog!' More than anything I think it was that infectious laugh of his. People were attracted to him like he was a giant-sized magnet or something." Dennis experienced the effects of this popularity first-hand when he too joined the Last Chance Motorcycle Club: he was nicknamed Offside in recognition of his famous brother Roadside. But then Dennis spent his childhood in the over-sized shadow of his younger brother by three years.

Ruby Blake likes to recall one particular scene when she thinks of her beloved third child, Randy. He was about twelve years old. It was a Saturday night and five or six relatives and friends had dropped in to play euchre. Randy declared it show time, and borrowing someone's shoe to use as a microphone, he was transformed into as fine an MC as Ed Sullivan ever was. Everyone was called to the stage: his father, Bill, did a number on his harmonica, an uncle played the spoons, someone else the drums on Ruby's potato pot, and of course everyone sang at the top of their lungs. Dennis howled with laughter but he was too shy to participate much.

The Blakes moved to Toronto from Newfoundland shortly after the first of their five children was born. It was the old story: Bill was a welder and he thought his prospects would brighten considerably in Toronto. The couple found a flat in the Queen-Lansdowne area, the central west-end, and then moved to larger places as they collected more children and more furniture. Bill was always

154

employed but his salary was not enormous. "I had to work too," says Ruby, "but I never left them with a babysitter, never." When the fourth child, Rick, came along, the family bought a house in the Borough of York, and Ruby, to meet expenses, had to get a full-time job. Bill transferred to the night shift so that he could look after the kids while Ruby worked at Eaton's warehouse during the day.

But the Blakes always had fun together. "I'd come home from work, make the supper and then we'd grab our skates and head for the rink at the Henry School. I'd leave the dishes right on the table," recalls Mrs. Blake. One weekend the entire gang went tobogganing and Ruby broke her tailbone. "I had to go to the doctor to get it straightened out." A common sight at five o'clock on Saturday mornings at the hockey arena was Momma Blake dressed in a ski jacket with her pyjamas prominently displayed underneath, rooting louder than anyone for whichever one of her kids was on the ice.

Randy was a particular favourite in the large, close family. Bill Blake recalls, "Randy was always a charmer, always had me wrapped around his little finger. He's the only one of our five kids who would phone me fifteen minutes after he was supposed to be in and say, 'Dad, I'm at the corner of so and so' — way the hell and gone out someplace — 'will you come and get me.' And I'd be stupid enough to go out and pick him up every time."

Dennis and Randy remember little but happiness in their childhood even though their boisterous mother could be pretty free with her hands when they were acting up. "She had a lot to put up with," says Dennis. The one thing they didn't appreciate about their father was the monthly haircuts he gave. "He'd tie us in a chair," remembers Dennis, "and go at it with hand clippers. Both of us swore we'd never get our hair cut when we grew up and Randy came pretty close to accomplishing that."

Randy didn't do all that well at school. He was good with his hands and was especially happy taking things apart, even if, as Dennis said, he couldn't get them back together again. He finally got his grade ten at age seventeen. But that was a struggle and he quit that year. Anyway he had a passion that was consuming all his energy and time.

"As early as I can remember," recalls his father, "Randy thought about nothing but motorcycles. Never anything about cars, always a bike." By the time he was nine, he knew the difference in detail between a Triumph and a Kawasaki, a Honda and a Harley Davidson. The day he was sixteen his father co-signed a loan for him at the bank and he went out and bought a used BSA. "That night he took it down in the basement, tore it apart just to see what made it tick and put it back together," recalls Dennis.

Ruby and Bill didn't object to Randy driving a bike; for one thing they knew that they'd never cure him of his compulsion. They were upset, however, when he joined a club. He had never been in trouble with the law as a youngster and they worried that if he got involved, there would be no way he could avoid it. For a biker, though, he managed to keep remarkably clear of the police. He was convicted of possession of marijuana in 1972 and 1974, and given a conditional discharge in the first instance and a two-hundred-dollar fine in the second, and in 1977 he was found guilty of impaired driving. But until 1979 he caused no serious trouble, and, of course, the rape charges had little to do with his being a biker. Now in Collins Bay Penitentiary, Randy often laments that if only he had kept to his own kind, his brother bikers, instead of hanging out with "hippies," he wouldn't be in the jam that he is.

Dennis says Randy could have joined any club he wanted to, but in the early Seventies he started riding and then partying with a group of about fifty guys who were talking about setting up their own. The Last Chance was established in 1974 and Roadside was a founding member. At age twenty he was one of the youngest full-fledged brothers in Toronto.* He always held positions of responsibility in the club; in 1979 he was elected road captain, which meant he had to chart and prepare the route for the club's all-important outings. A close friend of his and fellow club member, Jeff Ismail, explains why Roadside was so popular: "He's a big boy. If he wanted to, he could power-trip on people all the time. He's strong and he could punch-out people. But he's not like that. Not at all."

In the summer of 1975 Last Chance members went on a club run to North Bay. While they were looking for a place to stay, they ran into a group of the town bikers. Among them was a very large man — six feet four inches tall, weighing 335 pounds. Heavy Duty and his friends were most hospitable to the Toronto group; they led them to the best campsite, supplied them with quarts of oil and showed them around town. And during the evening entertainment was provided: Heavy Duty could sing and play the harmonica like no one Roadside had ever heard before. When the club returned to Toronto on Sunday evening, Roady stayed behind — the big man had promised to teach him to play "the harp."

Over the next few days Heavy Duty and Roadside worked hard on their music. On the fifth night they were drinking beer at a hotel where Heavy Duty was well known. He would join the band every

---

* Bikers are a very conservative lot. As well as despising blacks, hippies and bums, they believe the young should be neither seen nor heard.

now and then and sing a few numbers. During one, he called Roadside up on the stage. "After I got my nerve up I played my harmonica for the first time with a band, and Heavy Duty. When we finished, the crowd stood up, yelled and clapped for more. I could hardly believe it but I had his gift for playing the harp." From that day on they became partners in music. They called themselves the Road Heavy Blues Band and they played at hotels "as often as we could for as long as we could."

They had become the closest of friends. "We used to kid them and say that their exalted opinions of each other were rather exaggerated," says Dennis Blake. "But they were a truly amazing pair." Heavy Duty returned to Toronto with Roadside, and the next day the two set off on a trip west that was to have lasted two weeks. It took nine months.

Roadside wrote his family: "On our run to the West Coast, everything went fine: no breakdowns, no police, no hassles from citizens." But in British Columbia they knew there was a province-wide warrant out for Heavy Duty's arrest for passing bad cheques in Vancouver. He planned to turn himself in and have the matter cleared up, win or lose. The morning after the all-night party celebrating their arrival in Burnaby, B.C. Heavy Duty went to court. "Put the bacon and eggs on, I'll be back in an hour," he said. That afternoon he phoned. He wouldn't be home after all — the judge had sentenced him to three months right there and then.

Roadside got a job as a doorman at the Surrey Inn. After two and a half months his bike was up, he had saved a little money and he had a job waiting for Heavy Duty. They worked for three weeks at the Surrey Inn, helped out at the hotel's New Year's Eve party, and then decided it was time to go home. They thought they might as well go the long way, via San Francisco. Because it was in the dead of winter, they shipped their bikes back to Toronto by train, bought an old car and headed south. Randy wrote his mother that he thought the trip would take about two weeks.

Everywhere they stopped in the U.S. they left their imprint. Heavy Duty was not only huge but exceptionally loud and good-natured. And Roadside, at over six-foot-one, hair down to his waist, beard down to his chest, gold earrings, flashing gypsy eyes, and twenty multi-coloured tattoos — Randy's own favourite being "a real big eagle swooping down on a snake" — was by biker criteria about as handsome as they come. When Roadside and Heavy Duty pulled into the Last Chance clubhouse six months later, Roadside knew he would probably never have an adventure quite like that ever again.

When Roadside was arrested for rape in May of 1979, Heavy

Duty was devastated; over the years the two had remained the closest of friends. In November of 1982 Heavy, who had reached over four hundred pounds, died suddenly of a heart attack at the age of twenty-nine. Roadside, of course, could not be there for his funeral. It was the one time during his incarceration that he became seriously and unmovingly depressed.

As a teenager Randy was rather shy with girls and there weren't that many around. But his parents insist he always treated them with gentleness and respect. His father remembers the night Randy turned eighteen. He had gone to some tavern to celebrate the fact that he was at last of legal drinking age. On the way out some guy was beating up a girl and Randy stepped in to break it up. Apparently the assailant was a boxer and Randy knew it. Bill heard him in the washroom after he came in. 'I really got it, Dad,' he said. His two eyes were tiny black and blue slits, his cheeks were swollen like balloons and his mouth was a mess of cuts.

Randy himself admits to participating in the "splashes," the gang bangs going down at the club. "But the broads had to be willing. If they said no, I'd either leave or stop the action."

In 1973 Dennis introduced his brother to an old school friend he had known for some time. Dixie Bannon was tall, slender, with long dark hair. Two years older than Randy, she was not exactly pretty, indeed many of Randy's friends considered her quite homely. But he took one look and fell madly in love. "There was never anyone else for Randy but Dixie," says a friend. She became "his ol' lady," riding on the back of his bike, attending the club get-togethers when females were welcome, and most times accepting his nomadic lifestyle. He'd work for short periods, eight months here, four months there, as a truck driver, a roofer, a drywall installer, a shipper, but Randy made no bones about it: he didn't like a steady job and nobody was going to force him into one. "I got him out of bed every morning of his life and made him go to school," says his mother. "And when he did have a job and lived at home I made sure he was up. But after age eighteen, he had enough of me yelling at him in the mornings and he moved. Randy just didn't like to work at an ordinary job." He didn't mind fixing bikes, however, and once he even built a big Harley Davidson for a friend of his. He started to get into the business. "A registered Harley mechanic charges seventeen dollars an hour at Cycle World," he told a friend. "I do it a lot cheaper, like for half."

In the fall of 1977 Dixie told Roadside she was pregnant. He wasn't exactly overjoyed. "Well, Dixie, do what you want. Marriage is out of the question for me right now," he said. But when Chad was born on May 14, 1978, Randy was crazy about him. "The baby was small, only five pounds," says Ruby, "and I'll always remember Randy holding him in the palm of his one big hand." For a while Randy supported his family by working for a builder, putting in wallboard. But later that year he and Dixie were involved in a car accident. Randy suffered whiplash and couldn't work. Just before Christmas, 1978, he told her, "It will be better for you if I leave. You can get public housing and family allowance. And I can come and stay with you a couple of times a week." She took his advice and Randy moved into the house his good buddy Jeff Ismail had rented on Jeffcoat Drive in Rexdale.

The neighbours, terrified of suddenly finding bikers sprouting up in their midst, had taken up a petition to convince the landlord to evict his tenants. When Ismail heard about it, he approached the people who had signed and reassured them that he would be a good neighbour. "You won't find any nude women running out of the place or anything like that," he told them.

As well as Ismail, there were two other members of the Last Chance and two women living there; so Randy made the rec room his bedroom, although it was understood it was a temporary arrangement. Ismail wouldn't let Randy, or any of the others, walk into the house with their boots on. "I don't like dirt and I don't like someone coming into my house who is dirty. I'm a very clean person," he'd often say.

Ismail did like people, however, and he had many visitors at the Jeffcoat house. Next door lived Mr. and Mrs. Jack Goodenough, the parents of Larry Goodenough, a rough and tumble defenceman for the Philadelphia Flyers. Larry was visiting his parents during April of 1979, and since he had known Jeff Ismail for years — they had grown up together — he spent a lot of time at his house drinking and talking. On April 23, the night Claudine Harply claimed that Roadside raped her and twisted her leg until she passed out with the pain, Goodenough on at least two occasions visited the Ismail's garage where Randy was tinkering with his Harley. He had long discussions with Roadside about the virtues of a particular model of motorcycle. Goodenough did not testify because his wife did not want him involved and because Blake's lawyer, Harry Doan, did not subpoena him.

Jeff, Roadside and others would sometimes spend the evening at the Last Chance clubhouse in Woodbridge, a small town just outside of Toronto, and then drop in for a couple of beers at the Woodbridge Hotel. One night in early March Roadside lurched drunk out of the tavern smack into a knock-em-out brawl. A friend of his was being whomped by a bunch of guys, and Roady waded in to help him. The police finally broke up the melee. They took everyone to the police division and charged them with assault. Randy claimed they used the occasion to give him a good beating. He said they pulled out huge chunks of his beard, yanked at his hair and beat him all over his body. He asked a physician to take photographs of his cuts and bruises and then charged the cops with assault.*

Randy was released from jail on condition that he report twelve times a week to 51 Division in the city's central east-end. It meant that on most days he had to travel back and forth from the suburbs twice. It was a harassment that particularly irked him because at this point his Harley was acting up and he was without wheels.

One night he was sipping beer at the clubhouse when a big burly guy came over to him. "How you doing there, Roadside?" asked Bobby Caruso. Randy had met Caruso through a mutual friend at Christmas time and since then had talked to him on several occasions at the club. Caruso wasn't a member of Last Chance but outsiders were permitted to drop in and buy a few beers — it contributed to the club's coffers. Randy had never paid much attention to Caruso before — he thought of him as one of those phony bikers who talked up a big storm but who had about as much experience with a true hawg as his mother had. On this particular night, however, Bob said, "If you ever need a ride somewhere let me know. The shit-bag's working just fine." Randy's eyes lit up; he could see himself riding in comfort to the police station. After that he saw Caruso almost every day. At that time Dixie lived just around the corner from Caruso's parents' place, and Bob would drop in whenever Randy was there. He also liked to hang around the Jeffcoat house. Jeff Ismail didn't like Caruso one bit — he thought him crude and obnoxious. "Watch out," he warned Roadside, "Caruso and his buddies [Dempsey and Beatteay] are losers." Roady just laughed. He liked most people and he liked Bobby. For one thing they had a lot in common.

They were both brought up in Toronto, although Caruso's parents bought a home in Etobicoke during the 1950s, not far from where the Bells lived — as teenagers Caruso and Dave used to hang around the same plaza. Like Roadside, Bob had not got along very well at school and had left after grade ten. In the late Sixties he travelled around Canada — Williams Lake and Cornell, B.C., working in saw mills; Edmonton, Alberta, Prince George, B.C., doing a

---

* In May, 1979, Blake was found guilty of assault and causing a disturbance and was fined $100 or ten days in jail on the first charge and $250 or twenty-five days in jail consecutively on the second. He dropped the assault charges against the police.

variety of odd jobs. By 1971 he was back in Toronto working as a bouncer for various Yonge Street bars. It was at the Young Station Tavern that he first met Brian Dempsey, when Dempsey first arrived in Toronto. By 1975 Caruso was living with a young waitress named Donna Reid, whom he planned to marry. When she got pregnant, however, Caruso panicked and skipped town. Shortly after, he was convicted of armed robbery in Winnipeg and sentenced to two years imprisonment in Stony Mountain. "I was under a lot of stress, because of why I left Donna and that's why I got into trouble," he explained. He took some plumbing courses at Stony Mountain and continued with these through a Manpower program in Vancouver when he was released in May, 1977. By December, 1978, Caruso landed in Burnaby General Hospital with an illness doctors could not diagnose. His parents finally insisted that he return to Toronto and he was home for Christmas that year. After that he spent his time working as a day labourer a couple of times a week, teaching his dog to jump and generally having a good time partying. Roadside Blake knew that Bobby had something of a fair-sized record. But then he knew lots of guys with long records.

On a couple of occasions Caruso brought Brian Dempsey and John Beatteay to party at the clubhouse, and Randy met them there. In early May, Caruso invited him to visit 402 Lauder. "Come on. They're a great bunch of shitheads," he had said, and Randy had followed Bobby's car on his motorcycle. He had a real good time, and on May 5 he took Dixie to a party there. They didn't have a babysitter so Chad came along and they all slept over. The next time he visited 402 Lauder it was May 15, the last day he would taste freedom for a long, long time.

Randy was feeling mighty uncomfortable about Spudic's allegation that he and the others had raped her. He had been very, very drunk that night but he could vaguely remember that she had given him a blow job. So he knew something must have gone down. But when a few days later his lawyer told him that Claudine Harply had also accused him of raping her, he yelled, "Who the fuck is she?"

PART III

The Women

ELEVEN

Claudine

ALL MY YOUNG YEARS
ARE BEING WASTED

Claudine Harply has always considered herself unlucky when it comes to men.* It doesn't seem to matter how fabulous, how dreamy, the romance starts out to be, her lovers all end up cracking her ribs, blackening her eyes, breaking her arms, knocking her teeth loose. Most times she is forced to call the cops, who regularly charge her men with assault. That, of course, usually drives them away. And then it starts all over again: she meets some guy, often in a bar, who's wonderful to her for a while but then for reasons she can't comprehend, except that it usually has to do with alcohol, starts using his fists on her. But as Claudine often confided to sympathetic girl friends, even her own father had often flown into a rage and beaten her.

The occasion she remembers with most pain occurred the day she turned ten years old. She had received a beautiful two-wheel bike for her birthday, and after the kid next door had begged her for hours to let him ride it, she had reluctantly agreed. When her father spotted the boy riding around on it, he was furious. He started smacking Claudine, finally giving her a powerful kick which caught her between her legs. Blood began to flow as if she were having her first menstrual period.

---

* At the trial of Dempsey et al, Mr. Justice Patrick Galligan ruled that the media must maintain the anonymity of the victims involved. For that reason all names, including some place names, in chapters 11 and 12 have been changed. Several biographical details of no consequence to the events have also been altered.

But then Claire Harding says that right from babyhood her daughter, in some strange way, rejected her husband. Ted Harding was at sea in the navy for six months after Claudine was born in October, 1946. When he finally came home to Liverpool, his baby daughter took one look at him and began to scream her head off. The two never developed a close relationship.

Claire was only nineteen when she gave birth to her first child. None of her two brothers or three sisters had children at that point, so "they idolized her." Attention was lavished on baby Claudine. "She was such a beautiful little girl. We used to walk along the street and people would turn their heads and look at her. Honestly, it makes me sick when I think how her life has been so wasted," her mother says.

Ted Harding was a baker by trade. Several years after he was discharged from the navy, he opened a small grocery store. Even though more children arrived, two boys and a girl, all born exactly six years apart, both Ted and Claire had to work at the shop to make it profitable. On the weekends they liked to stop at the local pub for a pint or two. These evenings would often end in vicious fights. "Mom would always bring up things that had happened years and years ago," recalls Claudine. "Dad would fly into a rage and he'd start throwing the dishes around. Mom had a terrible temper too and I was always terrified that someone would get really badly hurt." A couple of times Claire did end up with a black eye and once Ted broke her leg.

The Hardings were exceedingly strict with their first-born as she grew into adolescence in the early 1960s, imposing rigid curfews and regulations to curb what they perceived was her wilful behaviour. And they insisted that she contribute to the household by babysitting.

One hot July Saturday, Claudine was looking forward to going to the movies with friends. Her parents were working during the afternoon and she was looking after the younger children. While she ironed the blouse she planned to wear that evening, her young brother began to taunt, "I'm telling on you for having friends in yesterday. You won't be able to go out tonight." "You little bugger," screeched Claudine. She grabbed the red-hot iron and thrust it on the boy's arm. As the boy howled, Claudine cried and pleaded with him not to tell their parents. Surprisingly the boy obeyed.

By the time Claudine reached sixteen, a group of native sons had put the city of Liverpool on the map in a way it had never been before. If the Beatles revolutionized the music of young people around the world, they had an overwhelming effect on the youth of their hometown. Rock groups sprang up like dandelions. Claudine could carry a tune fairly well and she and a girl friend sang with a rock group called the Marionettes. At one point they even went to London to cut a record. About all that came of it was a mention in the Liverpool paper, but music, particularly rock and roll, remained an important part of Claudine's life.

Claudine was a rather mediocre, disinterested student, and it was taken for granted that she would quit school when she was fifteen. She found work as a waitress at the Happy Days, which was reputed to serve the best Chinese food in Liverpool. She enjoyed this job because many of the rock stars would hang out there after an evening's gig. And because she was an exceedingly pretty young woman with long chestnut hair and green-grey eyes, she was popular among the musicians.

One night she spotted a well-dressed, slender young man who reminded Claudine of the actor James Dean. Carl Millington was a good inch shorter than Claudine, but he was so beautifully dressed, and so sweet, that she was immediately taken with him. Six months later Claudine discovered she was pregnant.

"My mother told me straight out: either I had to get married or I'd have to go away, have the baby and put it up for adoption," remembers Claudine. "She was worried about what the neighbours would think, not about me." The couple talked it over and decided that since they were in love, they'd get married. She was sixteen years old and he eighteen. About the only thing Claudine's parents knew about Carl was that he had been brought up by, and lived with, his aunt. At the wedding they were astonished to discover that the aunt was really his mother — Carl was ashamed of the fact that he was illegitimate and so hid her identity — and that she was a loud and profane drunk. "She showed up loaded and we near dropped," recalls Claire. After the wedding Claudine moved in with her belligerent, foul-mouthed mother-in-law. "She led me a dog's life," says Claudine.

To help the young couple out, Ted Harding gave Carl a job in his grocery store. It quickly became evident that he was too "bone-idle, lazy" to carry out his tasks. "Andy Capp had nothing on him," remembers Claudine. Carl blamed it on his asthma condition but Claudine thought that was nothing but a phony excuse. Even after the baby, Colin, was born on December 17, 1964, Carl steadfastly refused to work, and Ted finally fired him. Claudine was so furious about this that she left her husband and dreadful mother-in-law and took the baby to live at her parents' home. "I'm not going back to that house," she told her mom.

The last thing the Hardings wanted was the responsibility of an eighteen-year-old and her baby, and they agreed drastic action was called for. Claire came up with the idea of packing them off to Canada. "Surely Carl would have to work in Canada, there'd be no automatic pogey there," she told her husband.

In October, 1965, Claudine, Carl and baby Colin boarded the *Empress of Canada.* Their passage was paid by the Canadian government, eager at the time to promote white, Anglo-Saxon immigration. And they had a hundred pounds as start-up money, a gift from the Hardings.

Immigration officials had insisted that the couple begin their new life in the industrial city of Hamilton. The first thing Carl did was seek out the nearest welfare office. Claudine went to see the social worker. "You know, you're not doing me any favours by giving us welfare," she told her. "All he will do is collect and collect and collect. He will never work." Shortly after, Claudine found a job as a waitress and Carl looked after Colin, who was now two years old. They leased a small house and planned to rent out rooms to help pay the monthly expenses.

About four months after they arrived, Claudine and Carl went to visit four Irishmen, all bachelors whom they had met on the *Empress of Canada* and who had settled in Scarborough, a suburb of Toronto. Claudine thought to herself, "Now this is more like it." On their return to Hamilton the following Monday night, they opened the door of their house to discover all their furniture missing. They had not kept up the payments and it had been repossessed. At that very instant, Claudine said, "That's it. We're moving to Toronto."

The Irishmen had invited them to stay in their small basement apartment until they could find their own accommodation. What they didn't tell them was that they hadn't paid their rent and that they had long ago been served with an eviction notice. Only two days after Carl and Claudine arrived, the landlady and three very hefty sons knocked on the door at two in the morning and told the Irishmen that if they weren't out by morning, they would have their arms broken. Carl immediately had an asthma attack and had to be rushed to Scarborough General Hospital. Since neither Claudine nor any of the Irishmen had money for a hotel, she found herself in the middle of January on the streets of Toronto with a small child and nowhere to go.

Claudine turned to the police for help, and they installed her and Colin in a hostel for homeless women and children. Fortunately, a woman whom they had met on the ship over found them a furnished apartment in Scarborough which rented for eighty-five dollars a month.

The cycle began again. Claudine had no difficulty finding work at one point she had two jobs, as a waitress during the day at one restaurant and during the evening at another — but Carl was chronically unemployed. Claudine was sick to death of him. "I feel as though all my young years are being wasted," she wrote to her mother. She had become close friends with another waitress, Cathy McBride, and the two women began going out together after work.

Carl had always suffered from jealousy but as he and Claudine became more and more estranged, he grew excessively so. "He'd accuse me of doing this and that and start pounding me with his fists," recalls Claudine. One night he gave her two black eyes. Cathy said to her, "You don't have to take that. Why don't you leave him?" Cathy's mother owned a rooming house in West Hill and she agreed to take care of Colin while Claudine was at work. Claudine decided to spend the night at her friend's and then pick up the little boy the next day. She phoned Carl. "Where the hell have you been?" he screamed. "I'm going to beat the shit out of you." "Oh no you're not 'cause I'm not coming back, ever."

The next day Claudine went to collect her personal belongings and her child. Carl told her she could have neither. She contacted the police, and the officer who arrived told Claudine that she had a right to her clothing, but he said, "We can't do anything about your son because you were the one who deserted him." Claudine was shocked at this and told Cathy, "I'm going to fight him from hell and half acre to get my son back." She vowed that the very next morning she would contact a lawyer. But somehow she never quite got around to it.

Claudine and Cathy began to frequent Toronto's Yorkville "village," then at the height of its notoriety. One evening the two young women were having a coffee in a café when a fellow came over and introduced himself. "Howdy. My name's Mad Dog, what's yours?" He was a member of Satan's Choice Motorcycle Club and Cathy liked him immediately. The following Saturday evening the women ran into him again and he said to Cathy, "There's a helluva bash going down at the clubhouse. Why don't you two come with me?"

Claudine was surprised to discover that she knew half-a-dozen or so Satan's Choice members. They used to hang around the Red Barn restaurant where she worked as a waitress, but since they didn't wear their colours, she hadn't known they were bikers. "What the fuck are you doing here?" they yelled at her. "See'n what you're up to," she joked back. They all bought her drinks. Claudine's hair was dyed a light blonde at the time and she had taken special pains dressing that day. She was delighted and proud when she was told over and over how sexy she looked. She was having a real good time.

On a trip to the washroom she was stopped by a big bruiser of a guy, named Otto Stadnyk, who was decked out in full Nazi regalia.

"So who are you?" he asked Claudine.

"Who wants to know," she replied.

"Kinda of mouthy, ain't you?"

"It's not me who's the mouthy one."

"Who ya with?"

"Mad Dog."

"Mad Dog's got an old lady. He's with her."

"I'm with him too."

"Oh no you're not. A guy can't be with two broads. Maybe I otta get a splash going here."

At that very moment Bingo Bambu, one of the guys Claudine knew, took Stadnyk aside and cooled him out. Bingo explained to Claudine that a splash in biker parlance meant a gang bang. "You know you gotta be careful," he told her. "'Cause you're alone, Stadnyk could have insisted that you be fucked by anyone of the fifty guys here who felt like it." Claudine swore she'd never go back again. But Bingo Bambu had taken a particular fancy to her and asked her if she would come to a party at his house, which served as a kind of downtown clubhouse for Satan's Choice members. "Oh no," said Claudine. "I promise you nothing will happen 'cause you're with me." "Oh all right," she said.

It got to be known that Claudine was Bingo's lady, and she began hanging around his house every day. She wasn't crazy about Bingo and it didn't take her long to meet someone much more interesting.

Bill Harply was down in the basement fixing his Harley when Claudine first ran into him. He was a red-headed, Irish-looking guy, very polite and soft-spoken, and he wasn't wearing his colours. "You don't strike me as being the biker type," she told him. "Some of us are more quiet than others," he replied. She took to him right away.

She stayed over at Bingo's house that night. The next day he was travelling to Detroit to finalize an intricate deal involving the illegal importing of heroin. There was a huge party planned at the Satan's Choice clubhouse and Bingo told Claudine that even though he probably couldn't be there until the early hours of the morning, he'd arrange for someone else to take her. Bill Harply volunteered. Bingo never showed up and Bill and Claudine became lovers.

At the clubhouse Claudine had met Sue Simpson, who had just separated from her husband as well. The two decided to rent an apartment on Eastern Avenue. And about the same time, Bill Harply's parents discovered that he had joined the Satan's Choice and were so appalled they ordered him out of the house. He moved in with Sue and Claudine. Ironically, Otto Stadnyk, the very man who had almost had Claudine "splashed," turned out to be Bill's best friend. He introduced Otto to Sue and they began going out together. Both Harply and Stadnyk were unemployed at the time, and the apartment was used as an informal hang-out for club members. It wasn't long before the neighbours were complaining to the police.

During this time Claire Harding received a letter from her son-in-law. In it, Carl complained that Claudine had deserted him and the child, that she was hanging around bikers and "niggers" and taking all kinds of drugs. "If I don't get away from here, I'm sure I'll commit suicide," he wrote. Claire sent his and Colin's air fare in the next post.

Claudine was naturally upset that they were leaving, but Bill said to her, "Look, I really think a lot of you. You can always go over and visit Colin. And maybe if we stay together, we'll have a family of our own." But after the child left for England, Claudine had no further contact with him until she returned to Liverpool twelve years later. Claire Harding, who did keep in touch with her grandson, says, "In all those years, Claudine never asked about him, never sent him a Christmas card or a birthday present. She seemed to lose any motherly instinct she ever had for that child."

Bill Harply continued to ride with the Satan's Choice and sometimes he'd take Claudine with him. She liked motorcycles and in England had owned a 250cc Triumph automatic but she quickly grew tired of the club. On a couple of holiday weekends he took off without her and it hurt her. Not only that, on several occasions Bill and Claudine had been evicted from their premises because of the bikers hanging around their place. Then in January of 1970 she discovered she was pregnant.

Bill urged her to have an abortion but she said, "No, I've already given up one child for you, I'm not going to get rid of this one." At the urging of his parents, Bill finally agreed. But Claudine was not entirely satisfied. She was growing increasingly anxious about the number of unsavoury characters joining the Satan's Choice — Bill himself sponsored Cecil Kirby, who several years later was revealed as a notorious Mafia enforcer and murderer turned police informer — and she wanted Bill out of the club. She pleaded with him to quit. "No way," he told her.

Bill Walter Junior was born in September, 1970. He was a beautiful, healthy baby and any reservations Bill might have had about starting a family disappeared, so much so that after a fight at the clubhouse one night, he came home and told Claudine he was quitting the Satan's Choice. She was delighted.

Shortly after, Claudine received a divorce from Carl and she and Bill were married. The couple honeymooned in Europe, touring Switzerland, Germany and Belgium while Baby Billy stayed in Liverpool with his grandparents. It was a superb way to begin a marriage and the couple did prosper. They both made good money: he working for a computer company and she for a catering company, which meant they could save for a down payment on a house. He and Claudine often went out with friends. They liked to drink at the Knob Hill Hotel, and she would impress them by her agility with a pool cue. She truly loved her husband, for one thing their sexual relationship was superb, and her mother thought she would do anything to keep Bill happy.

A year after Billy was born, Claudine had an abortion at her husband's insistence. By 1973 she was pregnant again and Bill suggested she get rid of it. "No way, I'm not going through that again. I just don't think abortion is right." Claudine longed for a baby girl this time, but in October she gave birth to her third son, Peter. Bill had wanted another boy and he sent a card to the hospital that read, "Ha, ha, I won again."

They had saved about $3,500 as a down payment and began house hunting. They discovered that if they settled out of Toronto, they could get a house of the same quality for half the price. They bought a three-bedroom bungalow for $27,500 in Cookstown, about fifty kilometres north of Toronto. It meant that Bill had to commute to work, but he didn't mind driving. And Claudine, she was the happiest she had ever been in her life.

But there was an undercurrent of discontent that would grow more severe as the years passed. Bill hated his job. He was a relatively well-educated man, having completed his grade thirteen. He had joined a computer company after high school, and ended up in their manufacturing division assembling key punch machines. It was work he eventually found so boring that he'd sometimes grow nauseated just thinking about it. Finally he set out to get himself fired. After he took time off, showed up late, was insubordinate, he finally succeeded. Since by 1976 he had worked at the company eight years, he received almost four thousand dollars in severance pay, so he wasn't exactly in a hurry to get another job. It was at that point that his marriage began to crumble.

Claudine worked part-time as a waitress in Cookstown, and when Bill became unemployed he began dropping into the restaurant to pass time. It wasn't long before he was an integral part of the gang of young guys who frequented the place. Bill was buying at least one case of beer every day and Claudine also began to drink more and more heavily.

The conflict between the two didn't lessen when Bill finally enrolled in a six-month butchering course at George Brown College; in fact it grew worse. Bill would hang out at the El Mocambo Tavern every night and he'd come home at two or three in the morning drunk. The couple began to argue more and more.

On Monday, March 13, 1978, Claudine and Bill had a terrible fight. She complained bitterly that he hadn't been home all weekend. He said she was such a nagging bitch he couldn't stand the sight of her. "I'll do what I please in my own home and if you don't like it you can leave," he told her. Claudine responded by threatening him with a butcher knife. Bill managed to wrestle it off her and in the process cracked two of her ribs, blackened her eyes and cut her forehead so badly it required five stitches the next day. He flew out of the house in a rage that night and didn't come home the next two nights. On Wednesday Claudine took an overdose of sleeping tablets and was rushed to the hospital. When she was released the next day, Bill still hadn't shown up. A friend of Claudine's finally got hold of him. He told her, "I wish she would die. I'd be better off without her." At that point Claudine decided to call the cops. Twice before, neighbours, upset at the screaming coming from the Harply house, had sent for police, and the officers had wanted to press charges against Bill but Claudine had refused. "But now," she thought to herself, "I've had enough."

Bill finally arrived home Friday night at nine thirty. When Claudine phoned the police, she could tell from Bill's grin that he thought she was bluffing. They arrived moments later with a warrant for his arrest. He just glared at Claudine. "I told you I wasn't putting up with your bullying anymore," she said.

Bill's parents quickly arranged bail for him and he was released.* The following Sunday he phoned and asked if he could get his clothes. "Fine, as long as you don't cause any trouble," said Claudine. The kids were at the local arena skating when he arrived. Claudine continued to cook supper while he was in the bedroom packing. What she didn't know was that he was stuffing the green garbage bags full of the boys clothes as well as his own.

After a few hours a neighbour called and said, "Are your kids with you?" "No, they're still at the arena," replied Claudine. "Well,"

* Claudine was later persuaded by Bill's friends not to testify against her husband. The assault charges were dropped.

said the neighbour, "my kids are back and say Bill was there and took Billy and Pete away in a car." Claudine phone him at his mother's and he admitted he had them. "You are so smashed all the time, I just can't trust you to take care of them," he said. A friend of Claudine's advised her, "There's not going to be too many men who will want you with two kids to look after. You'll end up in public housing, leading a dog's life. If he thinks it's so easy bringing up two boys, let him find out." Claudine decided it would be best for everyone involved not to fight for the custody of her children and from then on she saw them only occasionally.

With no money and no transportation, Claudine found herself frighteningly isolated in the Cookstown house. Fortunately, a friend she had met years before, Lilly Barnes, came to visit her on Good Friday. Lilly thought Claudine looked a wreck. She hadn't been eating anything, she'd been drinking far too much, and she was popping Valium pills like they were jelly beans. Lilly invited her to come and spend a couple of weeks at her Toronto apartment.

The following Saturday, Claudine, Lilly and Lilly's boyfriend, Chris, went for a drink at The Stable in downtown Toronto. Lilly and Chris were regulars at the tavern, and soon a group of people they knew gathered at the table, among them two attractive young men, Ron Rusoff and Jim Elbourne.* Lilly invited them all back to her place and they partied all night. The next evening Ron and Claudine went out for dinner and soon they were seeing each other almost every day.

Claudine had mixed feelings about Rusoff. He was five years younger than she was and often "acted like a little boy." "He liked to think of himself as a big hood when actually he was nothing," she remembers. "I was scared of him because he was always bragging about the crimes he had committed and I never knew when he was serious and when he was joking." But Claudine needed him. Bill had rented the Cookstown house to someone else. He and Claudine had agreed on the divvying up of the furniture, but she had nowhere to store her portion. "I have a two-bedroom apartment and you can put it there," Ron told her. Claudine decided to move in with him.

On May 2, 1978, Rusoff and his friend Jim Elbourne told Claudine they were going up north to do some target shooting with Jim's 33 and that they would be back that evening. Only a few hours later Rusoff was back. He came to pick up Claudine who was visiting a

---

* These names have been changed to protect Claudine Harply's identity, but all details are entirely accurate.

friend. He was unusually quiet and looked pale. "What's the matter?" Claudine asked him. "I'll tell you later," he said. When they arrived back at his apartment, Ron drove the car into his underground parking spot. Claudine thought that was odd because he always kept the car outdoors in the visitors' area. When they got into the apartment, he developed a case of the jitters, walking all over the place, looking out the windows and over the balcony.

Claudine switched on the TV just in time for the six o'clock news. The lead story was a sensational one: a twenty-one-year-old college student had been gunned down that day as he looked after his father's TV and appliance store. The killer got away with only $150. Ron jumped and switched to another channel. Claudine said to him, "Is that what happened today?" "I never went into the store," he yelled. "Jim went in and I stayed out in the car. He came back and told me to get moving, that he thought he had blown some guy's lights out."

Claudine now says she didn't believe him. "He was always telling me these fairy tales and I was expecting that if this one was true that the police would be here any moment." But they didn't show up that night, and the next morning Rusoff said to Claudine, "I wasn't serious about what I told you last night." She quickly forgot about it.

One afternoon three weeks later, Claudine and Ron decided to do some shopping. In the underground garage Claudine had just got into the car when she saw someone come over and talk to Rusoff. Suddenly the man pulled out a gun and pressed it to Rusoff's forehead. In an instant some thirty police from the Emergency Task Force, many with high-powered rifles, descended on them. One of the cops shoved the nose of his automatic through the car window and pointed it directly at Claudine's head. Another officer grabbed her purse and asked her what her name was. "I was so frightened I couldn't even remember my own name." Claudine says at that point she had no idea why the police were there.

"Any weapons up there?" one of the officers asked her. "Not that I know of," she replied. The cop snapped back at her, "What do you mean not that you know of! Either there is or there isn't." "I don't know. I have no idea," she pleaded. "If anything happens to one of my men, I'll be down to get you." Claudine felt sick as a dog. "I was utterly terrified,' she says.

Later that day Jim Elbourne was charged with first degree murder and Ron Rusoff with second degree murder. Claudine was interrogated for six and a half hours, after which the police told her that she was very lucky that no charges were laid against her. She saw Ron once after he was released from prison and he told her,

"Elbourne wanted to kill you because he thought you would rat on us. I convinced him that you knew nothing."*

The combination of events — the separation from her husband, the "kidnapping" of her children, the traumatic episode with Rusoff — proved too much for Claudine. In July she swallowed a massive overdose of sleeping pills and was rushed to the hospital. That she had been hospitalized at Whitby Psychiatric Hospital for several months never came out during the gang rape trial of the Lauder gang.

During the time she had been living with Rusoff, Claudine was negotiating with her husband. She hadn't felt capable of working and desperately needed some money. Finally she signed away all rights to her house and any further support from Bill Harply and gave him permanent custody of her children, all for a mere $3,500 settlement. "Bill knew that he had me over a barrel and I really got dunged." However, she was able to set herself up in a pleasant apartment in Scarborough, and that summer she got a job as a bartender at a restaurant in the posh Manulife Centre. But after a month the person who had the job before her returned, and she found herself once again unemployed. It was another serious set-back for Claudine, and in October, 1978, frightened that she felt suicidal again, she checked herself into the psychiatric unit of North York General Hospital. After a week the doctors told her she was well enough to leave. They urged her, however, to cut down on her drinking, especially since she was continuing to take Valium.

There were many single and divorced people living in her apartment building, and Claudine made many good friends. She didn't have much money — she was receiving welfare at this point — and couldn't go out much, so most of her time was spent partying with her neighbours. After New Year's 1979 she decided she had better find a job. A girl friend suggested that she look downtown and that they meet afterwards at the Gasworks Tavern. The beer was cheap and there were lots of guys one could pick up. Claudine started drinking there every day. The odd time she'd be part of a group who would go back to somebody's place and party all night. It wasn't out of the ordinary, then, that she should drop into the Gasworks on April 23 before going to the Village People concert. Nor was it unusual that she should go back to Brian Dempsey's place to pick up a few joints. Indeed, a couple of days after the gang rape occurred, Claudine was back drinking at the Gasworks Tavern.

---

* On January 22, 1979, Jim Elbourne pleaded guilty to second degree murder and received a life sentence. Ron Rusoff turned Crown witness. His charge was reduced to accessory to murder after the fact, and he received a suspended sentence and was put on probation for two years.

TWELVE

Terri

SILVER WALKING BOOTS

C arl's Family Restaurant in Laurel Hill, Florida, was as Yankee as its owner, big Tom Roodyn, (the "Carl" in the name was a leftover from the founder, who drowned at age sixty-three while swimming off Longboat Key); hamburgers, bacon, lettuce and tomato sandwiches, blueberry pie, all clean and bland, were served up daily to the local citizenry and tourists. Theresa Roodyn, a slim and attractive woman in her mid-fifties, was sipping a cup of coffee and reading a wedding invitation, which her husband Tom had picked out of the batch of mail, when she was asked if she knew that her daughter had been raped and brutalized by six men in Toronto four years before. Cool as a cucumber, she glanced up and said, "No, I didn't, but it doesn't surprise me one bit. For years I've been expecting to hear that she's been murdered."

It wasn't that she didn't love Terri, she said, but her daughter had long been fascinated by motorcycle gangs and hoodlums of all sorts — "Terri liked those people and she liked the way they lived. She's a happy-go-lucky person who trusts everybody. And I always thought it would get her into serious trouble one day."

Theresa Roodyn maintains that her daughter had always lived in a world of make-believe inhabitated by those she considered exciting and eccentric characters. That's why Terri was so attracted to Harry Levison, a skinny, pimply young man who worked as a bartender and whom Terri had met in New Orleans in 1978. Theresa disliked him intensely. Terri kept talking about how Harry was going to become a mercenary, make lots of money and have thrilling adventures. The Roodyns didn't pay much attention — Terri was always making up apocryphal stories — until letters

177

began arriving from various African countries. Harry Levison had changed his name to Anthony Laferge and had been hired on as a kind of gunman paid to kill leftists guerillas. After that Terri's fascination with incendiaries in particular became an obsession; she read everything she could find on mercenaries and their bloody practices, and if pictures of decapitated and mutilated victims were included all the more interesting.

Terri's dream world naturally excluded the mundane — nine-to-five jobs, children or bourgeois possessions. "I've never known her to really work," says Tom Roodyn. She might had held down the odd job but they rarely lasted longer than a few weeks. The odd time she asked her mother for fifty dollars or so, but mostly she didn't "bum." "She never seemed to need money," said her mother. "We could never figure out why."

In adolescence she developed an itch for travel and hitchhiked everywhere. "She had these pointed silver boots, I called them her walking shoes," remembered her stepfather, Tom Roodyn, "and whenever she put them on, we knew she would soon disappear." During one of her periodic reunions with her mother, she worked as a waitress at the restaurant. One day she simply vanished, leaving all of her personal belongings behind. Mrs. Roodyn deliberated about whether she should phone the police but then decided against it. Terri's nomadic impulses had probably taken over again, she reasoned. Six months later Terri phone and asked her mother to send her clothes to an address in Toronto.

That kind of lifestyle was all right for the young, but as Terri approached thirty, Theresa thought it was time she settled down. "You got to think more like a squirrel who hides nuts away for his future," she told Terri. It wasn't a concern that loomed large in Theresa Roodyn's life, however. She only talked to her daughter about once a year — Terri didn't have a phone — and even then she never learned very much about what the younger woman was up to. Theresa didn't mind because Terri and her problems brought back to her an earlier painful life in Toronto, which she would very much like to forget.

It wasn't easy bringing up five young children with a husband who couldn't hold down a job, who was an incurable alcoholic, and who in his drunkenness would often be ugly, even cruel, to his wife and children. After seventeen years of poverty and abuse, Theresa had given up in despair and taken off for Florida. The children who had not already run away from their appalling home life were placed in foster homes or with friends. Terri had attended Warden Avenue Public School in Scarborough, a suburb of Toronto, but by the time she reached age twelve, the family had split up. She was sent to Peter and Ruth Dunn, friends of her father's family in Beaconsfield, Quebec. She started high school there but that didn't last for long; she had become as wilful and wild as her older siblings, two of whom were already in trouble with the police, and the Dunns simply couldn't handle her. By 1966 she was back in Toronto living with an old school chum, Cathy Lacroix, and Cathy's mother, Harriet.

Terri eventually was hired by a tool and machine manufacturer on the assembly line, but it wasn't a job she cared for. She found it tedious and depressing. "God, I hope I don't have to do this for the rest of my life," she told Cathy. "I would rather die." By that time she had something in her life that was much more interesting — motorcycles.

She was attracted to Sonny Hall from the first moment a friend introduced them. He wasn't a particularly big guy, but he was blond and blue-eyed and something of a big wheel in the Vagabond Motorcycle Club. He taught her not only everything about bikes — how to ride, how they functioned mechanically — but also the correct behaviour, the mores and manners, of being a biker's broad. She readily accepted the fact that men were god-like figures, kings of the universe, and women somewhat on the level of the club's mascot — a German shepherd puppy. George Hayes was a member of the Vagabonds in the late Sixties and he remembers Terri from those days. "She was very young, maybe sixteen or seventeen. Though she had a pretty good figure, she was slim and relatively tall, she wasn't very good looking. She had long straggly brown hair and not very good teeth. But there was something I admired about her. She was really gutsy. Sonny sometimes gave her a hard time, bossing her around, making her do things she didn't want to do, but she wouldn't just accept it like a lot of the broads around that clubhouse. She'd mouth him right back and I liked that."

By this time Cathy Lacroix and her mother were thoroughly sick of Terri's lifestyle, and after a fierce argument one evening, she walked out. Having no fixed address became a matter of routine for Terri over the next few years; there were times when a knapsack containing one or two T-shirts was all she owned in the world. Most times it didn't bother her; she simply never developed a taste for material goods.

In 1968 Sonny Hall disappeared suddenly, nobody seemed to know if he had gone travelling or gone to jail, and Terri took to hanging out at the Square Boy, a hamburger joint on Danforth Avenue frequented by bikers. It was there one evening that she met George Nikolopolous, who had just been discharged from the army. He was as dark as Sonny was fair, a hefty guy who didn't say all that much. But he seemed a fairly easygoing man, especially after the turbulent Sonny, and Terri needed him. They began going out together, a relationship that would last almost five years.

George had been thinking of getting involved with the Para-Dice Riders at that point. Terri encouraged him and it wasn't long before he was a full-fledged member. A snapshot taken at this time shows Terri and George sitting on a sofa in their apartment. Above their heads, mounted on the wall, are two rifles positioned one across the other in an X formation. On each side of the X is pinned up a T-shirt, the lettering on the larger one reading BORN TO RAISE HELL, and on the smaller one, GEORGE'S BAGGAGE. Even though Terri did all the talking, was even bossy, club protocol dictated that she be considered a mere possession of George's.

Donna Nikolopolous, the wife of George's brother Peter, became a kind of adopted sister to Terri. She says that Terri was enthusiastic about bikers because she so desperately needed to belong to a group of any kind. "I've never met anybody who craved love as much as Terri. I think she was starved for it in her childhood and she would do anything to make people take notice of her."

In 1969 George was sentenced to eighteen months in prison for his involvement in the robbery of a grocery store. When Terri flew to Florida to stay with her mother, George's family were angry with her. They felt this was the time George needed her the most; they had wanted her to visit him as often as possible.

Theresa Roodyn, feeling somewhat guilty about abandoning her daughter, tried to help her at that point. She worked in the restaurant as a cashier and waitress but Theresa also tried to get her to enrol in high school. She was only seventeen at this point and her mother told her it wasn't too late to get an education. But after ten months she suddenly disappeared. George had been released and she scurried back to Toronto to resume the relationship.

Terri worked off and on as a waitress or barmaid, and George did odd jobs, driving a truck, washing cars, working as a day labourer. Their lives still centred around the Para-Dice Riders, and during the warm weather most weekends they'd go on club outings. "I think she liked the biker life more than he did," says Donna. "There was something exciting about it that just turned her on."

George's parents bought a house in the east end of Toronto and invited him and Terri to live with them. Donna says the Nikolopolouses, old-fashioned Greek immigrants, didn't particularly like Terri, nor did they approve of the couple living together without being married, but they were so anxious that he not get in trouble again, they tolerated the situation. They were the kind of people who would do anything for their children. She took to calling them

Mom and Dad. "Terri desperately needed a family," says Donna. "I tried to like her for George's sake but it was hard." Says Peter, "She wasn't intelligent but she was street-wise." She was oblivious to any effect she might be having on people. "If you sat her down with some so-called intellectuals, they'd be talking about one thing, and she another, and it wouldn't bother her one bit. She was a very tough lady."

What upset Donna and Peter most about her was that they thought she was a "compulsive liar." "She used to tell the most ridiculous stories," Donna recalls. One day when George was away, Terri came into the house, very upset, weeping and heaving as though she was going to throw up. She told Donna the following story. She had been forced into the back of a van by a group of bikers. There, with a piece of sharp glass, they had engraved PDR (Para-Dice Riders) on both cheeks of her posterior. When George returned home, he quite naturally was furious, and swore he'd get even with whoever of his fellow club members had mutilated Terri. He was wise enough, however, to want to see for himself the damage done. Before he had the opportunity, she admitted she had lied. "What bothered me," says Donna, "is that George could have been done in if he had gone on a rampage for nothing. That's part of the biker's creed. She did things like that all the time, I think just to get attention."

In 1970 Terri gave birth to a baby girl. Donna says, "The day she got out of the hospital, she brought the baby to my house to show it off. Six weeks later she gave it up for adoption." For years Donna assumed it was George's child, but he insisted that it couldn't have been — the timing just wasn't right. "You know Terri, fucking anytime, any place. It could have been anybody's kid," he told his brother. In February, 1971, Terri had another baby, whom she named George Junior after his father. She kept that child slightly longer than the first but in the summer of that year he too was placed in a foster home and eventually adopted. "Terri just decided she didn't want the responsibility of a baby, and that was that," says Donna. Peter and Donna did keep in contact with their nephew, and on occasion would have him over to their place. During these visits George would drop by; the little boy didn't know he was his father and called him uncle. In 1976 Donna had invited George Junior over when Terri unexpectedly came in. "For some reason the kid said to her, 'I know you're my mom,' and he put his arms around her," recalls Donna. "I thought she might have felt something but she didn't bat an eyelash."

One of the reasons Terri gave her children up was that she was still obsessed with the idea of travel. In 1972 she abruptly left

George and went back to her mother's place in Florida. Not long afterwards she met the man she would marry.

Terri had always been addicted to the music of rock and roll; in her mind it validated her eccentric, self-centred lifestyle. Eric Spudic was a percussionist in the rock band Leg's End when Terri met him in a Sarasota bar one evening. He was quiet to the point of perversity and Terri was gregarious; they thought they complemented each other quite nicely. They were married in the summer of 1973 in Laurel Hill, Florida. A small reception was held at Carl's Family Restaurant.

Eric continued to play for Leg's End and when that group dissolved he plugged into others. Most were second-rate bands, playing grubby hotels and arenas in small towns such as Perry, Kentucky; Merryville, Louisiana; and Auburn, Alabama. Terri travelled with him, acting as a kind of manager-gopher. She ensured the sound system was set up properly, dealt with the people who paid them, and got hamburgers. It was an existence she liked: "We lived music," she told a friend. But after a very dry spell — Eric couldn't find a gig no matter how he tried — the couple decided to come to Toronto. They arrived in the spring of 1975 and stayed a year and a half.

They visited Peter and Donna Nikolopolous a great deal. "I think it was because we were among the very few respectable friends she had," says Peter. "When you're trying to impress your new husband, you can hardly introduce him to your good friend Pig Leg, or Raunchy Ronny, or Hard On Jack." The Nikolopolouses found Eric to be one of the quietest people they had ever met. "He'd come in and say hi and then that was it. He wouldn't say another word all evening." Donna saw a marked difference in Terri. "She had really mellowed out. She didn't seem to be nearly as wild as she had been. I rather liked her during that period."

While in Toronto, Eric worked as a clerk for Merrill Lynch Royal Securities and Terri was a reporter and file clerk for a credit bureau. She later took a much more lucrative job as a topless dancer at a particularly seedy tavern, according to her friends.

Terri and Eric had come to Toronto because they had heard that the music scene was booming there. But Eric couldn't find a band that wanted a percussionist no matter how hard he looked. By the winter of 1976 the Spudics decided that they wanted desperately to get back into music. They returned to Laurel Hill; Terri once again worked in her mother's restaurant, but Eric remained unemployed. "It wasn't that he couldn't find work, it was that he wouldn't look," Terri later told Donna Nikolopolous. The couple began to fight endlessly and in the summer of 1977 they split up. According to George, Eric told him, "I couldn't stand the way she never told the truth, she lied about everything."

After Terri received a letter from a girl friend telling her how wonderful New Orleans was, she packed her knapsack and left immediately. The reason her friend was so enamoured with the southern city was that she had made a friend of Doc Fergie, who could lay his hands on any kind of drug you wanted. And he'd sell it to you cheap. By this time, her friends say, Terri was obsessed by drugs; getting them was the focal point of her daily routine. She was especially fond of "downers," in particular Percodan and quaaludes, but she would partake of the more common varieties of drugs, LSD or speed, if the others weren't available. But by the spring of 1978 she was itching to travel again and hitchhiked to Toronto.

She stayed at the apartment of Jimmy Rich, who was ten years younger than she was, a former biker, but she visited Donna and Peter Nikolopolous often. On Victoria Day George arrived at his brother's apartment to discover that Terri was there. He introduced her to his bride-to-be, Ginny McKay. That summer Ginny was laid off her job and Terri wasn't working — a welfare cheque she received monthly was about all she needed — so the two spent a great deal of time together. Eventually Terri moved into the apartment which George and Ginny shared. When George was away driving a truck, the two women liked to go to the Young Station Tavern. "I don't think she went there to listen to the music so much as to simply drink. She was a great drinker. And she was a real tease with the men," says Ginny. "She usually went home with someone she picked up in the bar." Yet she told Ginny often that she thought vaginal intercourse was "dirty." "Screwing just screws up your vital organs," she said. She preferred oral sex, and she wore a T-shirt with the words GIVE HEAD TILL DEAD printed on the front of it. Ginny thought Terri was so preoccupied with drugs and sex that she concluded the young woman needed help and suggested that she go to a psychiatrist.

Ginny often watched Terri comb through the ashtrays in the apartment. She would painstakingly unravel the pathetic remains of roaches, until gradually she would collect enough marijuana to roll a small joint. "She was so obsessed with drugs. I've never seen anything like it," says Ginny. Terri began talking about how it was time to return to New Orleans to find Doc Fergie. One day Terri disappeared, in the process stealing fourteen dollars and two good dresses belonging to Ginny. "And I was on welfare at the time," Ginny complained.

Terri had returned to New Orleans, and when a friend of her's opened a tavern in Houma, Louisiana, called Ridout's Bar and Tavern in January, 1979, she got a part-time job there as a bartender. She also fell in love with Harry Levison, the would-be mercenary. Terri thought their relationship was one of the most satisfying she had ever had and when he left for Africa, she was devastated. Three months later in April of 1979, she set off again, hitchhiking over a thousand miles to Toronto. Dripping wet with rain, and smelling rather unpleasant, she knocked on the Nikolopolouses' door one night in early May and asked if she could stay for a while. Peter and Donna said okay but they made it plain that it was to be only a temporary arrangement. When she was still sleeping on their couch three weeks later, Peter couldn't stand it any longer and told Donna that Terri would have to go. On May 14 she went to the Young Station hoping she'd find somewhere to stay that night. There she met Richard Gillespie.

When, the next day, she described how she had been attacked and raped by seven bikers the night before, Donna just laughed. She didn't believe a word she said — Terri had told her too many phony horror stories before. "If you are going to give me that shit, get out of here," she yelled at her. It was only when the police started questioning her that she realized there might be something to Terri's accusations. Meanwhile Terri, the unceasing nomad, had once again hitchhiked back to New Orleans.

PART **IV**

The Rap

THIRTEEN

Aftermath

AN AWFUL WAY
TO LIVE

During their imprisonment, all six members of the Lauder Avenue gang have steadfastly maintained their innocence.

Of the six, Gillespie, Dempsey, Blake and Bell now admit that the accounts of what happened on April 23 and May 15, 1979, which were presented to the jury were to some extent concocted. Still, they insist that neither Claudine Harply nor Terri Spudic was raped. And since officials of Canada's federal penitentiary system consider remorse and the admission of guilt as a signal of a prisoner's progress towards rehabilitation, the Lauder gang's insistence that they did nothing illegal has remained a soiled spot on their records. John Beatteay sums up their attitude in a letter written in 1981: "If my parole depends upon my admitting guilt to a [parole] board of directors, I will be writing on this same stationery in 1993."

Richard Gillespie remained isolated and withdrawn during his incarceration at Warkworth Institution, seldom mixing with other inmates or participating in organized programs. As a result, his imprisonment continued longer than it might have. But finally, after serving three years and four months of his six-year sentence, he was released on parole to a halfway house in Toronto in May of 1983. He remains bitter and despondent and believes an enormous injustice was done to him and the other men. "It's fortunate that I'm not a weak person mentally. If I took everything seriously, I'm sure I would have had about twenty heart attacks by now. What happened to me could happen to any man who happened to be at the wrong place at the wrong time." He remains dubious that he will ever be able to function very well once on his own. He believes that the sentences received by him and the other members of the Lauder group are much more far-reaching than the actual time they will spend in jail. Given society's abhorrence for the nature of the crimes for which they have been convicted, their punishment, which will primarily take the form of social ostracism, will stretch far into the future. His experience at the Keele Community Correctional Centre, the halfway house, has reinforced this belief. On his arrival he was threatened by other ex-prisoners, who were determined to get the "rapehound." Shortly after, his room was broken into and he was so savagely beaten that his left lung collapsed. He was hospitalized for over a week and then released to the care of an uncle living in Toronto. Yet despite his pessimism, he still hopes that one day he will make his way by writing songs.

On May 26, 1983, the parole board voted to release David Bell. He was not the only one who was happy and relieved; his family was overjoyed. Eleanor and Andrew Bell have remained remarkably supportive, convinced that their son is innocent; so his transition into society was a much smoother one. "What I want to do now is forget the whole thing," he says. "I've matured a great deal in prison and I have no intention of letting anything like this happen again." Interestingly, Dave has resisted appeals to acquire a marketable trade. He is convinced he can still make it as a musician and has ignored concerns by prison authorities that it was that lifestyle that got him into trouble in the first place. He has had access to some musical training in prison and plans to work hard to become a performer.

In 1982 Robert Caruso was transferred from Kingston Penitentiary to Warkworth Institution. The indignation that so characterized Caruso' testimony at the trial has remained with him. "I didn't rape anyone. Period," he insists. Although his family were dubious at the time the charges were laid, he has now convinced them of his innocence and they have stuck by him. He has done well in prison. In fact, he is now so trusted by officials, he is allowed to leave the grounds while driving a truck (in the company of prison staff).

John Beatteay has also been transferred to Warkworth. He has become even more introverted, more sullen. His family worry that he is beginning to feel that his future is so "hopeless" that there is not much use paticipating in prison programs or even dreaming about his freedom. They hope that a taste of freedom, a day out of prison for example, may rekindle his desire to carry on. They are worried because they know that many of the Lauder gang have contemplated suicide.

Ruby and William Blake have seriously considered suing the federal Department of Correctional Services for what they consider has been outright discrimination against their son Randy.

Although he had a relatively minor criminal record and his part in the rapes no more excessive (the Blakes claim much less) than the others', he is the one member of the Lauder gang who has been incarcerated in the most restrictive of prisons. In February of 1983 he was transferred from Millhaven, the hard-core maximum security prison, to Collins Bay, a medium security facility but the most regimented in this category. His parents maintain that because of his exemplary conduct in prison, he should be given a much better break. They say that he has been discriminated against for one reason: he is perceived by authorities as a biker. "He might as well have a mark on his forehead," says his father. "No matter what he does, he won't be able to overcome it." And they firmly believe, like many others who have knowledge of his case, that he was not at Lauder the night that Claudine Harply was there.

Randy has done well in prison, completing several academic courses, and he hopes to eventually receive his grade twelve diploma. He plans to become a licensed auto mechanic. The Blakes are amazed at how he has taken his imprisonment in stride. "Even if he's having a low time, and he knows I'm coming, he'll come in there [the visiting room] in a happy mood for my sake," says Mrs. Blake. When Randy is released, Mrs. Blake is not so concerned that he won't be able to find a job or will be snubbed by his friends, as she is of continuous harassment by the police. "Once the police know he's in the street again, they'll all be watching. I'll be scared to death for him; I'm afraid they'd shoot him in the back in two minutes if they get the chance."

Brian Dempsey has been the one member of the Lauder gang who has continued to openly rebel, continued to thumb his nose at authority. In 1982 Brian wrote to a friend, "I'm being negative and bitter, I know. I'm so much the rebel because I know what happened and I know I should not be here; and I'll die trying to prove it. How's that for heavy shit. I get wound up for one reason and one reason only: I see no justification for my being here [in Kingston] and believe me, it's a 360 degree headache." Of all the Lauder gang, Dempsey alone has remained in Kingston Penitentiary, considered by all as the worst institution in the federal system. He has spent considerable time in solitary confinement, both as a form of punishment and at his own request. In a letter written in 1983, he explained his position, "I'm happier than I have been in a long time. I have simply told them to pack this joint in their anal canal. Perhaps that sounds a tad drastic but if you had lived here three years when you didn't want to come to this cesspool in the first place you'd know why I feel so good. I'm in the hole but that's my choice, that makes it my space." Brian Dempsey, however, has not lost his dream of becoming a great musician, as famous as Jimi Hendrix or Mick Jagger.

Most of the Lauder gang feel that their lives are in effect over, that they have been branded with an indelible stigma which will make them an anathema to society for years to come. Their only hope, and they consider it slight, is that the controversial legal principles that are still being debated in court will be resolved in their favour. But as Brian Dempsey says, "Given our past experience, we are not exactly holding our breath."

On March 22, 1982, two years and three months after the Lauder gang were found guilty, the Supreme Court of Ontario heard their appeal. An impressive slate of lawyers represented them: Clayton Ruby, Alan D. Gold, Brian Greenspan, Marc Rosenberg, Larry Feldman and Gerald Kluwak. All had established legal precedent in the past through criminal cases they had argued, particularly before supreme courts. Basically they insisted that justice was not served when the two cases involving Claudine Harply and Terri Spudic were tried together. They contended that the defendants should have had a choice of where each set of charges was heard, in county or supreme court. And they maintained that evidence pertaining to the Harply incident was not so similar to that of the Spudic case that the facts of both should have been presented to the jury at the same time.

The arguments of the defence counsel and the reply by the Crown attorney took up two full days of court time. At the end of the well-prepared and thoughtful deliberations, the three justices hearing the case took nine minutes to arrive at their decision: the appeal was denied. It took them four minutes to determine that the sentences should not be reduced. Clay Ruby for one was aghast at the swiftness with which the judges had reached a decision and became determined to take the case to the Supreme Court of Canada.

Up to this point all of the defendants had had their legal fees paid for by the Ontario Legal Aid plan. In October 1982 it was determined that there was not enough merit in the case to warrant an application before the Supreme Court of Canada. Therefore the six men would no longer be entitled to legal aid. Clay Ruby proceeded anyway. The only fees provided were the small amounts of money a few of the defendants could take from their prison savings.

Ruby presented the case and on December 21, 1982, the Supreme Court granted leave to appeal on two issues: similar fact evidence and the right to choose a trial in the county or superior courts. It was something of a victory, since in 1982 only 23 per cent of the cases submitted to the Supreme Court were considered important enough to the Canadian judicial system to merit a hearing by the high court.

What followed, however, was a fight of classic proportions between the defendants' counsel and the officials of the Ontario Legal Aid plan. At one point during the battle Ruby would call the bureaucrats' decisions "insensitive and stupid." He charged that the officials were "unbelievably arrogant" because they, despite what the Supreme Court had ruled, decided that the case had no merit. The official called the letters sent by Ruby "unprofessional and puerile." In the end the Supreme Court of Canada ordered that the men be granted legal aid — the first time in Canadian history that the high court had done this.

When the appeal is heard — in the spring of 1984, it is expected — the Supreme Court has two alternatives: the justices can deny the appeal or they can grant it, in which case the charges will be overturned and retrials ordered. If the latter occurs, the Crown attorney may not be able to proceed. Terri Spudic, who returned to the United States even before the original trial was concluded, was very reluctant to testify in the first place. Now living somewhere in north Florida, she has indicated that never again will she discuss what happened during the evening of May 15, 1979 — she says she simply wants to forget about it — and that under no circumstances will she take the stand again. Her lifestyle has not changed: she still runs with bikers, her wanderlust is unquenchable — her mother says that she never knows when Terri might call or from where. Her walking boots sit always at the door.

And Claudine Harply may not be mentally healthy enough to testify; her addiction to drugs and alcohol has intensified. In 1981 she spent six weeks in the Donwood Institute, a Toronto clinic which is highly respected for its treatment of addicts. Within days after leaving the institute, she was drinking again. Before she was sexually assaulted by the Lauder gang, she had attempted to commit suicide at least twice. Since the events of April 23, 1979, she has continued her drive towards self-destruction, attempting to do away with herself at least four times. Once she was pronounced dead on arrival at the hospital but she miraculously recovered.

She has been battered by the two men she has lived with since the April incident. The latest was charged with assault causing bodily harm, after he beat her and then forced her into a bathtub of scalding water. Curiously, Claudine has renewed her amorous relationship with the assailant.

She has not worked since the preliminary inquiry four years ago. And she is still receiving therapy for the injury to her leg that occurred the night of April 23, 1979.

After the trial Claudine continued to frequent the Gasworks Tavern even though many of the regular patrons snubbed her; they were friends of Brian Dempsey's and Bob Caruso's and they were upset that Claudine was a prime reason the two men were in jail. One night she got talking with two men and a woman whom she had met at the tavern before. Eventually they asked her back to a party at the Para-Dice Riders clubhouse. She agreed. "I was pretty bombed," she says. Once there, two women followed Claudine into the washroom and tried to get a valuable ring off her finger. When she refused to give it up, they beat her savagely. Her nose was broken, the caps on her three front teeth were knocked loose, her cheek was ripped by a knife, requiring eight stitches, and she was covered with bruises. Claudine felt that the women had assaulted her on orders from one or more of the Lauder gang but she was never able to prove it and they vehemently denied it. She didn't complain to the police because she was frightened club members would go after her again.

She did apply to the Ontario Criminal Injuries Board for compensation for pain and suffering received from both incidents, the beating by the women and the assault by the Lauder gang. Lawyers talked of compensation in the area of $15,000, and Claudine thought maybe she would set up a small retail shop or take a trip to Europe. But when the board heard her case in November, 1982, members asked some cutting questions. Why had she gone back to Lauder Avenue that night? Why had she drunk so much alcohol? Why did she continue to frequent the Gasworks? Why hadn't she complained immediately to the police in both instances? The police, who had been so eager for her to testify during the trial, were not so enthusiastic before the Criminal Injuries Board. The board finally awarded her $3,400, of which $1,200 was earmarked to pay her lawyer. She felt deeply betrayed. She says, "I will never be able to walk down the street without glancing over my shoulder. I will always be frightened that one of those guys will be after me. I have nightmares about it and it's an awful way to live. Yet sometimes when I think about them in prison, I feel sorry for them but then I feel more sorry for myself."

FOURTEEN

Epilogue

WHO ARE THE VICTIMS?

The researching and writing of this book has been a strange and sometimes distressing adventure. What was to be an analysis of how six men perpetrated the most degrading and cruellest of crimes — gang rape of helpless victims — and received their appropriate punishment at the hands of a sympathetic and competent justice system, has turned instead into a complex jigsaw puzzle. The sharp, clear perception I began with, dramatically expressed in the Toronto *Sun* headline — "Judge jails 'animals,' for 'gross' gang rapes" — now seems out of focus, warped. For in the end it was as difficult for me to believe the victims' account of what happened, as it was to credit the men's stories. One fact did emerge clearly: the jury was not presented with a true picture of what occurred on April 23 and May 15, 1979. And because of that, justice was not done. It's an unnerving conclusion for a feminist who intended to paint a picture of a typical gang rapist and who believes that rape is a horrible and insidious crime.

The forcible possession of a woman's body is a predominant theme throughout history. Sexually assaulting the female population was regarded as legitimate booty for a conquering army. The raping of a young virgin by marauding clansmen as a fair revenge for some slight done by an opposing tribe. The violation of a twelve-year-old black slave by the white master as merely something one did with one's property. Indeed, rape is the inferential action that stems from the concept preponderant still throughout society that woman is merely a possession of man. And gang rape is the magnification of this ugly male superciliousness. It is every gang of young punks, their language full of "fucks" and "cunts," their every movement menacing and bullying, their ridiculous sense of superiority reinforced by the playful punch on the arm of their comrades, one has met on the subway or street corner. I think Mr. Justice Patrick Galligan was most eloquent when he said, "A gang rape is an unspeakably gross repudiation of the most fundamental principles by which civilized people live in a free and open society."

Studies by social scientists indicated that anywhere from 23 per cent to 71 per cent of rapes were done by groups of two or more.* And, as would seem logical, the larger the group, the more severe the physical violence done to the victim. Finally, many of the rapists would probably not have committed such a crime singly; but among their peers they felt it necessary to prove they were "big shits."

Each member of the Lauder gang neatly fitted the portrait of a gang rapist painted by social scientists. All but one came from the lower middle class, they were not well educated, they spoke English, they were either Protestant or Roman Catholic, they were white, they were not successful in a career, and their average age was twenty-five — all statistics which corresponded exactly with the average. Some sociologists who have studied gang rape say there is something of a homosexual element in these acts: the mixing of their sperm in one woman's vagina has a certain symbolic significance to a group of rapists.** While I think actual sex with another man would have been repugnant to the Lauder gang, many of them were such close friends that they again seemed to fit the portrait. And there was one other important factor: a leader of such authority that he could spur the others on to commit crimes they would normally not commit. Brian Dempsey fills the bill. The Lauder gang seemed perfect specimens for my analysis.

On investigation, however, what I found, rather than hard facts, were illusions, like a row of painted veils, and as each one was put in place, the picture became more distorted.

Small details at first. Newspaper stories that left impressions that were so false as to be almost funny. For example, a Toronto *Sun* headline of November 18, 1972, reads, "Night of terror relived in nightmares: Mother." The image was that of a young woman as wholesome as apple pie describing her horrifying experience. Terri

---

* J. W. Mohr, "Sexual Behaviour and the Criminal Law, Part III," in *Rape and Attempted Rape, Preliminary Report*, Forensic Clinic (Toronto: 1965).

** W.H. Blanchard, "The Group Process in Gang Rape," *Journal of Social Psychology*, vol. 49 (1959), pp. 259-66.

Spudic was indeed a mother, twice, but she had given both children up for adoption months after they were born, and according to her friends, she was a liar, a frequent and devoted drug user, a vagabond.

Misconceptions that permeated the trial. For example, the impression that the accused were a gang of hard-core bikers when only one, Randy Blake, could conceivably be categorized as such, the references to times and events by the victims which on close scrutiny seemed improbable and therefore cast doubt on their entire testimonies.

The most significant illusion perpetrated, however, was that these men were treated with irreproachable fairness by the judicial system. As the defence lawyers and Crown attorney predicted, once Mr. Justice Galligan decided that the charges arising out of the Harply and Spudic incidents should be tried together, the Lauder gang's chances of being acquitted were extremely remote, if not nonexistent.

It seemed to me that dealing with the two sets of charges at the same time ran counter to the fundamental idea that one was innocent until proven guilty. As a layman, I have had difficulty understanding the legal precepts which allowed such a thing. First, did the crimes represent "a systematic course of criminal conduct"? Crown Attorney Rutherford implied that the Lauder gang had a habit of sending one of its members out to a bar to lure unsuspecting victims back to the house to be raped. That Harply and Spudic were only two women among a number. But there was no hard evidence of this; indeed the lifestyle of the Lauder gang was so chaotic, impulsive and aimless, it's hard to imagine how they could have organized themselves to plan such complicated action or indeed any patterned activity.

Second, were the facts surrounding the two sets of charges so similar that they were interchangeable? That would seem to be true if one took at face value the description of what went on April 23 and May 15 by the two victims. The testimony by two women who did not know each other did seem strikingly similar. But the men sang a far different song; each individual claimed that his actions during one night bore little similarity to those of the second night. Accordingly, the judge must have believed the two women's versions of the story at the beginning of the trial, before evidence for the accused was presented, in order to make his ruling on similar fact evidence. (Mr. Justice Galligan said he had read the transcript of the preliminary inquiry that included only testimony by Harply and Spudic and not the Lauder gang.) The defence lawyers argued that the least Galligan could have done to ensure fairness was to hear the accused's evidence in camera (in the absence of the jury) before he made his decision. Galligan decided that this was not necessary. And whatever the intent, the effect of trying the two cases together was to convict the accused before they even had a chance to tell their side of the story.

What resulted during the trial was the accumulation of a mass of detail relating to six individuals and two accusers. I think it must have been extremely difficult to single out each of the defendants and judge the evidence surrounding his involvement in a fair and unbiased manner. And indeed questions put to the judge by the jury during their deliberations indicated that they were very confused about details. In one instance the jurors were even unsure as to which of the accused had been charged with attempted buggery of Terri Spudic. The jury had understood that Dempsey, Beatteay and Bell had been charged when in fact it was Dempsey, Blake and Bell. Indeed, in the jurors' minds the stories of the accused must have melted into one sorry, degenerate mess.

A serious review of the evidence cannot help but throw into question the credibility of both Claudine Harply and Terri Spudic.

A story in the *Toronto Star* on November 18, 1979, headed "'I wasn't drunk,' woman tells rape trial of 6," went on at length to give Claudine Harply's account of her drinking that evening, how she had consumed only two beers at the house, and two or three beers after she had been raped. Nowhere did the article mention that her blood alcohol content at one in the morning was estimated at 360 milligrams of alcohol per 100 millilitres of blood, or four and half times the legal drinking limit, and that experts in alcoholism and addiction had testified that Harply must have been almost in a coma or even close to death, with the resulting distortion of memory and perception. If the Harply incident had been tried alone, that evidence would probably have resulted in the jury questioning the validity of her entire evidence to the point where they might have brought forth a not-guilty verdict.

I am convinced that Claudine Harply falsely identified Randy Blake as an attacker and the man who so badly twisted her leg. After interviewing many people, I believe he was not present at 402 Lauder Avenue during the evening of April 23, that the first time he visited the place was in early May, and that he is therefore serving six years in jail for a crime he never committed. Two people testified on Randy's behalf, but Crown Attorney Rutherford was able to emphasize contradictions in both their evidence. Randy had testified that on April 23, 1979, he returned home from signing in at a police station downtown at four thirty in the afternoon. Jeff Ismail, Randy's friend who rented the house where he was staying, had promised to install a water pump in a friend's car. The pump had been delivered earlier in the day by Dennis Blake, Randy's brother who worked as a driver for an auto parts supply company. Randy helped push the car from a nearby neighbour's house to Ismail's driveway. After that he worked on his motorcycle until one in the morning. He then went into the recreation room, watched some TV with Willy Austin, another resident, and then went to sleep. Crown Attorney Chris Rutherford was able to prove there was no invoice made out for the water pump, and this cast doubt on Randy's entire testimony. But there are many more people who swear they saw him that evening. As well as Jeff Ismail, there was Larry Goodenough, the hockey player; Doug Tokarski, another resident; Dennis Blake, Randy's brother; Jeoffrey Scott, a neighbour down the street; and the two women who also live at the Jeffcoat house. Blake's lawyer, Harry Doan, did not call them to testify even though most would have been willing to do so. As well, all the inhabitants of the Lauder Avenue house, the defendants and Charles Dempsey, Linda Brown and Jean Elgar, have steadfastly maintained that they did not meet Randy Blake until the first week of May, 1979.

If Randy Blake wasn't there, the man whose face she said she would never forget, by whom and how was her leg twisted? And was her leg twisted? The doctor who examined her had testified that "she had had a traumatic injury to the knee, which in most instances would be caused from a blow to the outer aspect of the knee," in other words, an injury consistent with a hard fall on the stairs or on the floor.

A doctor testified that Richard Gillespie was suffering from a serious bout of pneumonia that evening in April when he was supposedly raping Claudine Harply, and the jury believed that he was at the Hot Tub Club as he said. And finally, Brian Dempsey was hirsute in the extreme at the time he encountered Claudine Harply and clean shaven with neatly cut hair in his mug shot. How then did Harply pick three men, two of whom were probably not there, and one of whom was almost unrecognizable, from the photos presented by the police? If Harply was wrong in identifying her assailants, surely the remainder of her testimony should be called into question as well.

Harply testified that when she was pushed into the small front bedroom at about 8:10 p.m., there was no electricity turned on but that it was still light enough out for her to see her attackers quite clearly. But how could she have been so sure of their identity, since that evening the sun set at 6:55 p.m.? An hour and fifteen minutes later it must have been quite dark. Why had she not been able to identify the house on Lauder with its unusual purple colour, since she had had a chance to have a good look at it when she went to buy cigarettes the next morning? Why had she given Bobby Caruso her correct telephone number? Why had she told the hospital authorities that she didn't want the police called? There might very well have been reasonable answers to these and many other similar questions, but one wonders if the jury, faced with such an overwhelming amount of evidence, was able to consider each of these points in the detail it deserved.

While there were no major difficulties with Terri Spudic's evidence as there was with the identification of Blake and Gillespie in the Harply case, her testimony was riddled with contradictions and falsehoods. Some of these were not of great importance, but they do serve to cast a cloud of doubt over her version of events. For if she avoided the truth about inconsequential matters, quite likely she wouldn't be correct about something she had a stake in. She testified, for example, that she had worked for a year as a bartender in Ridout's Bar and Tavern in Houma. The Louisiana Liquor Licensing Authority, however, states that the place opened for the first time in January, 1979, only three months before Spudic arrived in Toronto. She testified that she had obtained a Harley Davidson 750 in 1977-78. She said she left it at Marty Leibowitz's house in Agincourt, a suburb of Toronto, and on her return in April, 1979, she sold it to him to obtain some needed cash. By this information, Spudic was able to deflect the defence counsels' implication that she came by the forty dollars she had on her on May 15 by illicit means, that is, prostitution. But Leibowitz, who was never called as a witness, claims he never knew of any such bike and says he certainly never bought one. Spudic also testified she never indulged in LSD or other drugs, yet she was a well-known user. Her friends insist she worked as a stripper in Toronto; yet on the stand she denied ever having worked in a tavern in that city. Her friends also maintain that she was an incorrigible liar with a penchant for spinning fanciful yarns, like the tale about the Vagabonds carving their initials on her posterior.

The contradiction in evidence pertaining to the events which occurred May 15 are of more significance. She claimed she returned to the Nikolopolous apartment of May 15 before she went to the Young Station Tavern and left two small gifts, a package of incense and a plant. Peter and Donna Nikolopolous claim that since Terri didn't have a key, there was no way she could have got into the apartment and in any case they found no sign of the plant or incense. She apparently indicated to Dr. Ronald Cyr that she had contracted gonorrhea three weeks before the rape and yet she adamantly refused to acknowledge that she had ever had venereal disease. For what purpose was the drug Atarax prescribed — for insect bites as Spudic claimed or to relieve anxiety, one of the "downers" that Terri enjoyed so much?

Finally, the forensic evidence was surprisingly incomplete. For example, why was no search for drugs done from samples of either Spudic's or Harply's blood? These findings would have indicated whether they had taken LSD or quantities of Valium on the day of the assaults. Coupled with large amounts of alcohol, such drugs would have an affect on the victims' ability to remember events clearly. And why were no smears taken of the rectum area, a usual process if buggery is alleged? The collection of such vital evidence should surely be considered standard procedure in a police investigation.

Lawyer Marshall Sack is certain that the jury realized that Spudic was lying on the stand. And, of course, the jurors had plainly heard the evidence of how intoxicated Harply must have been. Why then did they convict the Lauder gang? "They simply believed that something had happened to these women that they didn't want to happen, that they were violated against their wills," says Sack. The major reason for this conclusion was the detailed accounting by Harply and Spudic of events so similar as to be uncanny. But there were other factors as well. The gang's plan to present themselves as a group of innocent people may have indeed left them undifferentiated in the minds of the jurors — but as guilty, not innocent. The Lauder men were determined to sink or swim as a group, and they were successful. On the stand Dempsey and Caruso in particular exuded a macho arrogance that must have offended the sensibility of many of the jurors, male or female. While they never did learn of Brian's episodes with Elaine Lagroix and Lucia Sun Manten, they might have sensed the chauvinistic attitude of Dempsey which so often landed him in hot water. As well, the Lauder gang were represented by divided counsel. Finally, the jurors probably realized that while the victims might not have been telling the whole truth, the defendants' stories were pure fabrication.

As mentioned, most of the Lauder gang now admit their account of events was a lie, although they are still adamant that no rape took place either on April 23 or May 15, 1979. They say they thought the jury would never have swallowed the truth because it meant believing that young women such as Spudic and Harply would agree willingly to group sex. They decided that the only chance they had was to make up a logical sequence of events. That was to prove false, of course.

Having interviewed all but two of the Lauder gang about what happened on May 15, I was able to piece together the following account. Since all were in different institutions and forbidden to communicate with each other — and given the censorship of mail and regulations concerning visitors — the possibility that together they concocted the story is remote.

After the group arrived home from the Lansdowne hotel, Dave Bell was so smashed he went to bed. (All of the Lauder gang are so adamant that Bell played no part in the action that night that I tend to believe them.) Shortly after, Spudic and Gillespie arrived. They sat around chatting with Dempsey, Beatteay and Blake for a while, and then Terri and Richard retired to the small basement room. There Spudic performed fellatio on Gillespie. While they were in the process of this, Brian Dempsey shoved his head through the doorway of the small room and winked at Spudic. She indicated that it would be his turn next. While she was performing oral sex on him, Beatteay and Blake came into the room. Beatteay passed out immediately and played no further role. Blake and Dempsey continued for several hours to "have a good time" with Spudic, and she willingly performed oral sex on each again. Blake, however, eventually felt a little uncomfortable and went upstairs. "Dempsey began to smack her bottom a little, and she began to say things like 'Watch it, I'm not into that.' I thought I had better split at that point." Dempsey denies that he hit Spudic even playfully. He does admit to having had sex with her, however. Dempsey fell asleep soon after beside the air mattress. About three in the morning Bobby Caruso came to Lauder Avenue and it was he who deeply offended Terri Spudic. He began to use insulting biker language, forced himself on her to some degree, although the others say not in an overly rough manner as the absence of bruises would indicate. It was Caruso who insisted on vaginal intercourse and it was Caruso who stole her last forty dollars. (Caruso steadfastly maintains that he did not force Terri Spudic to do anything against her will.) In the morning she was indeed upset: her money had disappeared, she felt lousy from the drugs and booze consumed the night before and she was furious at the way Caruso had treated her. Shortly before she left, she performed fellatio on Dempsey who she sensed was the leader of the gang and might protect her from Caruso.

This contrasts sharply with Spudic's account in which she claimed she did not willingly participate in any sexual activity. But of all the versions this one coincides most closely with the statements given to the police by the Lauder gang when they were first arrested. Bell revealed that he saw Spudic for the first time the morning after as she was performing fellatio on Dempsey. She was naturally upset at this point, and Bell confirmed that. Blake acknowledged that he had indeed been in the basement area that night; when he woke he was lying at the bottom of the stairs but he couldn't recall how he got there. All told the police that Caruso had not come to the Lauder house until the early hours of the morning and it was at that point that he made contact with Spudic. Terri herself recalled that two men whom she didn't recognize came into the room early in the morning and raped her. One fitted the description of Caruso.

What happened during the night of April 23, 1979, has not emerged in quite so vivid detail, primarily because the event occurred a month and a half before the Lauder gang's arrest and their recollection of what happened that night was blurred by the passage of time. And, of course, they had had a great deal to drink. A party went on into the wee hours of the morning; Harply participated in fellatio and intercourse with Dempsey, Caruso and Beatteay. Chuck Dempsey recalls sitting in the kitchen playing bridge with Linda and Jean when Harply came in dressed in a towel. Chuck Dempsey claims she then pulled open the towel and said, "It's your turn next." The men remain adamant that Harply willingly engaged in all these activities. Claudine Harply, on the other hand, still maintains that her version of events as she told the jury is exactly what happened that night.

I think that one can safely conclude at this point that the jury was not given a true account of what occurred on either April 23 or May 15, 1979.

There are those who would say that doesn't matter much, that a form of justice, albeit a little rough around the edges, was achieved anyway, that the Lauder men got what they deserved given the kind of lifestyle they engaged in and the fact that they lied on the stand. They will insist that it doesn't much matter that Blake probably wasn't there for one of the crimes and that Bell probably didn't participate in either — they are guilty by association.

Feminists emphasize that every woman has a right to spurn a man's sexual advances no matter what activity has gone on before. Given these men's unhealthy attitudes towards women, they obviously have a propensity to rape. Coupled with that is the evidence of two women on two different occasions who claim they were sexually brutalized by the same six men. In the face of this, these feminists would say, the inconsistencies in testimony and the indication of loose moral character on the part of the victims simply don't matter. Rough justice is good enough.

I feel that's too simplistic an approach to the Lauder gang dilemma. This was not a case of a gang of hoodlums jumping a teenage girl and raping her in the bushes. This was a social encounter between people who held roughly the same moral values; the women, I believe, understood very well the code of behaviour by which these men operated. They talked the same language, they admired the same masculine and feminine attributes, they both had past experiences which should have prepared them for what might have happened at Lauder Avenue. This is not to say that these men should be allowed to sexually assault a woman at will. But these circumstances, and the fact that so much doubt was cast on the women's evidence, should surely have been taken into account in the punishment. These men have not simply been given prison sentences for six, nine or twelve years. They have been branded as gang rapists, which these days is truly a terrible stigma — and a dangerous one in prison society. As feminists persuade the population as a whole to react with greater abhorrence to sexual assault, the more care our judicial system should take in ensuring that anyone who is labelled a sexual offender is truly guilty.

And there are other important questions which this trial and the subsequent convictions raise.

In their 1977 book *Rape: The Price of Coercive Sexuality*, Lorenne Clark and Debra Lewis skilfully criticized the Metro Toronto Police Department for not treating seriously enough the complaints of many women who claimed they were raped.* They backed up their allegations with statistics which showed that a large number of complaints were classified as "unfounded" and were not investigated with any thoroughness. These findings caused something of an uproar, not only among the police, but also in the Ontario attorney general's office. Law enforcers were determined to rectify the situation and it became a priority to investigate rape cases. "You knew you'd chalk up points if you successfully dealt with a rapist, and a gang of rapists would be even better," a former detective told me. And there is some indication that the police might have been somewhat overzealous in their approach to the Lauder gang. For example, there is the fact that the day after the raid, the media ran stories claiming seven members of the Last Chance had been arrested for gang rape and that 402 Lauder Avenue was the headquarters of the motorcycle club. Since all three Toronto newspapers published this erroneous information it seems it must have come from the police. While this may merely have been an error, the Lauder gang felt strongly that the police were attempting to paint them in the worst light possible.

---

* Lorenne M. G. Clark and Debra J. Lewis, *Rape: The Price of Coercive Sexuality* (Toronto: Women's Educational Press, 1977).

One might also ask if the preparation which Crown Attorney Chris Rutherford gave his two key witnesses might not have been unfair to the Lauder gang, especially given that both cases were tried together. It seems to me that the line between proper preparation of witnesses and actual coaching could be rather thin. Harply would say, "He [Rutherford] helped me get my facts together. I wouldn't have remembered half the stuff without his help." Rutherford is considered by almost everyone to be a most conscientious and capable Crown Attorney. However, prolonged dealings with any witness, even though completely proper, could affect the witness's evidence.

But this book is an indictment of a lifestyle as much as it is a criticism of the judicial system. Both the victims and the accused where children of the Sixties moulded by the philosophic underpinnings of rock and roll, and the drugs and the nihilism which much of the music encouraged. It's no coincidence that one of Brian Dempsey's great heroes was the late Jimi Hendrix, whose indulgence in drugs of all kinds led to his early death at age twenty-seven. Hendrix's music is heavy with macho sentiments of the most obscene variety ("Fuck her in the ass, suck me little woman in your little pussy," rants one song). In their most formative years, Brian and others lapped up this ugly and sadistic chauvinism until it became a predominant thread in their makeup. It was part of a general scorn for the ethics and morality, the niceties, of their society which developed in their teenage years from a number of influences expressing an age-old misogyny. They would be rude to whom they liked, they would disdain working at any steady job. Living off the avails of society — welfare or unemployment, or even stolen credit cards — they would indulge in booze and drugs as much as they liked because their music, the one thing that meant more to them than any other, told them that their lifestyle was not merely acceptable but even heroic.

The quintessential victim, Claudine Harply, and the nomad, Terri Spudic, were part of the same generation and the same lifestyle. Rock and roll was a special part of both women's lives; Harply, who once aspired to follow the example of Liverpool's best-known native sons, was on her way to a rock concert the night of the assault, and Terri was married to an itinerant rock and roll drummer. Both lead lives that inevitably steer towards tragedy. Harply has attempted suicide on many occasions; Spudic's mother said she would not be surprised if her daughter was found murdered one day.

Interestingly, the women in this saga, Jean Elgar and Linda Brown as much as Claudine Harply and Terri Spudic, enjoyed the by-products of the women's liberation movement. They could cast aside the traditional roles of wife and mother, could indeed experience exactly the lifestyle they chose. The question that has to be asked, however, is, what attitude, what philosophy regarding their role in society, did they substitute? In the end their freedom was merely an illusion, for they were in bondage to men in a way their mothers would never have dreamed of.

There is something fundamentally irresponsible about all of the characters. And this cavalier approach to life has had tragic consequences — Brian's baby was burned to death in a fire started by careless smoking. Indeed, the only innocent victims in this story may be the families. Claudine Harply has relinquished the care of her three sons to others. Terri Spudic abandoned her two children altogether. Linda Brown, Roadside Blake, John Beatteay, Brian Dempsey and Bob Caruso have all had children who for one reason or another have been denied a secure unbringing by at least one parent. The parents of the convicted men — all of whom are ordinary, hard-working people — have also suffered immensely. They too must bear the stigma of rape, even though they continue to believe in their sons' innocence, and they fear for the safety of their sons in the prison system. Yet they feel deeply sorry for the women. They wonder how these children, moulded in the exuberant, rebellious yet hopeful Sixties, could have become so lost.

Bassett

MAGGIE SIGGINS

This telling biography of John Bassett provides a fascinating behind-the-scenes look at the world of politics, publishing, business and sports in which Bassett has wheeled and dealed for over four decades. Maggie Siggins interviewed more than 200 of Bassett's friends, family, business associates, critics and enemies to piece together a public career that includes masterminding the rise and fall of the Toronto *Telegram* and the building of a media empire.

"*Bassett*'s information on the sports-newspaper-and-TV business world is first-rate, indeed excellent." — Larry Zolf, *Montreal Gazette.*

"This is an important book because it documents the cynicism and opportunism which too often prevail among our publishing and broadcasting moguls." — *Globe and Mail.*

Long Way from Home

The Story of the Sixties Generation in Canada

MYRNA KOSTASH

Long Way from Home is an extraordinary book about the extraordinary Sixties — a decade of upheaval and change for the generation of Canadians who had grown up amidst the comfort, security and political complacency of the Fifties. Everything was held up for questioning and a new way of life evolved, with its own language, music, ideas, values: flower power, love-ins, drugs and anti-war demonstrations.

Myrna Kostash, a well-known writer and journalist, researched the story of the Sixties generation — her generation — by crossing Canada several times, interviewing hundreds of people to discover why and how the Sixties profoundly affected their lives.

"A social document of rare clarity and insight." — June Callwood.

"This is a welcome document of a decade that needs to be recorded before it is forgotten." — *London Free Press.*

The Flying Bandit

HEATHER ROBERTSON

The Flying Bandit is a fast-paced account of the life and times of one of Canada's most notorious and best-loved bank robbers. Based on Ken Leishman's private journals, Robertson's book brings back to life all his legendary front-page exploits and spectacular heists.

"Entertaining and highly readable." — *Winnipeg Free Press.*

"A fabulous story." — *Windsor Star.*

The Life and Death of Anna Mae Aquash

JOHANNA BRAND

Who killed Anna Mae Aquash and why? The startling story of a Canadian victim in the secret war between the FBI, the RCMP and the American Indian Movement.

"This book should force the government to insist on a full-scale investigation." — *Toronto Star.*

Sweethearts

The Builders, the Mob and the Men

CATHERINE WISMER

In this study of organized crime involvement in legitimate business, Catherine Wismer zeroes in on the mobsters, extortionists, hit men and builders who moved in on Toronto's thriving high-rise apartment business during the Sixties.

"A very human chronicle of a shabby period in modern Toronto labour history." — *Globe and Mail.*

"A real-life tale of violence and union corruption — Wismer excels in describing the social and political atmosphere of Toronto ... and in explaining why the city was ripe for development at such a breakneck pace." — *Toronto Star.*

Achevé d'imprimer
en février mil neuf cent quatre-vingt-quatre
sur les presses de l'Imprimerie Gagné Ltée
Louiseville - Montréal.
Imprimé au Canada